my **revision** notes

AQA A-level

ECONOMICS

Steve Stoddard and David Horner

HODI
EDUCA
AN HACHE

Hachette UK's policy is to use papers that are natural, renewable and recyclable products and made from wood grown in sustainable forests. The logging and manufacturing processes are expected to conform to the environmental regulations of the country of origin.

Orders: please contact Bookpoint Ltd, 130 Park Drive, Milton Park, Abingdon, Oxon OX14 4SE. Telephone: (44) 01235 827720. Fax: (44) 01235 400454. Email education@ bookpoint.co.uk Lines are open from 9 a.m. to 5 p.m., Monday to Saturday, with a 24-hour message answering service. You can also order through our website: www. hoddereducation.co.uk

ISBN: 978 1 4718 6587 9

© David Horner and Steve Stoddard 2016

First published in 2016 by
Hodder Education,
An Hachette UK Company
Carmelite House
50 Victoria Embankment
London EC4Y 0DZ
www.hoddereducation.co.uk

Impression number 10 9 8 7 6 5 4 3 2 1
Year 2020 2019 2018 2017 2016

Cover photo reproduced by permission of Alex Tihonov/Fotolia

Typeset in Bembo Std Regular, 11/13 pts. by Aptara, Inc.

Printed in Spain

A catalogue record for this title is available from the British Library.

Get the most from this book

Everyone has to decide his or her own revision strategy, but it is essential to review your work, learn it and test your understanding. These Revision Notes will help you to do that in a planned way, topic by topic. Use this book as the cornerstone of your revision and don't hesitate to write in it — personalise your notes and check your progress by ticking off each section as you revise.

Tick to track your progress

Use the revision planner on pages 4 and 5 to plan your revision, topic by topic. Tick each box when you have:

- revised and understood a topic
- tested yourself
- practised the exam questions and gone online to check your answers and complete the quick quizzes

You can also keep track of your revision by ticking off each topic heading in the book. You may find it helpful to add your own notes as you work through each topic.

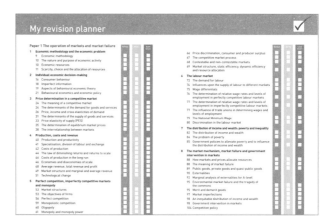

Features to help you succeed

Examiners' tips and summaries

Expert tips are given throughout the book to help you polish your exam technique in order to maximise your chances in the exam. The summaries provide a quick-check bullet list for each topic.

Typical mistakes

The authors identify the typical mistakes candidates make and explain how you can avoid them.

Now test yourself

These short, knowledge-based questions provide the first step in testing your learning. Answers are at the back of the book.

Definitions and key words

Clear, concise definitions of essential key terms are provided where they first appear.

Key words from the specification are highlighted in bold throughout the book.

Revision activities

These activities will help you to understand each topic in an interactive way.

Debates

Debates are highlighted to help you assess arguments and use evidence appropriately.

Exam practice

Practice exam questions are provided for each topic. Use them to consolidate your revision and practise your exam skills.

Online

Go online to check your answers to the exam questions and try out the extra quick quizzes at **www.hoddereducation.co.uk/myrevisionnotes**

My revision planner

REVISED   TESTED   EXAM READY

Exam practice answers and quick quizzes at
www.hoddereducation.co.uk/myrevisionnotes

Countdown to my exams

- Start by looking at the specification — make sure you know exactly what material you need to revise and the style of the examination. Use the revision planner on pages 4–6 to familiarise yourself with the topics.
- Organise your notes, making sure you have covered everything on the specification. The revision planner will help you to group your notes into topics.
- Work out a realistic revision plan that will also allow you time for relaxation. Set aside days and times for all the subjects you need to study, and stick to your timetable.
- Set yourself sensible targets. Break your revision down into focused sessions of around 40 minutes, divided by breaks. These *Revision Notes* organise the basic facts into short, memorable sections to make revising easier.

REVISED ☐

2–5 weeks to go

- Read through the relevant sections of this book and refer to the exam tips, summaries, typical mistakes and key terms. Tick off the topics as you feel confident about them. Highlight those you find difficult and look at them again in detail.
- Test your understanding of each topic by working through the 'Now test yourself' questions in the book. Look up the answers at the back of the book.
- Make a note of any problem areas as you revise, and ask your teacher to go over these in class.
- Look at past papers. They are one of the best ways to revise and to practise your exam skills. Write or prepare planned answers to the 'Exam practice' questions in this book. Check your answers online and try out the extra quick quizzes at www.hoddereducation.co.uk/myrevisionnotes
- Use the revision activities to try out different revision methods. For example, you can make notes using mind maps, spider diagrams or flash cards.
- Track your progress using the revision planner and give yourself a reward when you have achieved your target!

REVISED ☐

One week to go

- Try to fit in at least one more timed practice of an entire past paper and seek feedback from your teacher, comparing your work closely with the mark scheme.
- Check the revision planner to make sure you haven't missed any topics. Brush up on any areas of difficulty by talking them over with a friend or getting help from your teacher.
- Attend any revision classes put on by your teacher. Remember, he or she is an expert at preparing people for examinations.

REVISED ☐

The day before the examination

- Flick through these *Revision Notes* for useful reminders — for example, the exam tips, summaries, typical mistakes and key terms.
- Check the time and place of your examination.
- Make sure you have everything you need — extra pens and pencils, tissues, a watch, bottled water, sweets.
- Allow some time to relax and have an early night to ensure you are fresh and alert for the examinations.

REVISED ☐

My exams

A-level Economics Paper 1

Date:...

Time:...

Location:...

A-level Economics Paper 2

Date:...

Time:...

Location:...

A-level Economics Paper 3

Date:...

Time:...

Location:...

1 Economic methodology and the economic problem

Economic methodology

Economics is the study of how the world's scarce resources are allocated to competing uses to satisfy society's wants.

As a social science, Economics attempts to adopt a scientific methodology for observing the behaviour of individuals and groups and then makes predictions based upon these observations. For example, how many more units of a product might an individual buy if the price of that product is reduced by 25%?

Positive economic statements

Positive economic statements are objective statements that can be tested against facts to be declared either true or false. A positive economic statement does not necessarily have to be true.

> **Positive statement**: an objective statement that can be tested against the facts to be declared either true or false.

Normative economic statements

Normative economic statements are subjective opinions or value judgements that cannot be tested against facts. These often concern views about what individuals, firms or governments *should* do, based upon people's ethical, moral or political standpoint. Some economists view such statements as being the concern of the field of politics rather than economics. However, much of economic policy rests on normative judgements about the 'right' levels of, for example, taxes, minimum wages or the amount of government intervention in markets.

> **Normative statement**: a subjective opinion, or value judgement, that cannot be declared either true or false.

> **Typical mistake**
>
> A positive statement need not necessarily be factually true. It simply needs to be capable of being tested to be declared true or false.

Now test yourself

TESTED

1 Which of the following would be classed as a normative economic statement?
   A   An increase in price usually leads to a fall in the quantity demanded of a good.
   B   The government should spend more money on improving public transport.
   C   A reduction in income tax will lead to more people choosing to work.
   D   An increase in price usually leads to a rise in the quantity supplied of a good.

Answer on p. 226

The nature and purpose of economic activity

Needs, wants and economic welfare

REVISED

The main purpose of economic activity is to satisfy society's needs and wants.

A **need** is something that humans require to survive, such as food, shelter and warmth. A **want** is something not essential for survival, but which people feel improves their standard of living, or **economic welfare**, e.g. a new car.

Economic welfare refers to the standard of living, or general wellbeing, of individuals in society. Satisfying society's needs and wants in terms of material and non-material things leads, in general, to increased economic welfare. Increasing real gross domestic product (GDP) per capita is pursued in order for average living standards to increase, as this allows people to be able to satisfy more of their needs and wants. There is debate, however, about whether people feel genuinely happier simply by having more of their wants satisfied.

> **Need**: something which humans need to survive, e.g. food, shelter and warmth.
>
> **Want**: something which people feel improves their standard of living but is not required for survival.
>
> **Economic welfare**: the standard of living or general wellbeing of people in society.

Economic resources

A country's economic resources are known as the **factors of production**. Four are usually identified:
- **Capital:** man-made physical equipment used to make other goods and services. This includes machinery and computer equipment.
- **Enterprise:** entrepreneurs are individuals who take a business risk in combining the other three factors of production in order to produce a good or service.
- **Land:** all naturally occurring resources such as minerals, the sea, fertile land and the environment. These can be further divided into renewable and non-renewable resources.
- **Labour:** people involved in production, sometimes referred to as human capital.

> **Factors of production**: a country's productive economic resources, divided into capital, enterprise, land and labour.

Typical mistake

Don't confuse the term 'capital' for 'money' in economics. Money is classed as financial capital.

Now test yourself

TESTED

2 Which of the following would be classified as land by an economist?
   A a sewing machine
   B a taxi driver
   C oil in the North Sea
   D a laptop computer

Answer on p. 226

Exam tip

The four factors of production can be memorised using the acronym CELL, standing for capital, enterprise, land and labour.

Scarcity, choice and the allocation of resources

The basic economic problem

REVISED

The **basic economic problem** is that of scarcity, i.e. that economic resources are limited relative to society's wants. This means that choices must be made when deciding how to allocate these resources. In so doing, the three fundamental economic questions must be considered:

1 **What to produce and in what quantities?** Goods are usually divided into consumer goods and capital goods. Consumer goods are those that give satisfaction to consumers, such as pizza or a fridge freezer. Capital goods are those used to produce other goods, including machinery and IT equipment.

2 **How should goods and services be produced?** The basic production decision is between labour-intensive methods (where a high proportion of human capital is used compared to capital) or capital-intensive methods (the opposite).

3 **To whom should goods and services be allocated?** This choice affects the degrees of equity and equality in society. Decisions about who in society gets what will be determined by the economic system that prevails. Two extreme forms of economic system are:

- **The free market or capitalist economy.** Decisions are made solely by the interactions of consumers and firms, with no government intervention.
- **The command or centrally planned economy.** Decisions are made solely by the planning department of governments.

> **Basic economic problem**: scarce economic resources compared with society's unlimited wants.

Now test yourself

TESTED

3 Why do individuals, firms and governments have to make choices about what to produce?
4 How might decisions about the three fundamental economic questions differ between a free market economy and a centrally planned economy?

Answer on p. 226

Opportunity cost

REVISED

In making any choice regarding how to allocate scarce resources, something must be given up. This is the concept of **opportunity cost**, i.e. that scarce resources have competing uses. It means that when someone chooses one use, they must forgo the next best alternative use.

> **Opportunity cost**: the cost of the next best alternative that you give up when you have to make a choice.

Now test yourself

TESTED

5 John bought a German saloon car for £10000 2 years ago. A new car would cost £13000. He could sell his German saloon car for £8000. What is the present opportunity cost of keeping his car?
   A £10000   C £3000
   B £13000   D £8000

Answer on p. 226

Economic goods and free goods

Economic goods are those that use up scarce economic resources in their production. These include most consumer goods.

Free goods are unlimited in their supply and availability, such as sunlight or air, and thus the opportunity cost of consuming them is zero.

> **Economic good**: a good that has an opportunity cost in consumption because it uses up scarce resources.
>
> **Free good**: a good that does not have an opportunity cost in consumption because it does not use up scarce resources.

Production possibility diagrams

A **production possibility curve (PPC)** is a diagram which depicts the maximum combinations of two goods that can be produced by an economy, assuming all resources are fully employed and used efficiently. Figure 1.1 shows a PPC.

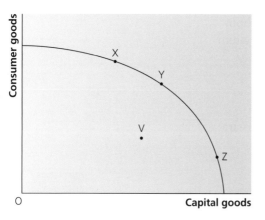

Figure 1.1 A production possibility curve (PPC)

Any point on the production possibility curve, e.g. X, Y or Z, implies that all factors of production are fully employed. An economy operating at point V must therefore be operating inefficiently, with unused resources, e.g. unemployed labour or idle machines.

Shifts of the PPC

Factors leading to shifts of the PPC, outwards or inwards, are driven by changes in the quantity and efficiency (quality) of the factors of production.

Factors causing an outward shift of the PPC

- Technological improvements that lead to increased productivity of capital equipment.
- Discovery of new resources, e.g. oil and gas.
- Improvements in education and training that lead to a more productive workforce.
- Changes that lead to an increase in working population, e.g. increases in immigration or a raised retirement age.

Factors causing an inward shift of the PPC

- Disasters such as earthquakes or floods that devastate productive resources.

> **Production possibility curve (PPC)**: a diagram which shows the maximum possible output combinations of two goods in an economy, assuming full employment of efficient resources.

> **Exam tip**
>
> Production possibility diagrams may also be referred to as production possibility frontiers (PPFs) and production possibility boundaries (PPBs).

> **Typical mistake**
>
> Do not confuse an increased utilisation of factors of production with economic growth. An increased utilisation of factors of production moves the economy to a point closer to the PPC, whereas economic growth leads to an outward shift of the PPC.

- Wars.
- Global warming/climate change, which may lead to loss of farmland, rising sea levels and more extreme weather.
- A prolonged recession, which may lead to permanent loss of productive capacity if businesses close down and/or workers lose skills.

Using a PPC diagram to show opportunity cost

The PPC in Figure 1.2 shows the maximum combinations of consumer goods and capital goods that can be produced with a given set of factors of production.

The diagram shows the concept of opportunity cost — as more capital goods are produced, more consumer goods must be given up. An increase in the amount of capital goods from OM to OS leads to a loss of output of consumer goods from OL to OR.

A subsequent increase in production of capital goods from OS to OV leads to a proportionately larger fall in production of consumer goods from OR to OT.

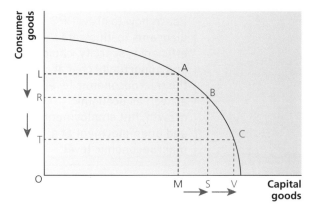

Figure 1.2 The production possibility curve and opportunity cost

Using a PPC diagram to show economic growth

Production possibility diagrams can also be used to show **economic growth**.

The PPC in Figure 1.3 again shows the maximum combinations of consumer goods and capital goods that can be produced with a given set of factors of production. We will assume that the economy is producing at point A on the current PPC.

An improvement in technology, or any of the factors that lead to an outward shift of the PPC, means that there has been an increase in the productive capacity of the economy. This will lead to the entire PPC shifting outwards. Production at point E is now possible, leading to increased potential output of both capital goods and consumer goods.

> **Economic growth**: an increase in the productive capacity of an economy over time.

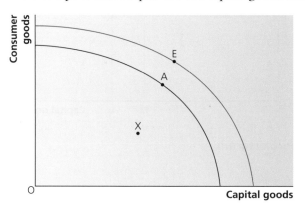

Figure 1.3 The production possibility curve and economic growth

> **Typical mistake**
>
> A movement from point X to point A is not economic growth — it is simply an economy making fuller use of its existing, previously unemployed, resources.

Economic efficiency and production possibility diagrams

The two main types of economic efficiency are **productive efficiency** and **allocative efficiency**. Productive efficiency is concerned with how well society uses its scarce resources to maximise outputs of goods and services.

At the level of a whole economy, productive efficiency occurs when maximum output is produced from the available factors of production, which would be at any point on the PPC. By definition then, any point that lies inside the PPC is productively inefficient.

The concepts of productive efficiency and productive inefficiency are shown in the PPC diagram in Figure 1.4.

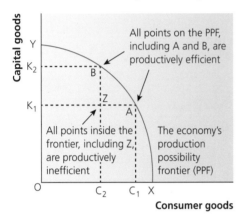

Figure 1.4 Productive efficiency and the PPC

Allocative efficiency exists when an economy's factors of production are used to produce the combination of goods and services that maximises society's welfare. The PPC shows all possible efficient combinations of goods and services that can be produced, but does not specify an allocatively efficient point. The allocatively efficient point on the PPC is the one that best reflects society's preferences for particular goods and services.

> **Productive efficiency:** when maximum output is produced from the available factors of production and when it is not possible to produce more of one good or service without producing less of another.
>
> **Allocative efficiency:** when an economy's factors of production are used to produce the combination of goods and services that maximises society's welfare.

> **Exam tip**
>
> Learn how to draw PPC diagrams to illustrate efficiency, scarcity, choice and opportunity cost at the microeconomic level as well as economic growth, full employment and unemployment at a macroeconomic level.

Now test yourself

TESTED

6 With reference to the figure:
  (a) What is the significance of point Z?
  (b) Explain why points A and B can be considered productively efficient.
  (c) How might point Y be achieved in the future?
  (d) Explain how the diagram can be used to show the concept of opportunity cost.
7 Explain the effect on a PPC of the following:
  (a) improvements in soil fertility resulting from the use of chemicals
  (b) a decrease in population size due to falling birth rates
  (c) technological improvements in capital equipment
  (d) increased government spending on education and training

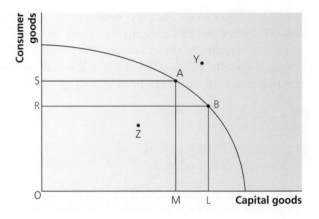

A PPC diagram

Answers on p. 226

Exam practice

1 Which statement is true?
  A A positive economic statement never contains words such as 'should' or 'ought to'.
  B A positive economic statement is one that can be tested against the facts.
  C A normative statement never contains words such as 'will' or 'does'.
  D A normative statement can be scientifically proven. [1]
2 Scarcity in an economy means that:
  A there is a misallocation of resources
  B there are no free goods
  C people must make choices
  D it is not possible to maximise economic welfare [1]
3 When money is used as a medium of exchange:
  A trade is likely to increase
  B specialisation and the division of labour are impossible
  C barter becomes more widespread
  D prices must increase [1]
4 Which of the following is a factor of production?
  A a loan from a bank
  B profits made by businesses
  C labour productivity
  D a computer [1]
5 The diagram shows an economy's production possibility curve. Which of the following combinations of consumer goods and capital goods is achievable with current factors of production?
  A only A
  B only B and C
  C A, B, C and D
  D only A, B and C [1]

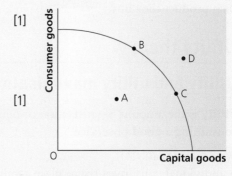

A PPC diagram

Answers and quick quiz 1 online

ONLINE

Summary

You should have an understanding of:
- The meaning of the term 'economics'.
- Basic economic methodology.
- The nature and purpose of economic activity.
- The difference between needs and wants.
- Positive and normative economic statements.
- The meaning of scarcity and how this leads to choices having to be made.
- The four key factors of production: capital, enterprise, land and labour.

- The difference between consumer goods and capital goods.
- The concept of opportunity cost and its significance for individuals, firms and governments.
- The difference between economic goods and free goods.
- Production possibility curves and how to draw them correctly.
- How to use PPCs to illustrate opportunity cost, efficiency and economic growth.

2 Individual economic decision-making

Consumer behaviour

Rational economic decision-making and economic incentives

REVISED

Traditional, neoclassical economic theory assumes that consumers always act rationally, seeking to maximise satisfaction for every pound spent on each product they buy.

Utility theory

REVISED

Utility and utility maximisation

Utility is the amount of satisfaction or benefit that a consumer gains from consuming a good or service.

We assume that:
- individual consumers try to place a value on a good or service equal to the satisfaction they perceive it will bring. They may try to give this an actual monetary value, e.g. £5
- consumers aim to maximise utility per pound spent and so will compare their perceived satisfaction with the price of the good or service
- **rational consumers** will consume a good or service only if the perceived satisfaction is greater than, or equal to, the price

> **Utility:** the amount of satisfaction or benefit that a consumer gains from consuming a good or service.
>
> **Rational consumer:** an assumption of traditional economic theory that consumers act in such a way as to always maximise satisfaction, or utility, when they spend money on goods and services.

Now test yourself

TESTED

1 A rational consumer will always try to:
  A   spend all of their income
  B   maximise their earnings
  C   take the views of others into account
  D   maximise their total utility

Answer on p. 226

Marginal utility

Marginal utility is the satisfaction gained from consuming an additional unit of a good or service.

> **Marginal utility:** the satisfaction gained from consuming an additional unit of a good or service.

> **Exam tip**
>
> The concept of the margin and marginal analysis underpins many ideas in A-level microeconomics. We will return to it many times throughout this book.

Table 2.1 shows what happens to marginal utility when an individual consumer buys more of a good or service, such as a cup of coffee.

Table 2.1 Marginal utility from consuming cups of coffee

Number of units	Total utility	Marginal utility
1	8	8
2	15	7
3	20	5
4	23	3
5	24	1

In Table 2.1, the total utility from consuming additional cups of coffee continues to increase, up to a value of 24 at 5 units, but the marginal utility from consuming additional cups falls, down to 1 for the fifth cup.

> **Exam tip**
>
> In reality it is likely that individual consumers' perceptions of utility differ between quantities of different products, but this does not necessarily undermine the theory.

Diminishing marginal utility

As illustrated in Table 2.1, when individuals consume more units of a good or service, the additional units give successively smaller increases in total satisfaction. This is the concept of **diminishing marginal utility**. For example, once an individual consumer has drunk their first cup of coffee, their thirst or need for a boost of energy will largely have been satisfied, so that additional cups do little extra to satisfy these requirements.

The concept of diminishing marginal utility is a way of deriving an individual's downward-sloping demand curve for a good or service, as shown in Figure 2.1.

Diminishing marginal utility: as individuals consume more units of a good or service, the additional units give successively smaller increases in total satisfaction.

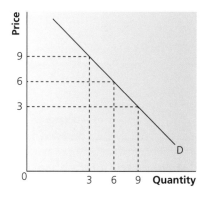

Figure 2.1 Diminishing marginal utility and the individual demand curve

For the first units of a good or service in Figure 2.1, an individual is happy to pay a relatively high price. For example, the individual is prepared to pay £9 for the third unit, but only £6 for the sixth unit and £3 for the ninth unit. As marginal utility declines, the price the consumer is willing to pay for additional units decreases.

TESTED ☐

2 What is the marginal utility to a consumer from the fifth pancake?

Quantity of pancakes	Total utility
3	200
4	260
5	300
6	330
7	330

A 60   C 30
B 40   D 0

Answer on p. 226

Imperfect information

The field of behavioural economics recognises that humans are unlikely to always act rationally in the face of every decision they make. One reason for this is that consumers face imperfect information. This means that they rarely possess all the information required to make fully informed decisions. Imperfect information makes it difficult for economic agents to make rational decisions and is a potential source of market failure.

Sources of imperfect information

REVISED ☐

- Economic agents can be faced with too little information or too much information, or find themselves knowing more or less information than other parties to a transaction.
- Information can also be presented in such a way as to exclude some people and be meaningful to others, e.g. technical or legal jargon.
- There can be costs involved in acquiring information that deter people from doing so — for example, house surveys, mechanical checks on cars, thorough checks/references on new employees, etc.

Consider how imperfect information might lead to a misallocation of resources in the case of merit goods and demerit goods.

Asymmetric information

REVISED ☐

Asymmetric information is a form of imperfect information when one party (usually the seller) has more/superior information than another (usually the buyer). Examples include:

- the market for so-called 'lemons' where a second-hand car salesman knows more about the quality of a car he is selling than the buyer does
- where an individual may know more about their credit-worthiness than the bank from which they are attempting to secure a loan

Both examples lead to an imbalance of power, where one party can exploit the other, resulting in market failure. Uncertainty also leads to a lack of trust between agents, which may mean that a mutually beneficial exchange does not occur.

> **Asymmetric information**: a source of information failure where one economic agent knows more than another, giving them more power in a market transaction.

> **Exam tip**
>
> Sources of imperfect and asymmetric information challenge traditional assumptions of economics regarding rational consumer behaviour.

Aspects of behavioural economic theory

Behavioural economics is a relatively modern field of economic theory which recognises the social, moral and psychological factors that determine the behaviour of economic agents. It differs from traditional economic theory in the sense that it questions the assumption of individuals as rational decision makers. People may therefore not behave as traditional textbooks suggest.

Bounded rationality

REVISED

Bounded rationality is the idea that people may try to behave rationally, but their ability to do so is severely restricted, for three main reasons:
- The human mind has limited ability to process and evaluate information.
- The available information is incomplete and often unreliable (and rapidly out of date).
- The time available to make decisions is limited.

Therefore, even with the best intentions, individuals end up 'satisficing', or accepting sub-optimal outcomes.

> **Bounded rationality**: when people try to behave rationally but are restricted by factors such as lack of time to make decisions.

Bounded self-control

REVISED

Bounded self-control is when individuals have good intentions but lack the self-discipline to see them through, e.g. regular gym attendance, losing weight, giving up smoking or saving for the future.

As a result of bounded rationality and bounded self-control, people are therefore 'predictably irrational' — a term coined by leading behavioural economist Dan Ariely, demonstrating predictable biases in decision-making.

> **Bounded self-control**: when individuals lack the self-discipline to see their rational good intentions through.

Now test yourself

TESTED

3 Which of the following is not a reason for bounded rationality in individual decision-making?
   A too much information for the human mind to process
   B incomplete and unreliable information
   C limited time to make decisions
   D up-to-date information

Answer on p. 226

Rules of thumb

REVISED

Rules of thumb, sometimes known as heuristics, are 'thinking shortcuts' individuals use to make decisions, given the problems of bounded rationality. For example, consumers may choose the same hot drink in a coffee shop each time they visit because they have enjoyed it on previous visits. This saves the consumer the time and effort of having to make comparisons on every visit.

> **Rules of thumb**: thinking shortcuts, or informed guesses, that individuals use to make decisions in order to save time and effort.

Anchoring

REVISED

Anchoring is the tendency of individuals to rely on particular pieces of information, especially in situations where they lack knowledge or experience. For example, a consumer choosing between car insurance premiums online may focus on price as the key point of comparison rather than the features, excesses and exclusions of individual policies.

> **Anchoring:** the tendency of individuals to rely on particular pieces of information when making choices between different goods and services.

Availability

REVISED

The **availability bias** is when people make judgements about the probability of events by recalling recent instances, e.g. rushing out to buy barbecues and sun cream on the first sunny day of the year, or stockpiling snow shovels and path-clearing salt following a particularly harsh winter. Availability serves as a mental shortcut if an example comes to mind easily, e.g. recalling a family member who lost their retirement savings in the last recession, therefore discouraging personal saving.

> **Availability bias:** when people make judgements about the probability of events by recalling recent instances.

Social norms

REVISED

The concept of **social norms** recognises the influence of others upon individual decision-making, for example encouraging passengers to put pressure on drivers not to drive too fast or under the influence of alcohol. Equally, people may be influenced to drink or smoke by social friendship or work groups. Social norms link strongly into economic policies that use knowledge of behavioural economics, concerning, for example, the wearing of seatbelts, reducing smoking in public places and using mobile phones while driving. Social norms can be used to increase charitable donations — hence examples of donations on 'telethons' such as Children in Need and Comic Relief.

> **Social norms:** when individuals are influenced by others when making decisions.

Altruism and fairness

REVISED

The biases of **altruism and fairness** mean that people are motivated to 'do the right thing'. Therefore, giving to charity, doing voluntary work or paying extra to support Fairtrade initiatives may be seen as irrational in traditional, neoclassical economic theory. However, individual consumers can genuinely gain a sense of satisfaction and extra utility from acting in these ways. Critics of altruism and fairness argue that people simply fear 'being judged', especially in a world where information flows freely, such as via social media.

> **Altruism and fairness:** individuals are motivated to do the right thing, even if this means paying more for a good or service.

Now test yourself

TESTED

4 Which of the following is not a bias in individual decision-making?
  A altruism
  B anchoring
  C marginal utility
  D availability

Answer on p. 226

Behavioural economics and economic policy

An understanding of the insights provided by behavioural economic theory can help governments and other agencies devise policies that more effectively influence economic decisions. This may involve influencing the ways in which individuals' choices are 'framed' as well as 'nudging' people towards more desirable courses of action.

Exam tip

There are now many interesting, accessible books written on the subject of behavioural economics. Ask your teacher for recommendations.

Choice architecture

REVISED

Choice architecture refers to how choices may be influenced by the way they are presented to the decision maker, in order to achieve desired outcomes. For example, countries with governments that require people to opt out of organ donation generally have a significantly higher percentage of the population willing to donate than countries where people are required to opt in.

Choice architecture: influencing consumer choices by the way the choices are presented.

Framing

REVISED

Framing is a form of choice architecture that influences choices by the way words and numbers are used, e.g. presenting life insurance premium payments as 'less than £3 per day' sounds more palatable than £1,000 per year. Gym membership adverts often using clever framing.

Framing: influencing consumer choices by the way words and numbers are used.

Nudges

REVISED

Nudges are another form of choice architecture that aim to influence consumer behaviour via the use of gentle suggestions and positive reinforcement, such as the 'five-a-day' campaign to encourage greater consumption of fruit and vegetables. Nudges can be a means of changing people's behaviour in a socially desirable manner without taking away freedom of choice. They can be a more cost-effective alternative to the use of laws, bans or regulation and can complement traditional policy methods — for example, seatbelt laws are costly to enforce, but using adverts to reinforce a social norm means this issue now needs little enforcement.

Nudges: influencing consumer behaviour via the use of gentle suggestions and positive reinforcement.

Default choice

REVISED

Default choices are an additional form of choice architecture which set socially desirable choices as the default option, making it an effort to choose otherwise. They have been used, for example, in organ donation and pension enrolment. In each case, the default choice would be to opt in and so individuals would have to actively elect to opt out. Unsurprisingly, the use of default choices in each case has led to significant increases in opt-in rates.

Default choice: influencing consumer behaviour by setting socially desirable choices as default options.

Mandated choice

REVISED

Mandated choice is a stronger form of choice architecture where people are required by law to make a choice. For example, in many countries people are required to make a decision about organ donation as part of their driving licence or passport application.

Mandated choice: where people are legally required to make a choice.

Restricted choice

Restricted choice is another way of influencing people's choices, recognising that too much choice can sometimes 'paralyse' individuals from making an effective choice, for example with savings, pensions or ice-cream flavours! Therefore, giving a limited number of options may be better.

> **Restricted choice:** giving consumers a limited number of options when making a choice.

Now test yourself

5 Which of the following would be considered a form of choice architecture?
   A giving consumers an unlimited choice of options
   B clearly illustrating the full annual cost of health insurance
   C giving consumers extensive nutritional information on food packaging
   D giving consumers a limited choice of options

Answer on p. 226

Exam practice

1 A traditional economic assumption about consumer behaviour is:
   A bounded rationality
   B asymmetric information
   C utility maximisation
   D altruism   [1]

2 What is the marginal utility to a consumer from the fourth packet of crisps?

Quantity of packets of crisps	Total utility
1	100
2	260
3	400
4	500
5	560

   A 160
   B 140
   C 100
   D 160   [1]

3 Economic policy that takes behavioural theory into account is least likely to involve:
   A obliging consumers by law to opt in or out of organ donation
   B taking account of consumer altruism
   C giving consumers a limited range of pre-selected options
   D setting out all possible options   [1]

4 With the help of a diagram, explain how the availability bias might lead to individuals over-estimating their requirement for snow-clearing equipment following a snowy winter.   [9]

5 With the help of a diagram, explain how mandating choices towards pension opt-in might influence the market towards more desirable outcomes.   [9]

6 Evaluate the effectiveness of policies that take account of behavioural economics in attempting to resolve market failures.   [25]

Answers and quick quiz 2 online

Summary

You should have an understanding of:

- The assumptions of traditional neoclassical economics regarding rational decision-making.
- How consumers make rational decisions about how much of various products to consume on the basis of utility theory and the hypothesis of diminishing marginal utility.
- How, in reality, consumers are faced with imperfect information when making decisions.
- The significance of asymmetric information.
- How behavioural economic theory challenges the fundamental assumption of traditional economic theory of consumer rationality.
- The meaning of bounded rationality and bounded self-control.
- Some key biases in decision-making: rules of thumb, anchoring, availability and social norms.
- How altruism and perceptions of fairness influence consumer decisions.
- How insights provided by behavioural economists can help governments and other agencies influence economic decision-making.
- The meaning and examples of choice architecture, framing, nudges, default choices, restricted choice and mandated choice.

3 Price determination in a competitive market

The meaning of a competitive market

A **market** is a situation in which buyers and sellers come together to engage in trade. In the modern age, a market does not have to occur in a physical location, with e-commerce now playing an increasingly important role in the exchange of goods and services.

A **competitive market** occurs when there are a large number of potential buyers and sellers, all individually powerless to influence the ruling market price. This price, known as the **equilibrium price**, is determined by the interaction of market demand and market supply.

The determinants of the demand for goods and services

Demand refers to the quantity of a good or service that consumers are willing and able to buy at given prices in a particular time period. Economists are concerned with **effective demand**, i.e. desire for a product backed up by the ability to pay, rather than an unfulfilled want.

> **Demand**: the quantity of a good or service that consumers are willing and able to buy at given prices in a particular time period.
>
> **Effective demand**: consumers' desire to buy a good, backed up by the ability to pay.

> **Market**: a situation in which buyers and sellers come together to engage in trade.
>
> **Competitive market**: a situation where there is a large number of potential buyers and sellers with abundant information about the market.
>
> **Equilibrium price**: the price at which the planned demand of consumers equals the planned supply of firms.

The law of demand and the shape of the market demand curve

REVISED

The law of demand states that as the price of a good or service falls, the quantity demanded increases. This inverse relationship between the price and quantity demanded of a good or service is shown in Figure 3.1. In analysing the effect of a change in price on quantity demanded, we usually assume that all other possible determinants of demand are held constant. Economists refer to this assumption as 'ceteris paribus'. An increase in the quantity demanded resulting from a fall in price is known as an extension of demand, whereas a fall in quantity demanded resulting from an increase in price is known as a contraction of demand.

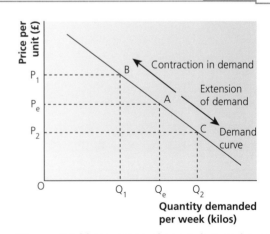

Figure 3.1 Movements along a demand curve

Using graph paper, construct a demand curve to show the information shown in the table.

Price of coffee (£ per kilo)	Quantity of coffee demanded per week (kilos)
18	150 000
15	200 000
12	250 000
9	300 000
6	350 000
3	400 000

Shifts of a demand curve

A mistake that students often make is in confusing a movement along a demand curve with a shift of the whole demand curve. As previously explained, the only variable that leads to a movement along a given demand curve is a change in price of that good or service. Factors that may lead to a shift in the position of the demand curve are referred to as the **conditions of demand**.

These include:
- **Real disposable incomes:** the incomes of individuals after the effects of inflation, **taxation** and benefits are taken into account.
- **Tastes and preferences (fashions):** the popularity of goods and services is often influenced by changes in society's preferences and may be influenced by the media, advertising and technological change.
- **Population:** the size, age and gender composition of the population will affect the market size for many products.
- **Prices of substitute products: substitute** products are those in competitive demand that may be seen as close alternatives to a particular good or service.
- **Prices of complementary products: complementary** products are those in joint demand, i.e. demanded together with other goods or services.

If any of these factors changes, then the demand curve for the good or service in question will change. This leads to either a rightward or a leftward shift of the demand curve, as shown in Figure 3.2. A rightward shift is known as an increase in demand, whereas a leftward shift is known as a decrease in demand. A rightward shift means that a greater quantity of a good or service is demanded at any given price, whereas a leftward shift means that a lower quantity of a good or service is demanded at any given price.

> **Conditions of demand:** factors other than the price of the good that lead to a change in position of the demand curve.
>
> **Taxation:** a charge placed by the government on various forms of economic activity. Most taxes are on forms of income and types of spending.
>
> **Substitute:** a good that may be consumed as an alternative to another good.
>
> **Complement:** a good that tends to be consumed together with another good.

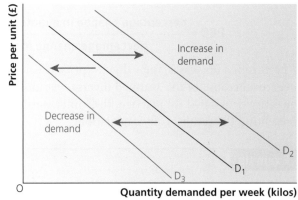

Figure 3.2 Shifts of the demand curve

Revision activity

Assume that it becomes more fashionable for people to drink coffee, which leads to an increase in demand at every given price. Draw a new demand curve on your previous graph based on the information below:

Price of coffee (£ per kilo)	Original quantity of coffee demanded per week (kilos)	New quantity of coffee demanded per week (kilos)
18	150 000	180 000
15	200 000	230 000
12	250 000	280 000
9	300 000	330 000
6	350 000	380 000
3	400 000	430 000

Now test yourself

TESTED

1 What would be the effect of the following on demand for cars in the UK?
   (a) an increase in petrol prices
   (b) a decrease in car parking fees
   (c) a fall in rail fares
   (d) an increase in fuel efficiency of cars

Answer on p. 226

Price, income and cross elasticities of demand

Price elasticity of demand (PED)

REVISED

Price elasticity of demand refers to the responsiveness of the quantity demanded of a good or service to a change in its price.

The formula is stated as:

$$PED = \frac{\text{percentage change in quantity demanded}}{\text{percentage change in price}}$$

Apart from a few cases, the value for price elasticity of demand is negative because of the assumed inverse relationship between price and quantity demanded. In practice, the minus sign tends to be ignored when presenting the result of any calculation.

> **Price elasticity of demand:** the responsiveness of quantity demanded of a good to a change in price.

Exam tip

It is worth memorising the percentage change formula as you will be required to use it frequently.

$$\text{Percentage change} = \left(\frac{\text{change}}{\text{original value}}\right) \times 100$$

Key values and diagrams

Price inelastic demand

When demand for a product is price inelastic, the value of PED is between 0 and 1, ignoring the minus sign.

Example — a 50% increase in the price of petrol leads to a 10% fall in quantity demanded. So:

$$PED = \frac{-10}{+50} = -0.2$$

The change in price has led to a smaller percentage change in the quantity demanded.

Price elastic demand

When demand for a product is price elastic, the value of PED is greater than 1, ignoring the minus sign.

Example — a 10% reduction in the price of cars leads to a 15% increase in quantity demanded. So:

$$PED = \frac{+15}{-10} = -1.5$$

The change in price has led to a larger percentage change in the quantity demanded.

Figures 3.3(a) and 3.3(b) illustrate an inelastic and elastic section of a demand curve.

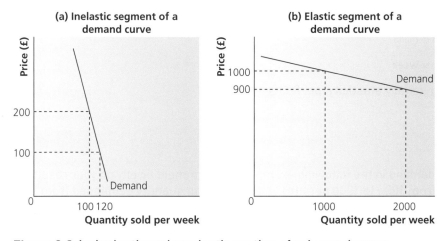

Figure 3.3 An inelastic and an elastic section of a demand curve

Unitary elastic demand

When demand is unitary elastic, the value of PED is exactly 1, ignoring the minus sign. The demand curve is a rectangular hyperbola, as shown in Figure 3.4.

Example — a 20% increase in the price of a mobile phone leads to a 20% decrease in quantity demanded. So:

$$PED = \frac{-20}{+20} = -1.0$$

The change in price has led to the same percentage change in quantity demanded.

Perfectly inelastic demand

When demand for a product is perfectly price inelastic, the value of PED is 0. The demand curve will be vertical, as shown in Figure 3.4.

Example — a 10% increase in the price of a carton of milk leads to no change in quantity demanded. So:

$$PED = \frac{0}{+10} = 0.0$$

The change in price has led to no change in quantity demanded.

Perfectly elastic demand

When demand is perfectly elastic, the value of PED is infinity. The demand curve will be horizontal, as shown in Figure 3.4.

Example — an extremely small increase in the price of a product leads to the quantity demanded falling to zero.

The change in price has led to an infinitely large change in quantity demanded.

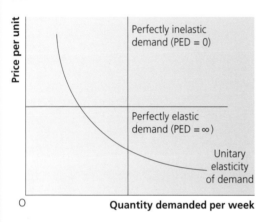

Figure 3.4 Demand curves showing unitary elasticity, perfectly inelastic and perfectly elastic demand

Now test yourself

2 Calculate the price elasticity of demand in the following examples and comment briefly on your results:
   (a) A rise in the price of petrol from 100p to 120p per litre leads to a fall in quantity demanded from 50 to 45 litres per week.
   (b) A fall in the price of games consoles from £250 to £200 leads to a rise in quantity demanded from 100 to 150 per day.
   (c) A rise in the price of racing bicycles from £2400 to £2640 leads to a reduction in quantity demanded from 60 to 40 per month.

Answer on p. 226

Price elasticity of demand and total revenue

The price elasticity of demand of a product determines what happens to consumer spending (and therefore total revenue) following a price change.
● If demand is price elastic, a reduction in price leads to an increase in total revenue.
● If demand is price inelastic, a reduction in price leads to a decrease in total revenue.
● If demand is price elastic, a price increase leads to a reduction in total revenue.
● If demand is price inelastic, a price increase leads to an increase in total revenue.

Exam practice answers and quick quizzes at **www.hoddereducation.co.uk/myrevisionnotes**

Now test yourself

3 The initial price of tea bags is £1.50 per box and quantity demanded is 3000 boxes per week. Following a sales promotion, price is reduced to £1.20 per box and quantity demanded becomes 3300 per week as a result. Calculate both the change in total revenue and the price elasticity of demand.

4 If demand for holidays to the Maldives is price elastic, what will happen to total revenue if holiday companies increase their prices for holidays to this destination?

5 If an increase in the price of milk leads to a rise in total revenue, what can be concluded about price elasticity of demand?

Answers on p. 226

Determinants of price elasticity of demand

The following factors will influence the price elasticity of demand for a good or service:

- **Availability of close substitutes:** if a very close substitute exists for a product, an increase in its price will lead to consumers buying more of the substitute. If one or more close substitutes exist, this will tend to make demand for the product price elastic. If there are few close substitutes, demand will be more inelastic.
- **Percentage of income spent on the product:** if a product accounts for a relatively large percentage of a consumer's income, such as a new car, a change in price of, say, 50% is likely to have a significant impact upon disposable income. Therefore demand for such products will tend to be price elastic. However, the same proportional price change for a relatively inexpensive product such as a loaf of bread will not have the same overall impact upon disposable income and so consumers are likely to be less sensitive to changes in price. Therefore demand for such products will tend to be price inelastic.
- **Nature of the product:** if a product is seen as a necessity, or perhaps even has addictive qualities, demand will tend to be price inelastic, as few alternatives will exist from the viewpoint of the consumer. However, if a product is seen as a luxury, i.e. something that a consumer can do without, demand will tend to be price elastic.
- **Time period:** the longer the time period following a price change, the easier it is for a consumer to adjust their spending patterns or research alternatives, and for more alternatives to become available. In the very short run, motorists may feel obliged to pay whatever price they are charged per litre of fuel, and so demand will be more price inelastic. In the long run, motorists may be able to switch to alternative fuels or more fuel-efficient cars, use public transport or move closer to work. This will make demand for a product more price elastic in the long run.
- **Broad or specific market definition:** a broad market category, e.g. food, is likely to have price inelastic demand, whereas a specific product in a market segment, e.g. baked beans produced by a particular firm, is likely to have more price elastic demand.

Income elasticity of demand (YED)

Income elasticity of demand measures the responsiveness of demand to a change in real income. The formula is:

$$\text{YED} = \frac{\text{percentage change in quantity demanded}}{\text{percentage change in real income}}$$

> **Income elasticity of demand:** the responsiveness of demand for a good to a change in consumers' real income.

Key values

For YED the sign is important. If the value is positive, i.e. greater than 0, the product is a normal good. This means a rise in income will lead to an increase in demand. If the value is negative, i.e. less than 0, the product is an inferior good. This means a rise in income will lead to a fall in demand.

Income elastic demand

When demand for a product is income elastic, the value of YED is greater than +1.

Example — a 10% increase in real income leads to a 20% increase in demand for foreign holidays. So:

$$YED = \frac{+20}{+10} = +2.0$$

The increase in real income has led to a greater percentage increase in demand. Income elastic products are often referred to as luxury goods.

Income inelastic demand

When demand for a product is income inelastic, the value of YED is between 0 and +1.

Example — a 10% increase in real income leads to a 2% increase in demand for cartons of milk. So:

$$YED = \frac{+2}{+10} = +0.2$$

The increase in real income has led to a smaller percentage increase in demand. Income inelastic products are often referred to as basic goods or necessities.

Negative income elasticity

When demand for a product is negative income elastic, the value of YED is negative, i.e. less than 0.

Example — a 20% increase in real income leads to a 10% fall in demand for a supermarket's value brand of baked beans. So:

$$YED = \frac{-10}{+20} = -0.5$$

The increase in income has led to a fall in demand. Negative income elastic products are referred to as inferior goods.

Now test yourself

TESTED

6 In each of the following cases, calculate the income elasticity of demand and comment upon your answer:
   (a) A 7% increase in real incomes causes a 21% fall in demand for a supermarket's own brand of chocolate biscuits.
   (b) A 10% increase in real incomes causes a 25% increase in demand for holidays to Barbados.
   (c) An 8% fall in real incomes leads to a 32% fall in demand for fillet steak.

Answer on p. 226

Cross elasticity of demand (XED)

REVISED

Cross elasticity of demand measures the responsiveness of the demand for a product following a change in price of another product.

The formula is:

$$XED = \frac{\text{percentage change in quantity demanded of product A}}{\text{percentage change in price of product B}}$$

> **Cross elasticity of demand**: the responsiveness of the demand for a product following a change in price of another product.

Key values

For XED the sign is again important.

A positive value indicates that products A and B are substitutes, i.e. a rise in the price of product B leads to an increase in demand for product A.

A negative value indicates that products A and B are complements, i.e. a rise in price of product B leads to a fall in the demand for product A.

Example — a 20% increase in the price of cod leads to a 10% fall in the demand for chips. So:

$$XED = \frac{-10}{+20} = -0.5$$

The two products are therefore complements.

Now test yourself

TESTED

7 In each of the following cases calculate the cross elasticity of demand and comment upon your answer:
   (a) A 20% rise in the price of butter leads to a 15% rise in the demand for margarine.
   (b) A 10% rise in the price of strawberries leads to an 8% fall in the demand for fresh cream.

Answer on p. 226

The determinants of the supply of goods and services

Supply refers to the quantity of a good or service that firms plan to sell at given prices in a particular time period.

> **Supply**: The quantity of a good or service that firms plan to sell at given prices in a particular time period.

The law of supply

REVISED

The law of supply states that as price increases the quantity supplied will increase. This positive relationship is shown in Figure 3.5. Firms are assumed to want to maximise their profits and so a higher price gives an incentive for firms to increase production.

As with demand, a change in price will lead to a movement along an existing supply curve. An increase in price will lead to an increase in quantity supplied, known as an extension in supply. Conversely, a decrease in price will lead to a decrease in quantity supplied, known as a contraction in supply.

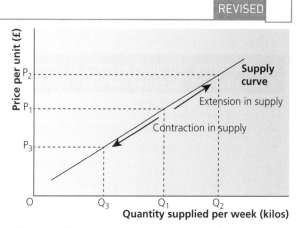

Figure 3.5 Movements along a supply curve

Revision activity

Using graph paper, construct a supply curve to show the information in the table.

Price of coffee (£ per kilo)	Quantity of coffee supplied per week (kilos)
18	400 000
15	350 000
12	300 000
9	250 000
6	200 000
3	150 000

Shifts of a supply curve

REVISED

Several non-price factors may lead to a shift of the supply curve. These are known as the **conditions of supply**:

- **Production costs:** these include wage costs, raw material costs, energy costs, building rent and interest on borrowing.
- **Productivity of labour:** this refers to the output per worker per hour. This can be affected by the amount of training offered and the quality of capital equipment used by workers.
- **Taxes on businesses:** these include excise duties, VAT and business rates.
- **Production subsidies:** these are government grants to firms to encourage greater production.
- **Technology:** improvements in technology may lead to increased productivity of firms.

If any of these factors changes, then the supply curve for the good or service in question will change. This leads either to a rightward or leftward shift of the supply curve as shown in Figure 3.6. A rightward shift is known as an increase in supply, whereas a leftward shift is known as a decrease in supply. A rightward shift means that a greater quantity of a good or service is supplied at any given price, whereas a leftward shift means that a lower quantity of a good or service is supplied at any given price.

Conditions of supply: factors other than the price of the good that lead to a change in position of the supply curve.

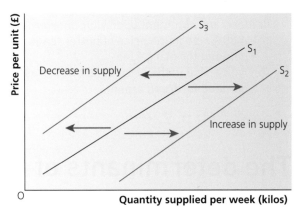

Figure 3.6 Shifts of a supply curve

Revision activity

Assume that warm weather leads to a better coffee harvest than expected, which leads to an increase in supply at every given price. Draw a new supply curve on your previous graph (see the Revision activity above) based on the information below.

Price of coffee (£ per kilo)	Original quantity of coffee supplied per week (kilos)	New quantity of coffee supplied per week (kilos)
18	400 000	430 000
15	350 000	380 000
12	300 000	330 000
9	250 000	280 000
6	200 000	230 000
3	150 000	180 000

Price elasticity of supply (PES)

Price elasticity of supply measures the responsiveness of the quantity supplied of a good or service to a change in price.

The formula is:

$$PES = \frac{\text{percentage change in quantity supplied}}{\text{percentage change in price}}$$

> **Price elasticity of supply:** the responsiveness of the quantity supplied of a good or service to a change in price.

Key values and diagrams

REVISED

Price elasticity of supply will always have a positive value because of the direct relationship between price and quantity supplied.

Price inelastic supply

When the supply of a product is price inelastic, the value of PES is between 0 and 1.

Example — a 20% increase in the price of barley leads to a 5% increase in quantity supplied. So:

$$PES = \frac{+5}{+20} = +0.25$$

The change in price has led to a smaller percentage change in quantity supplied. The supply curve will be relatively steep, as shown in Figure 3.7.

Price elastic supply

When the supply of a product is price elastic, the value of PES is greater than 1.

Example — a 5% fall in the price of carpets leads to a 10% fall in quantity supplied. So:

$$PES = \frac{-10}{-5} = +2.0$$

The change in price has led to a greater percentage increase in quantity supplied. The supply curve will be relatively shallow, as shown in Figure 3.7.

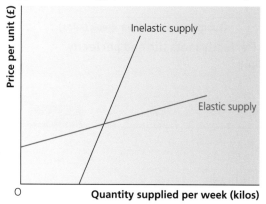

Figure 3.7 Inelastic and elastic supply

Unitary elastic supply

When the supply of a product is unitary elastic, the value of PES is exactly 1. In this case, the supply curve is any straight line drawn through the origin, as shown in Figure 3.8.

Example — a 15% increase in the price of table salt leads to a 15% increase in quantity supplied. So:

$$PE = \frac{+15}{+15} = +1.0$$

The change in price has led to the same percentage change in quantity supplied.

Perfectly inelastic supply

When the supply of a product is perfectly inelastic, the value of PES is zero.

Example — a 5% increase in the price of copper leads to zero increase in the quantity supplied. So:

$$PES = \frac{0}{+5} = 0$$

The change in price has led to zero change in the quantity supplied. The supply curve is vertical as in Figure 3.9.

Perfectly elastic supply

When the supply of a product is perfectly elastic, the value of PES is infinity.

Example — a 2% increase in the price of a downloadable song leads to an infinitely large increase in quantity supplied.

The supply curve for perfectly elastic supply is horizontal as in Figure 3.9.

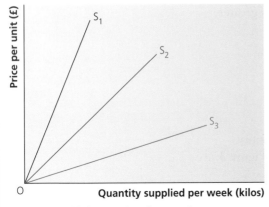

Figure 3.8 Unitary elastic supply

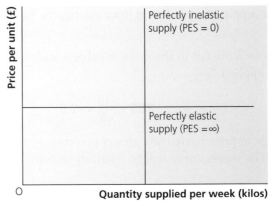

Figure 3.9 Perfectly inelastic and perfectly elastic supply

Determinants of price elasticity of supply

REVISED

The following factors will influence the price elasticity of supply for a good or service:

- **Time taken to expand supply:** if it is difficult or time consuming to increase production, e.g. building a new oil refinery, then supply will tend to be more price inelastic.
- **Size of spare capacity:** firms with machinery, factory space or labour that is not fully utilised will be more able to expand production in the short run. Supply will therefore tend to be more price elastic.
- **Available stocks:** firms with stocks of finished or partly finished goods will be able to respond relatively quickly to a price increase and so supply will tend to be more price elastic.

- **Ease of switching production:** if firms can easily adjust the way they use their factors of production, such as capital and labour, to respond to changes in prices, then supply will tend to be relatively price elastic. However, if a firm has highly specialised equipment and employees, supply will tend to be relatively price inelastic.

The determination of equilibrium market prices

The equilibrium market price and quantity are determined by the interaction of the market demand and supply curve for a particular good or service, as shown in Figure 3.10.

When the quantity demanded equals the quantity supplied in a market for a particular product, the market is in a state of equilibrium. The market will continue to be in a state of equilibrium until one of the conditions of demand or supply changes.

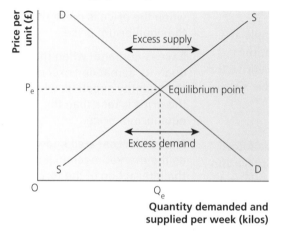

Figure 3.10 Equilibrium price and quantity

Revision activity			
Construct a demand curve and a supply curve on graph paper based on the information in the table. Find the equilibrium price and quantity on your diagram.	**Price of coffee (£ per kilo)**	**Quantity of coffee demanded per week (kilos)**	**Quantity of coffee supplied per week (kilos)**
	18	150 000	400 000
	15	200 000	350 000
	12	250 000	300 000
	9	300 000	250 000
	6	350 000	200 000
	3	400 000	150 000

Market disequilibrium

REVISED

Market **disequilibrium** occurs when the quantity demanded does not equal the quantity supplied. This is illustrated in Figure 3.11.

Market disequilibrium: a situation where the quantity demanded does not equal the quantity supplied.

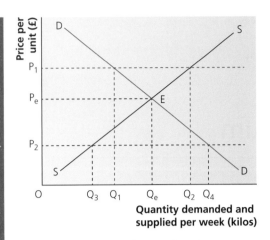

Figure 3.11 Excess demand and excess supply

If the price is above the market equilibrium price of P_e, for example at P_1, then there will be **excess supply**. As shown in the diagram, the quantity demanded is only at Q_1, whilst the relatively high price encourages a greater quantity to be supplied at Q_2. The amount of excess supply is thus $Q_2 - Q_1$.

If the price is below the market equilibrium price of P_e, for example at P_2, then there will be **excess demand**. As shown in the diagram, the quantity demanded is at Q_4, whilst the low price leads to less incentive for firms to supply the product, leading to a lower quantity supplied at Q_3. The amount of excess demand is thus $Q_4 - Q_3$.

Eventually, **market forces** will lead to the excess supply or excess demand being resolved. In the case of excess supply, firms will be forced to reduce their prices, leading to a contraction along the supply curve and an extension along the demand curve, eliminating the excess supply and restoring equilibrium at price P_e and quantity Q_e.

In the case of excess demand, firms are able to increase their prices, leading to an extension along the supply curve and a contraction along the demand curve, eliminating the excess demand and restoring equilibrium at price P_e and quantity Q_e.

> **Excess supply**: when the quantity supplied exceeds the quantity demanded, when the price is more than the equilibrium price.
>
> **Excess demand**: when the quantity demanded exceeds the quantity supplied, when the price is less than the equilibrium price.
>
> **Market forces**: also known as the market mechanism — the interaction of the forces of demand and supply.

Now test yourself

TESTED

8 If the current price is above the free market equilibrium price, state whether there is excess demand or excess supply.
9 Explain how equilibrium would eventually be restored by market forces in question 8, above.

Answers on p. 226–7

Changes in equilibrium price

REVISED

A change in the market equilibrium price may be caused by either a shift of the demand curve or a shift of the supply curve (resulting from a change in the conditions of demand or supply).

An increase in demand

An increase in demand, e.g. for a normal good following an increase in real incomes, would lead to a rightward shift of the demand curve. This would also lead to an increase in equilibrium price and quantity as shown in Figure 3.12.

A decrease in demand

A decrease in demand, e.g. for a normal good following a fall in real incomes, would lead to a leftward shift of the demand curve. This will also lead to a decrease in equilibrium price and quantity as shown in Figure 3.13.

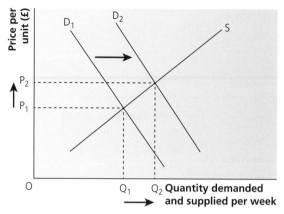

Figure 3.12 An increase in demand

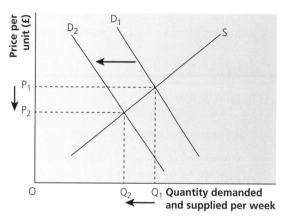

Figure 3.13 A decrease in demand

An increase in supply

An increase in supply, e.g. for coffee following a good harvest, would lead to a rightward shift of the supply curve. This will also lead to a decrease in equilibrium price and an increase in quantity as shown in Figure 3.14.

A decrease in supply

A decrease in supply, e.g. for coffee following a poor harvest, would lead to a leftward shift of the supply curve. This will also lead to an increase in equilibrium price and quantity as shown in Figure 3.15.

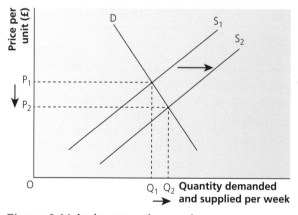

Figure 3.14 An increase in supply

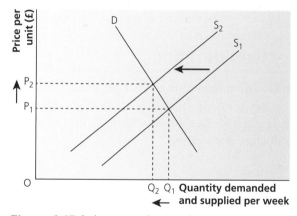

Figure 3.15 A decrease in supply

Now test yourself

10 Using a supply and demand diagram in each of the following cases, explain what happens to the equilibrium price and quantity.
   (a) The market for UK seaside holidays following a rise in real incomes.
   (b) The market for copper following the discovery of more efficient mining techniques.
   (c) The market for petrol following the development of new fuel-efficient cars.
   (d) The market for mobile phones following an increase in labour productivity.

Answer on p. 227

The interrelationship between markets

Shifts of demand and supply curves arise not only from changes in market conditions for the product in question, but also from changes in associated markets. They can also be caused by changes of prices of goods in joint demand, joint supply, composite demand, or derived demand.

Joint demand

REVISED

Products in **joint demand** are also known as complementary goods, i.e. goods that tend to be demanded together, such as cars and fuel. Therefore, as demand for cars increases, so will demand for fuel.

This is the opposite effect to goods that are substitutes, or in competing demand, which can be used as an alternative to another good. For example, as demand for cars increases, the demand for public transport may decrease.

> **Joint demand**: goods that tend to be demanded together, i.e. complementary goods.

Joint supply

REVISED

Joint supply exists when the production of one good also leads to the production of another good. An obvious example is the production of beef and leather, both arising from cattle farming.

> **Joint supply**: when the production of one good leads to the production of another good.

Composite demand

REVISED

Composite demand exists when a good is demanded for more than one distinct use. Therefore an increase in the demand for one of the distinct uses reduces the supply available for other uses.

> **Composite demand**: when a good is demanded for more than one distinct use.

Derived demand

REVISED

Derived demand exists when a particular good or factor of production is necessary for the provision of another good or service, e.g. an increase in the demand for healthcare is likely to lead to an increase in the demand for doctors and nurses.

> **Derived demand**: when a particular good or factor of production is necessary for the provision of another good or service.

Now test yourself

TESTED

11 Give an example of each of the following:
   (a) joint demand
   (b) joint supply
   (c) composite demand
   (d) derived demand

12 Which one of the following best describes the relationship between the demand for coach travel and the demand for coach drivers?
   A joint demand
   B complementary demand
   C competitive demand
   D derived demand

Answers on p. 227

Exam practice

1 The demand curve for games consoles will shift to the right following:
A a fall in wages of games console manufacturers
B an increase in indirect tax on games consoles
C a rise in consumers' real incomes
D a fall in games console manufacturers' spending on advertising [1]
2 The supply curve for milk will shift to the right following:
A an increase in advertising by the milk industry
B a reduction in subsidies to milk producers
C technological improvements in milk production
D an increase in population [1]
3 Which of the following would lead to a rise in the price of petrol?
A improvements in oil extraction technology
B a reduction in supply of oil from Middle Eastern countries
C an increase in demand for cars
D an increase in demand for biofuels [1]
4 The price elasticity of demand for most normal goods is:
A zero
B between zero and –1
C positive
D negative [1]
5 An increase in the incomes of UK consumers leads to an increase in demand for foreign holidays but a fall in demand for holidays in the UK. The reason for this is:
A Foreign holidays have a high price elasticity of demand while holidays in the UK have a low price elasticity of demand.
B There is a negative cross elasticity of demand between foreign holidays and UK holidays.
C Demand for foreign holidays is income elastic whereas demand for UK holidays is income inelastic.
D Holidays in the UK are an inferior good while foreign holidays are a normal good. [1]
6 Which of the following would lead to an increase in total revenue?
A a decrease in the price of a good with price inelastic demand
B a decrease in the price of a good with price elastic demand
C an increase in the price of a good with price elastic demand
D an increase in the price of a good with unitary elastic demand [1]
7 With the help of a diagram, explain what would happen in the market for cars following an increase in the price of petrol. [8]

Answers and quick quiz 3 online ONLINE

Summary

You should have an understanding of:
- The meaning of a competitive market.
- The nature of the demand curve.
- The determinants of demand.
- The nature of the supply curve.
- The determinants of supply.
- How to calculate price elasticity of demand and how to interpret the results.
- The factors influencing PED.
- The relationship between PED and total revenue.
- How to calculate income elasticity of demand and how to interpret the results.
- The difference between normal goods and inferior goods.
- How to calculate cross elasticity of demand and how to interpret the results.
- The difference between substitutes and complements.
- How to calculate price elasticity of supply and how to interpret the results.
- The factors influencing price elasticity of supply.
- How changes in price lead to movements along demand and supply curves.
- How changes in the conditions of demand and supply cause shifts of the demand and supply curves for particular products.
- How equilibrium price and quantity is determined.
- Excess demand and excess supply and how market forces will eventually eliminate these disequilibrium situations.
- The possible interrelationships between different markets.

4 Production, costs and revenue

Production and productivity

Production

REVISED

The term 'production' refers to the total output of goods and services produced by an individual, firm or country. It also describes the process of converting inputs of raw materials and the services of the various factors of production, such as labour and capital machinery, into outputs.

> **Production:** the total output of goods and services produced by an individual, firm or country.
>
> **Productivity:** a measurement of the rate of production by one or more factors of production.

Productivity

While the term 'production' relates to the total output produced, **productivity** is a measurement of the rate of production by one, or all, of the various factors of production. It is thus a measure of how efficient an individual worker, firm or country is at generating output. Productivity may be defined as the output per factor of production employed per unit of time. If one hairdresser can complete 10 haircuts per day, whilst another can complete 12 in the same time, the latter is more productive. Similarly, if a football striker averages 1.5 goals per game over a season, he or she is more productive than one who averages 0.8 goals per game.

Measurement of productivity

The formula for measuring productivity is:

$$\text{Productivity} = \frac{\text{total output per period of time}}{\text{number of units of factor of production}}$$

Thus, the formula for labour productivity would be expressed as:

$$\text{Labour productivity} = \frac{\text{total output per period of time}}{\text{number of units of labour}}$$

Labour costs tend to be the most significant part of total costs for many firms and so **labour productivity** is an important determinant of how competitive firms and individual countries are.

> **Labour productivity:** output per worker per unit of time.

TESTED

Now test yourself

1 Explain the difference between production and productivity.
2 Calculate the daily productivity of a coffee shop with 3 members of staff who make and sell 450 cups of coffee per day.

Answers on p. 227

Improvements in labour productivity can arise from more and better education and training and from increased motivation. Advances in technology, leading to workers being equipped with the latest capital equipment, can also lead to increased labour productivity. Specialisation and division of labour also facilitate more effective use of specialist capital equipment, which can lead to further increases in labour productivity.

Specialisation, division of labour and exchange

Specialisation

REVISED

Specialisation involves an individual worker, firm, region or country producing a limited range of goods or services. Examples of specialisation at each level include:

● an individual worker specialising as a tax accountant
● an individual firm specialising in accountancy, e.g. PwC
● an individual region specialising in investment banking, e.g. the City of London
● an individual country specialising in the provision of financial services, e.g. the UK

Division of labour

REVISED

Specialisation at the level of the individual worker is referred to as the division of labour.

Adam Smith, in his very famous book *The Wealth of Nations*, published in 1776, described the division of labour among groups of workers in a pin factory. Smith argued that, without specialisation, one worker making pins from start to finish might make 20 pins per day, while ten workers specialising in the individual tasks involved might be able to make 48,000 pins per day.

The importance of exchange

REVISED

Specialisation and the **division of labour** are only viable if an efficient system of **exchange** exists so that, for example, a tax accountant is able to exchange his services for payment so that he can buy food and pay his rent.

Similarly, a country such as the UK can only specialise, to a large extent, in financial services if it is able to exchange this output for other goods and services that it is less able to produce efficiently, such as food and key raw materials.

Throughout most of history, and still in some parts of the world today, exchange has relied upon a system known as barter. Barter involves the exchange of goods and services for other goods and services. A system of exchange involving money as a medium of exchange avoids the need for barter; money also has the benefit of being easily divisible, unlike a particular good.

> **Specialisation**: where an individual worker, firm, region or country produces a limited range of goods or services.
>
> **Division of labour**: specialisation at the level of an individual worker.
>
> **Exchange**: where one thing is traded for something else, e.g. an hour's work is given in return for a set rate of pay.

The benefits of specialisation and division of labour

REVISED

● Repetition of a limited range of activities can increase skill and aptitude, leading to a worker becoming an expert, e.g. a neurosurgeon.
● Reduced time spent moving between different tasks or workstations means increased productivity.
● As tasks are broken up into smaller ones, it becomes efficient to use specialist machinery.
● Division of labour allows people to work to their natural strengths, for example physical strength, technical skill or the ability to communicate.

The significance of the short run versus the long run

REVISED

When considering costs of production, economists often distinguish between the **short run** and the **long run** in terms of periods of time. The short run is usually defined as the period of time in which at least one factor of production is fixed in terms of the number of units a firm can use. This helps to define its capacity, or scale of output. In the short run, the most likely factors of production to be fixed are land or capital equipment, while access to labour tends to be more flexible, though not entirely. In the short run, then, firms will have some fixed costs of production for which they must pay even if they do not produce any output, along with variable costs of production that change with the level of output.

In contrast, the long run can be defined as the period of time over which a firm can vary all the factors of production it uses and thus may increase or reduce its scale of output.

> **Short run**: a period of time in which the availability of at least one factor of production is fixed.
>
> **Long run**: a period of time over which all factors of production can be varied.

Costs of production

Fixed and variable costs

REVISED

When an entrepreneur combines the various factors of production to create output and seek a profit, these factors of production incur costs.

Costs are the expenses a business must pay to secure the services of the factors of production and to obtain raw materials. A firm's total costs are made up of fixed costs and variable costs.

Fixed costs

Fixed costs do not vary directly with output in the short run. Examples may include:
- rents on business premises
- buildings insurance
- quarterly heating and lighting bills
- salaries of senior staff
- annual marketing and advertising budget

Average fixed costs (AFC), however, fall as output increases because the firm is able to spread the fixed costs over an increasing volume of output, as shown in Figure 4.1. This is a key incentive for firms to increase their output.

$$AFC = \frac{\text{total fixed costs}}{\text{output}}$$

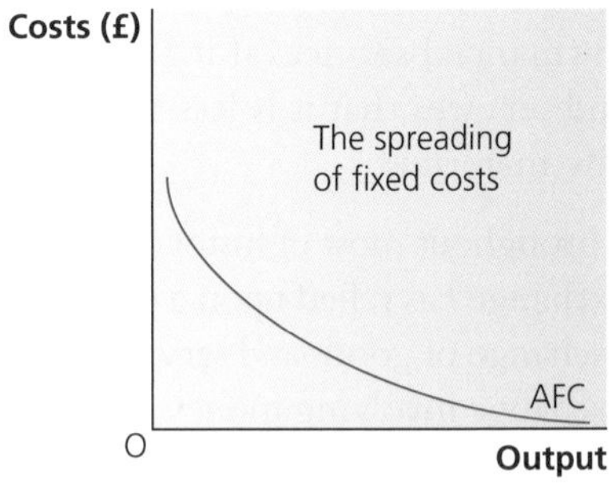

> **Fixed costs**: costs of production that do not vary with the level of output in the short run.

Figure 4.1 **Average fixed cost curve slopes downwards**

Variable costs

Variable costs are those that vary directly with the level of output. Examples may include:
- raw materials
- packaging
- wages of casual staff
- fuel for delivery vehicles
- distribution costs

> **Variable costs**: costs of production that vary with the level of output.

As shown in Figure 4.2, average variable costs (AVC) initially fall in the short run, but begin to rise at higher levels of output as more units of factors of production (probably labour) begin to overcrowd fixed factors of production. This leads to bottlenecks and disruptions to production. A good analogy here is a busy restaurant kitchen that becomes overcrowded with chefs and other staff; employees get in each other's way, leading to increased wastage and reduced productivity.

$$AVC = \frac{\text{total variable costs}}{\text{output}}$$

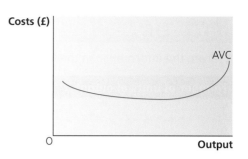

Figure 4.2 Average variable costs

Now test yourself

TESTED ☐

3 Which of the following would be considered a variable cost of production in the short run?
A heating and lighting
B building rent
C salaries of senior staff
D packaging costs

Answer on p. 227

> **Exam tip**
>
> Make sure you know the difference between the short run and the long run and between fixed costs and variable costs.

Total costs (TC)

REVISED ☐

Total costs are made up of total fixed costs and total variable costs of production:

Total costs (TC) = total fixed costs (TFC) + total variable costs (TVC)

Average total costs, or costs per unit of output, are found by dividing total costs by the output being produced:

$$\text{Average total cost (ATC)} = \frac{\text{total costs (TC)}}{\text{output}}$$

And, as shown in Figure 4.3:

Average total costs (ATC) = average fixed costs (AFC) + average variable costs (AVC)

> **Total cost**: the addition of fixed costs and variable costs at a given level of output.
>
> **Average total cost**: total costs of production divided by the number of units of output.

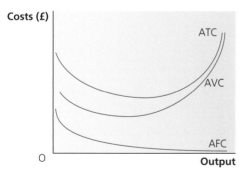

Figure 4.3 Adding average fixed costs and average variable costs to show average total costs

Now test yourself

4 From the information in the table, what is the total cost of producing 4 units of output?

Number of units of output	Average fixed cost (AFC) (£)	Average variable cost (AVC) (£)
1	60	40
2	30	30
3	20	20
4	15	25

A £40
B £100
C £160
D £200

Answer on p. 227

Marginal cost

Marginal cost is the addition to a firm's total costs from making an additional unit of output. Linked to the law of diminishing marginal returns explained later in this chapter, as increasing units of variable factors of production are added to a fixed factor in the short run, marginal cost of production initially declines and then begins to rise. This is because as units of factors of production, e.g. labour, become increasingly less productive, the wage cost per unit of output will begin to rise.

The shape of the marginal cost curve, along with all short-run cost curves, is shown in Figure 4.4.

> **Marginal cost:** the addition to a firm's total costs from making an additional unit of output.

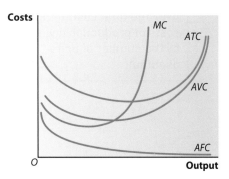

Figure 4.4 Short-run cost curves

The law of diminishing returns and returns to scale

Diminishing returns

In the short run, where at least one factor of production is fixed in supply, costs may be influenced by **the law of diminishing returns.**

> **The law of diminishing returns:** when additional units of variable factors of production are added to a fixed factor, marginal output or product will eventually decrease.

This concept can be explained easily if we take a fairly simple example of a busy restaurant kitchen, as additional chefs are employed over a busy period. In the short run the chefs (labour) are the variable factor, while the fixed factor is assumed to be the kitchen (capital). As increasing numbers of customer orders come in, the first few workers are likely to contribute increasing returns in the form of increasing productivity as they work effectively together as a team. They benefit from increased specialisation and division of labour, e.g. chefs focusing on a limited range of tasks such as sauces or desserts, and little time is lost from chefs moving between different types of task.

However, as the kitchen becomes busier and more chefs are employed, the chefs may begin to get in each other's way, leading to reduced productivity as more mistakes occur. This is the law of diminishing returns in action.

Figure 4.5 shows the law of diminishing returns as additional units of labour are added to a fixed factor such as land or capital. After the employment of the fifth chef, the addition of each successive chef adds less to total product than previous chefs and thus marginal product diminishes.

> **Typical mistake**
>
> Students often confuse diminishing returns, a short-run phenomenon, with diseconomies of scale or decreasing returns to scale, which are strictly long-run phenomena.

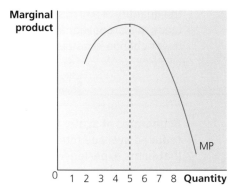

Figure 4.5 Marginal product increases and eventually decreases as diminishing returns set in

Now test yourself

TESTED ☐

5 From the following table, identify the number of workers at which diminishing marginal returns begin to occur.

Number of workers	Total returns (units of output)
1	10
2	22
3	35
4	42
5	47

A 4
B 2
C 3
D 1

Answer on p. 227

Costs of production in the long run

Returns to scale

In the long run, where all factors can be variable, costs are likely to be influenced by increasing or decreasing returns to scale. **Returns to scale** refer to the relationship between increases in the quantity of a firm's inputs and the proportional change in output.

There are three possible scenarios:
- **Increasing returns to scale:** where an increase in the quantity of a firm's inputs leads to a proportionally greater change in output, e.g. a 5% increase in labour leads to a 10% increase in output.
- **Constant returns to scale:** where an increase in the quantity of a firm's inputs leads to a proportionally identical change in output, e.g. a 5% increase in labour leads to a 5% increase in output.
- **Decreasing returns to scale:** where an increase in the quantity of a firm's inputs leads to a proportionally lower change in output, e.g. a 10% increase in labour leads to a 5% increase in output.

> **Returns to scale:** the relationship between increases in the quantity of a firm's inputs and the proportional change in output.
> **Increasing returns to scale:** where an increase in the quantity of a firm's inputs leads to a proportionally greater change in output.
> **Constant returns to scale:** where an increase in the quantity of a firm's inputs leads to a proportionally identical change in output.
> **Decreasing returns to scale:** where an increase in the quantity of a firm's inputs leads to a proportionally lower change in output.

Economies and diseconomies of scale

Economies of scale

Economies of scale are the benefits that can arise as a firm increases its output, leading to reduced average total costs. These cost reductions reflect improvements in productive efficiency. They may give a firm a competitive advantage in the market in which it operates by enabling it to pass on lower prices to consumers and/or generating higher profits that might be re-invested or passed on to shareholders.

> **Economies of scale:** the reduced average total costs that firms experience by increasing output in the long run.

There is a range of potential economies of scale available to firms, depending on the specific features of the industry in which the firm operates, and several may be available at once. For example, the cost of laptop computers has tended to come down steadily as manufacturers such as Apple, HP and Lenovo exploit economies of scale in production and pass these cost savings on to consumers. Figure 4.6 shows that, as a firm increases its output from O in the long run, average costs begin to fall up to output Q_1, due to the effect of one or more economies of scale.

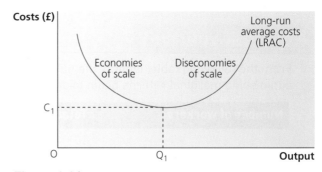

Figure 4.6 **Long-run average cost curve**

Internal economies of scale

Internal economies of scale are those that come about as a result of the growth of the firm itself, and include:
- **Financial economies of scale.** The larger and more reputable a firm is, the more likely it is that banks and other lenders will deem it credit-worthy and a less risky recipient of loan funds. This will lead to it being offered cheaper loans with lower rates of interest, which reduce its costs. On the other hand, smaller, less well-known firms tend not to be able to access the cheapest costs of borrowing, as they are perceived to be more risky. Purchasing economies, where larger firms

> **Internal economies of scale:** reductions in long-run average total costs arising from growth of the firm.

Exam practice answers and quick quizzes at **www.hoddereducation.co.uk/myrevisionnotes**

can take advantage of bulk-buying discounts, are another example of financial economies of scale. This means that firms such as the large supermarkets can exert significant buying power when purchasing groceries from suppliers that a smaller, convenience store cannot do.

● **Technical economies of scale.** Larger businesses can generally afford the latest, specialist capital equipment, which is often very expensive. For example, the world's biggest car manufacturing firms such as Toyota and the Volkswagen Group have the financial resources to invest in bespoke assembly lines that increase productivity and reduce average costs of production. A smaller manufacturer such as Aston Martin would not find it cost effective to invest in such technology, so its unit costs are likely to be higher.

● **Marketing economies of scale.** Larger firms are likely to have huge advertising budgets, for example Marks and Spencer's typically lavish TV marketing campaigns around Christmas. However, because of the large volume of sales made by Marks and Spencer, the firm can spread this budget over a larger output than a smaller retailer. This can give larger firms a significant competitive advantage.

● **Managerial economies of scale.** Larger firms can afford to recruit the highest-profile chief executive officers (CEOs) who tend to attract substantial salaries but also tend to be the most effective in increasing profits through a combination of increasing revenues and reducing costs. Furthermore, larger firms can take greater advantage of the division of labour. Large financial services firms, such as PwC, can afford to have specialist managers in areas such as audit, tax and corporate finance, leading to increased productivity and competitive advantage in these areas. A smaller firm of accountants may be forced to provide a more general service, relying on personal service as a source of competitive advantage rather than cost efficiency.

> **Revision activity**
>
> Explain how any two economies of scale may be applied to the sea fishing industry.

External economies of scale

REVISED

External economies of scale occur when firms benefit from the growth of the industry in which they operate. For example, the development of a successful financial services industry centred on the City of London has meant that firms in London have benefited from easier access to specialised labour and infrastructure, such as transport links to the centre of the financial district.

> **External economies of scale**: reductions in long-run average total costs arising from growth of the industry in which a firm operates.

Diseconomies of scale

REVISED

Diseconomies of scale occur when an increase in a firm's output ceases to yield a reduction in average costs and begins to lead to an increase in average costs of production. This is shown in Figure 4.6 at output levels beyond Q_1. Research suggests several possible sources of diseconomies of scale, arising mainly from problems of managing large businesses:

● **Coordination and control.** As a firm becomes larger, it becomes more difficult to monitor what all resources are doing and how they are deployed. This is likely to lead to increased wastage and loss of quality, leading to increased costs.

● **Communication.** As a firm grows in size, particularly if it is a multinational company operating on different continents in different time zones, it can become difficult to communicate effectively with all offices and staff, leading to ineffective decision making and delays in action. Furthermore, management theory suggests that employees are more likely to feel like 'small fish in a big pond' in larger businesses, leading to a lack of motivation and productivity.

> **Diseconomies of scale**: increases in average total costs that firms may experience by increasing output in the long run.

> **Exam tip**
>
> It is worth being aware of a few examples of very large businesses that have suffered from diseconomies of scale. Large supermarkets and banks have arguably been affected in recent years.

The minimum efficient scale of production

The **minimum efficient scale (MES)** is the lowest level of output at which average total costs of production are minimised.

In Figure 4.6 the minimum efficient scale occurs at output Q_1. The significance of the MES is that in industries where the MES occurs at a large scale of output, only large firms will be able to achieve this. Once achieved, this can act as a significant barrier to entry for any potential new competitors in an industry, leading to the dominance of one or a small number of powerful firms. However, the efficiency benefit may be an argument in favour of large firms with monopoly power, and in favour of mergers or takeovers in order to achieve this level of output. Consider the tendency in recent decades for mergers between large car manufacturers and European airlines, for example. The concept of the MES has a bearing on competition policy, which is explored in Chapter 8.

> **Minimum efficient scale (MES):** the lowest level of output at which average total costs of production are minimised.

> **Exam tips**
>
> You should understand the significance of the minimum efficient scale for the structure of an industry and barriers to entry.
> The concept of minimum efficient scale may be used as an argument in favour of large, dominant firms, since firms may need to be large to achieve maximum economies of scale.

Now test yourself

TESTED

6 An industry has a high minimum efficient scale relative to the total scale of the industry. This is likely to lead to:
   A   a highly concentrated market
   B   a highly competitive market
   C   low barriers to entry
   D   diminishing marginal returns

Answer on p. 227

Average revenue, total revenue and profit

Marginal revenue (MR), total revenue (TR) and average revenue (AR)

A firm's **total revenue** is found by multiplying price (P) × quantity sold (or demanded) (Q):

$$\text{Total revenue (TR)} = \text{price (P)} \times \text{quantity (Q)}$$

Figure 4.7 shows how total revenue changes as price changes. At a price of £500, 20 products are demanded per week, giving a total revenue of £10000. If price is reduced to £300, 60 products are demanded per week, giving a total revenue of £18000. In order to calculate **average revenue**, total revenue is divided by the quantity sold:

$$\text{Average revenue (AR)} = \frac{\text{total revenue (TR)}}{\text{quantity (Q)}}$$

Note that average revenue is the same as price, as a simple examination of the above two formulae reveals. Thus the average revenue shows the quantity demanded at each price, which means that the demand curve can also be said to be the average revenue curve.

> **Total revenue:** the money a firm receives from selling its output, calculated by price x quantity sold.

> **Average revenue:** total revenue divided by units of output. Equal to price in a firm that sells one product at a fixed price.

7 What is the average revenue of a firm that sells 800 units of a product for a total of £56 000?

  A £7
  B £77
  C £70
  D £700

Answer on p. 227

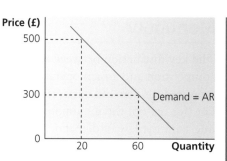

Figure 4.7 Total revenue, average revenue and the demand curve

Marginal revenue

REVISED ☐

Marginal revenue is the addition to a firm's total revenue from selling an additional unit of output. The formula can be stated as:

$$\text{Marginal revenue (MR)} = \frac{\text{change in total revenue}}{\text{change in output}}$$

> **Marginal revenue:** the addition to a firm's total revenue from selling an additional unit of output.

Market structure and marginal and average revenue

Perfect competition

REVISED ☐

As explained in more detail in Chapter 5, a perfectly competitive firm is characterised by:

- a large number of buyers and sellers
- no firm is large enough to influence the market price — each is a 'price taker'
- perfect knowledge of the market
- no barriers to entry to or exit from the market
- each firm sells an identical product

The result of these particular conditions is that firms in perfect competition face a perfectly elastic demand curve, as shown in Figure 4.8. At the ruling market price P_1, the firm can sell all the units of output it can produce. This constant price means that both average revenue (AR) and marginal revenue (MR) are constant, as shown in the left-hand figure.

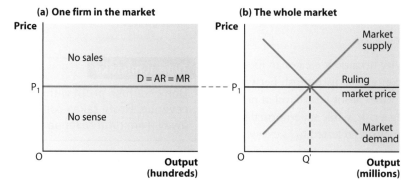

Figure 4.8 A perfectly competitive firm faces horizontal demand, average and marginal revenue curves

> **Exam tip**
>
> Note the relationship between the market and the individual firm in perfect competition. The individual firm is obliged to take the ruling market price.

Monopoly

The key distinction between the demand curve for a firm in perfect competition and a firm operating as a pure monopoly is that a pure monopolist's demand curve is effectively the entire market demand curve. For this reason, the monopolist's demand curve is downward-sloping. In line with the law of demand, the monopolist has to reduce price to bring about an increase in quantity demanded. The monopolist's demand curve is also its AR curve.

However, the monopolist's MR curve slopes downwards twice as steeply as the AR curve, as shown in Figure 4.9. Because the market demand or average revenue curve falls as output increases, the firm's marginal revenue curve must be below the average revenue curve.

> **Exam tip**
>
> Note that the monopolist's demand (AR) curve is effectively the market demand curve and hence is downward-sloping.

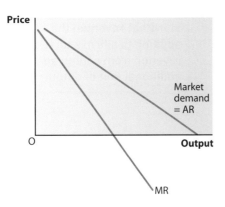

Figure 4.9 A monopolist faces downward-sloping demand, average and marginal revenue curves

Now test yourself

TESTED

8 Explain why a monopolist faces downward-sloping average revenue and marginal revenue curves, while a firm in perfect competition faces horizontal ones.

Answer on p. 227

Profit

Profit is the difference between total revenue and total costs. In other words:

Total profit = total revenue – total costs

If this figure is negative, the firm is making a loss.

Profit is an important driver of business activity because it creates an incentive for entrepreneurs to take a business risk. Economists distinguish between **normal profit** and **supernormal profit**. Normal profit is the level of profit required to reward the entrepreneur for taking a risk, while supernormal profit is the profit over and above normal profit, sometimes referred to as excess profit.

> **Profit**: the difference between total revenue and total costs.

> **Typical mistake**
>
> Don't confuse profit with revenue. Profit takes costs away from total revenue.

> **Normal profit**: the minimum level of profit required to reward the entrepreneur for taking a risk and therefore to stay in a particular line of business.
>
> **Supernormal profit**: profit over and above normal profit, sometimes referred to as abnormal or excess profit.

Technological change

Technological change arises out of inventions and innovations. It can have significant impacts upon firms and industries, including upon methods of production, productivity and efficiency. It can lead to the development of new products and new markets and the destruction of existing markets.

Invention is the creation of a product or process, while **innovation** is the improvement or development of an existing product, bringing it to market.

The effects of technological change on a firm's long-run costs of production are shown in Figure 4.10. Long-run average total costs are reduced, reflecting dynamic efficiency.

Invention: the creation of a product or process.

Innovation: new products and production processes that are developed into marketable goods or services.

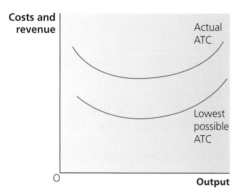

Figure 4.10 The effects of technological change on a firm's long-run costs of production

Technological change can make some markets more competitive, e.g. in the case of the internet, while it can make others less competitive if the technology is protected by a patent, which effectively gives a legally backed monopoly for up to 20 years.

Creative destruction

REVISED

Linked to technological change is the concept of **creative destruction**. Firms that have previously enjoyed monopoly power could easily see this eroded by the development of new 'disruptive' technologies that effectively create new markets or revolutionise old ones. Throughout time, developments such as the engine, the telephone and the internet have significantly transformed the way businesses work. More recently, internet-based firms that make use of specific platforms or apps have used disruptive technology to undermine the monopoly power of existing firms. Examples include eBay, Amazon, Apple, Uber and Just Eat.

Creative destruction: where technological change leads to the development of new, 'disruptive' products which render existing products obsolete.

Now test yourself

TESTED

9 Complete the following table, assuming each football sells for £5 and that variable costs are constant at £2 per unit.

Quantity of footballs sold	Total revenue (£)	Total fixed costs (£)	Total variable costs (£)	Total costs (£)	Profit (£)
10	A	100	H	L	P
20	B	E	I	M	Q
30	C	F	J	N	R
40	D	G	K	O	S

Answer on p. 227

Exam practice

1 Which of the following is most likely to lead to increased labour productivity in an industry?
   A an increase in the number of firms in the industry
   B a reduction in wages paid in the industry
   C an increase in new capital equipment in the industry
   D an increase in demand in the industry   [1]
2 Calculate the productivity of the four firms in the following example and complete the table.   [4]

Firm	Total output (units)	Number of employees	Productivity (output per employee)
A	140	7	
B	350	25	
C	88	11	
D	261	9	

3 Explain why specialisation and the division of labour may increase productivity.   [4]
4 With the aid of a diagram, explain what happens to a firm's fixed and variable costs in the short run. [6]
5 Explain why a firm's costs of production may be influenced by diminishing returns in the short
   run and increasing returns to scale in the long run.   [9]
6 With the aid of a diagram, explain possible reasons for the shape of a firm's average total cost
   curve in the long run.   [9]
7 Explain how the airline industry might benefit from economies of scale.   [9]
8 Discuss whether technological change has made markets more or less efficient.   [25]

Answers and quick quiz 4 online

ONLINE

Summary

You should have an understanding of:
- The distinction between production and productivity.
- How to calculate labour productivity.
- The meaning of specialisation and the division of labour.
- The need for exchange in allowing for specialisation and division of labour.
- The distinction between the short run and the long run in economics.
- The law of diminishing returns.
- The difference between increasing, constant and decreasing returns to scale.
- The difference between fixed and variable costs of production.
- The difference between marginal, average and total costs and reasons for the shape of their curves.
- The difference between short-run and long-run costs.

- How the price and productivity of factor inputs affect firms' costs of production and choice of factors of production to use.
- Economies and diseconomies of scale.
- The difference between internal and external economies of scale.
- The concept of the minimum efficient scale of production.
- Marginal, average and total revenue and the relationship between these.
- The meaning of profit and the difference between normal and supernormal profit.
- The difference between invention and innovation.
- How technological change can affect methods of production, productivity, efficiency and firms' costs of production and the structure of markets.
- How the process of creative destruction is linked to technological change.

5 Perfect competition, imperfectly competitive markets and monopoly

Market structures

The term **market structure** refers to the number and size of firms within a market for a particular good or service and the extent to which they compete with one another.

Some markets are supplied by a large number of small firms, for example commodities such as wheat. Other markets are supplied by one firm, or a small number of firms, for example internet search engines such as Google.

> **Market structure:** the number and size of firms within a market for a particular good or service.

The spectrum of competition

REVISED

By far the best way to appreciate this idea is to consider the spectrum of competition. As shown in Figure 5.1, this ranges from **perfect competition** at one end to **pure monopoly** at the other end.

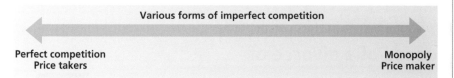

Figure 5.1 **A spectrum of competition**

In theory, perfect competition is the most competitive form of market structure. Few examples exist of such markets, but the workings of the stock market, or some agricultural markets such as wheat farming, have been considered examples of perfect competition.

Pure monopoly exists when one, and only one, firm supplies the market and it is the least competitive form of market, in theory. Again, there are few examples in reality, although the Royal Mail used to have a legally enforced monopoly for the delivery of letters.

> **Perfect competition:** a market structure that has a large number of buyers and sellers who have perfect information about the market, identical products and few, if any, barriers to entry.
>
> **Imperfect competition:** any market structure that is not perfect competition.
>
> **Pure monopoly:** When only one firm supplies the market.

The objectives of firms

An objective is a target or aim. Firms may have a range of possible objectives.

Profit maximisation

REVISED

The main objective of firms is assumed to be **maximising profit**, i.e. making the maximum positive difference between costs and revenues. A basic assumption of economic theory is that entrepreneurs are encouraged to take business risk and start trading if they believe a profit can be made. There are several benefits to firms of maximising profits. Making large profits can enable firms to:
- re-invest funds into developing new products that lead to them to gain more customers
- pay out higher returns to shareholders which may encourage more people to buy shares in the company, or help boost the share price

> **Profit maximisation:** when a firm seeks to make the largest positive difference between total revenue and total costs.

> **Exam tip**
>
> Unless told otherwise, assume that the primary objective of firms in economic theory is to maximise profits.

Profit maximisation occurs when a firm's total revenue (TR) exceeds total costs (TC) by the greatest amount. The profit-maximising rule for firms in all market structures is also stated as the level of output where marginal cost (MC) = marginal revenue (MR). This means that the cost of producing the last unit is equal to the revenue gained from selling that last unit.

As shown in Figure 5.2, as MC meets MR from below, at output M_1, profit is maximised. While MC is also equal to MR at output M, crucially this is the *profit minimisation* or loss maximisation level of output, as the cost of every unit of output up to this point has exceeded the addition to total revenue. Between output M and M_1, the addition to total revenue exceeds the addition to total cost.

Exam tip

Note that the profit-maximising rule for every firm in each type of market structure is MC = MR.

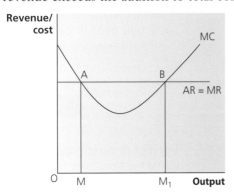

Figure 5.2 The profit-maximising rule for a firm in perfect competition

The possible consequences of a divorce of ownership from control

REVISED

In modern management theory, the **divorce of ownership from control** that exists in large firms may mean that profit maximisation is not always achieved. Large corporations may be predominantly owned by shareholders who are separate from the day-to-day running of the business, having bought shares in various businesses on the stock market as a form of financial investment. On their behalf, the businesses are run by a board of directors who may not hold any shares.

Divorce of ownership from control: the separation that exists between owners of the firm (shareholders) and directors in large public limited companies.

This separation of ownership from control may lead to conflicting objectives, with the directors pursuing their own objectives, and with profit maximisation, the assumed shareholder objective, not being a top priority.

Objectives of directors, who run the business on a day-to-day basis, may include:
- **Growth maximisation:** since growth of a firm may serve to boost the profile and CV of senior managers, including more column inches in publications such as the *Financial Times*. It may also reduce the threat of takeover by other firms, contributing to a 'quiet life' for senior executives.
- **Sales revenue maximisation:** as executive pay and bonuses may be linked to annual sales revenue rather than profit, this is likely to lead to a firm not targeting profit maximisation as its primary objective.
- **Satisficing:** given that it is likely to be extremely difficult in practice to produce at the precise output at which MC = MR, firms are more able to target a satisfactory, sub-optimal level of profit rather than a maximal one. This is shown in Figure 5.3. Profit maximisation occurs at a single, specific output, Q_1, which will be hard to achieve. A satisfactory level of profit (P_{sat}) that most shareholders will be happy with can be achieved at any level of output between Q_2 and Q_3. Note

that managers will be also operating with imperfect information and shareholders will be subject to asymmetric information about the intentions and objectives of the managers, making **satisficing** a realistic view of what happens.

Satisficing: making do with a satisfactory, sub-optimal level of profit.

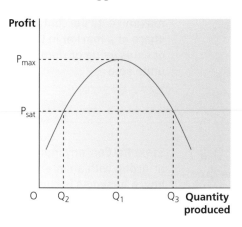

Figure 5.3 Profit satisficing

Now test yourself

TESTED

1 Outline as many reasons as you can why large businesses may not always be able to maximise profits.

Answer on p. 227

Sales maximisation

REVISED

This occurs when firms' sales revenue is at a maximum. Sales maximisation occurs at the level of output at which the sale of one more unit would not add to overall revenue. This can help the firm benefit from economies of scale.

Exam tip

Don't confuse profit maximisation with sales revenue maximisation.

Survival

REVISED

A large proportion of new businesses fail in the first few years of operation. In its early stages of life, therefore, a key objective of a firm might simply be to survive the critical period before it establishes a customer base and repeat sales, and is able to cover its costs.

Growth

REVISED

Once a firm has survived the critical first few years of its life, its owners are likely to pursue an objective of growth. This will involve a firm increasing its output and scale of operations, possibly in terms of expanding its productive base and the size of its workforce. Growth means that a firm may be able to take advantage of various economies of scale outlined earlier in Chapter 4. This objective will also help a business fend off any takeover bids from rival companies.

Increasing market share

Linked to the objective of growth is one of **increasing market share**. Having the highest market share for a particular product can give a firm the benefits of monopoly power outlined later in this chapter, although this may also attract attention from the government, which may fear that such firms could abuse their power.

> **Increasing market share:** when a firm seeks to maximise its percentage share of a market in terms of sales value or number of units sold.

Stakeholder objectives

The preceding objectives assume that all firms are predominantly interested in achieving financial objectives. A more modern view is that firms may achieve financial and non-financial objectives at the same time. Firms are seen to be looking to satisfy the needs of a range of business **stakeholders**. Firms may take the view, for example, that looking after the needs of their employees is at least as important as maximising profit. If there is a genuine commitment to doing this, this may show the firm in a good light, which may lead to it being seen as a good place to work.

> **Stakeholder:** any individual or group with an interest in how a business is run.

Now test yourself

2 A newly started business is most likely to aim for which of the following objectives in the short run?
   A   sales maximisation
   B   stakeholder objectives
   C   survival
   D   growth

Answer on p. 227

Perfect competition

Understanding perfect competition

'Perfect' does not necessarily mean 'best' in this sense. It means an extremely competitive market, made up of a large number of small firms, with each firm being too small to influence the market price on its own. Indeed, firms which exist in a perfectly competitive market are described as **price takers**, since they are obliged by market forces to accept the market equilibrium price, or risk going out of business.

> **Price taker:** a firm that is unable to influence the ruling market price and thus has to accept it.

Assumptions of perfect competition include:
- few, if any, barriers to entry to a market
- consumers and firms have complete, or perfect, knowledge of all the products supplied by firms, as well as their prices
- products are identical, or homogeneous

The impact of these features is that any firm that tries to sell its product at a price higher than the market equilibrium will not make any sales, since consumers will know about the cheaper alternatives and, since all products are identical, have no loyalty to any particular firm. Therefore all firms must accept the market price if they are to remain in the market.

Price determination in highly competitive markets

We can show how perfect competition works using supply and demand analysis, shown in Figure 5.4.

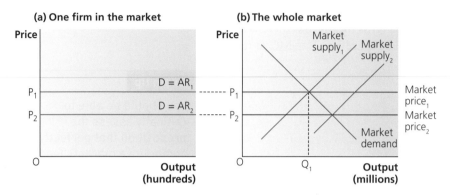

Figure 5.4 Price determination in highly competitive markets

Figure 5.4(b) shows a highly competitive market, with firms supplying this market earning supernormal profits. Initial market equilibrium price is P_1 and market output is Q_1. This leads to each individual firm facing price P_1, as in Figure 5.4(a). Because of the key features of highly competitive markets, if other firms become aware that the existing firms in the market are earning supernormal profits, which they can easily do because of the existence of perfect information, they will enter the market easily due to the low, possibly non-existent barriers to entry.

This will have the effect of increasing overall supply in the market, as shown in Figure 5.4(b), which leads to a rightward shift of the market supply curve. This reduces the equilibrium price to P_2 as output increases beyond Q_1. This increase in supply and reduction in price will occur up to the point at which only normal profit is made, meaning that only the most competitive firms survive in the market.

In the short run it is possible for a firm to be making a loss, normal profit or supernormal profit. The latter case is shown in Figure 5.5.

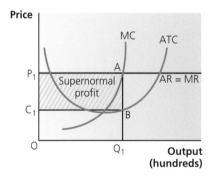

Figure 5.5 Short-run profit maximisation under perfect competition

Exam tip

While there are few, if any, real-world examples of perfect competition, in both product and labour markets, the model provides a yardstick for judging the extent to which markets perform efficiently or inefficiently, and the extent to which a misallocation of resources occurs.

Perfect competition in the long run

Because of the particular features of perfect competition, perfectly competitive firms will be able to make only normal profit in the long run. Any supernormal profit will encourage firms to enter the industry, increasing market supply, while firms making losses will leave the market in the long run. The overall effect is to leave only those firms making normal profit in the market. This situation is illustrated in Figure 5.6, with individual firms producing at the profit-maximising output Q_1 and price P_1. In the long run, firms in perfect competition are both productively efficient and allocatively efficient. Productive efficiency occurs where firms produce at the lowest point on their ATC curve, at point X in Figure 5.6. Allocative efficiency occurs where price = marginal cost (abbreviated as P = MC), meaning that the price consumers pay for a good or service equals the cost of producing the last unit of output. This means that there is an optimum allocation of society's resources. In Figure 5.6, P = MC at the profit-maximising output Q_1.

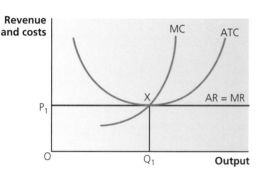

Figure 5.6 Long-run profit maximisation under perfect competition

Now test yourself

TESTED

3 Which of the following is not a feature of a perfectly competitive market?
  A large number of buyers and sellers
  B perfect information
  C product differentiation
  D no barriers to entry

Answer on p. 227

Advantages of perfect competition

REVISED

Economists usually agree that a highly competitive market functions well in 'static' terms, achieving productive and allocative efficiency.

● **Productive efficiency.** Highly competitive markets help to achieve productive efficiency. This occurs when goods and services are produced at minimum average cost, or when minimum inputs are used to produce maximum outputs. Any firm that does not achieve this will lose its market share to rival firms which can produce the same product more cheaply. For example, in the market for barbers, where few barriers to entry exist and there is little to differentiate one from another, any barber that does not minimise its costs and hence price is likely to struggle to retain customers.

● **Allocative efficiency.** Highly competitive markets will lead to firms producing what consumers demand since, if they do not, they will lose market share to firms that are producing the most desired products. This leads to consumer sovereignty, i.e. the consumer is 'king' (or queen!). Again, in the market for barbers, if a supplier does not offer haircuts that customers desire at a competitive price then it will lose sales to rival barbers.

Productive and allocative efficiency are the components of **static efficiency**, i.e. efficiency measured at a point in time.

Static efficiency: efficiency measured at a point in time, comprising productive efficiency and allocative efficiency.

Monopolistic competition

Monopolistic competition is a form of imperfect competition where a large number of producers sell products that are differentiated from one another, by branding or quality, for example. Barriers to entry and exit are relatively low.

Monopolistic competition has the following main characteristics:
- a large number of producers
- similar products which are differentiated from one another, e.g. by branding or quality
- barriers to entry and exit are relatively low

Examples may include independent fast-food takeaways, plumbers and hairdressers.

Monopolistic competition: a form of imperfect competition with a large number of firms producing slightly differentiated products.

Exam tip

Don't confuse monopolistic competition with monopoly. The characteristics of monopolistic competition place it closer to perfect competition than monopoly in terms of market structure.

Short run

REVISED

The short-run profit-maximising situation facing a firm in monopolistic competition is very much like that of the monopolist, with some brand loyalty leading to a downward-sloping demand curve, as shown in Figure 5.7. The monopolistically competitive firm maximises profit where MC = MR, at output Q_1, leading to an equilibrium price of P_1. In the short run the individual firm is able to make supernormal profit equal to the shaded area.

Exam tip

Remember that the profit-maximising level of output for all forms of market structure occurs where MC = MR.

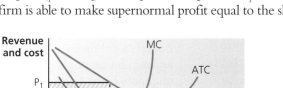
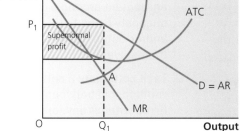

Figure 5.7 A firm in monopolistic competition in the short run

Long run

REVISED

In the long run, individual firms in monopolistic competition will make only normal profit. Low barriers to entry will mean that new firms can enter the industry relatively easily, attracted by the supernormal profits made by some firms. The effect of this is to reduce the demand (D = AR) for the individual firm as new entrants take some market share. The end result is that the D = AR curve is just tangential to the firm's ATC curve, meaning normal profit is made at the profit-maximising output Q_1. Figure 5.8 illustrates a firm in monopolistic competition in the long run.

Figure 5.8 A firm in monopolistic competition in the long run

Oligopoly

Oligopoly market structures are forms of imperfect competition where, in general, a small number of relatively powerful firms compete for market share. Such markets tend to be highly concentrated. Firms in oligopoly are interdependent, which means they take into account the likely actions of other firms in the industry when deciding how to behave.

> **Oligopoly:** a market structure dominated by a small number of powerful firms.

> **Exam tip**
>
> Oligopolistic markets can vary in relation to the number of firms, degree of product differentiation and ease of entry.

Concentration ratios

REVISED

Concentration ratios indicate the total market share held by the largest firms in the industry. For example, a concentration ratio of 5:80 in the supermarket industry would indicate that the largest five firms held 80% of the total market share.

> **Concentration ratio:** a measurement of how concentrated a market is — the total market share held by the largest firms in a market.

Collusive and non-collusive oligopoly

REVISED

Collusion occurs when firms work together to determine price and/or output. This reduces the uncertainty that may exist among firms in the industry regarding pricing and output decisions of rivals. A **cartel** is an example of a collusive arrangement where oligopoly firms agree to fix prices and/or output between themselves. The Organization of the Petroleum Exporting Countries (OPEC) is a famous example of a cartel.

Collusion between firms can be either tacit or overt. **Tacit collusion** is where firms appear to be organising prices and/or output between themselves without a formal agreement having been made, while **overt collusion** involves a more formal, open agreement.

When collusive agreements are made, consumers are essentially presented with an effective monopoly and the associated benefits and drawbacks outlined later in this chapter. In addition, collusive agreements allow inefficient firms to survive.

> **Cartel:** a collusive agreement among a group of oligopoly firms to fix prices and/or output between themselves.
>
> **Tacit collusion:** a collusive relationship between firms without any formal agreement having been made.
>
> **Overt collusion:** a collusive relationship between firms involving an open agreement.

The kinked demand curve model of oligopoly

REVISED

The kinked demand curve model of oligopoly is a useful illustration of the **interdependence** and uncertainty facing firms in this form of imperfect competition and why oligopolistic markets tend to have stable prices and non-price methods of competition.

> **Interdependence:** how firms in competitive oligopoly are affected by rival firms' pricing and output decisions.

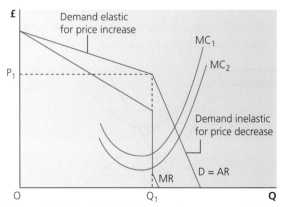

Figure 5.9 The kinked demand curve model of oligopoly

If an individual firm produces at Q_1 in Figure 5.9, selling at price P_1, it perceives its demand curve as being relatively elastic if it raises its price and inelastic if it cuts its price. This is because the firm expects rival firms not to follow a price rise but to follow a price cut. If the firm increases its price and rivals do not follow suit, it will lose some, but not all, market share. If the firm cuts its price, other firms will have no option but to follow — this will lead to a small expansion of market size but no increase in market share for the individual firm. Since a price increase or decrease is perceived as being likely to reduce revenue and subsequent profit for the individual firm, each firm understands its best strategy to be holding price at P_1 and quantity at Q_1.

Price stability in oligopoly can be explained further if it is understood that the marginal revenue (MR) curve is twice as steep as the average revenue (AR) curves above and below the ruling market price P_1. The kinked D = AR curve gives rise to a discontinuous MR curve, meaning that the individual firm can be in profit-maximising equilibrium where MC = MR for a range of MC curves, such as those shown in Figure 5.9. This means that firms in oligopoly tend to prefer non-price forms of competition.

> **Exam tip**
>
> The kinked demand curve model of oligopoly provides a useful illustration of the interdependence and uncertainty facing firms in this form of imperfect competition.

Non-price competition

REVISED

Methods of non-price competition include:
- product differentiation, e.g. marketing, packaging, advertising and branding
- customer service, e.g. point of sale and after-sales service
- loyalty products, e.g. loyalty cards, warranties and guarantees

Monopoly and monopoly power

Monopoly

REVISED

A pure monopoly exists when there is a single supplier of a good or service, which therefore has 100% market share. As with perfect competition, there are few examples of pure monopoly in reality. Economists study these theoretical models in order to examine the performance of firms in real life compared with these extreme examples. Tesco, with a market share in the groceries market of around 30%, and Google, with a market share of around 90% of internet traffic, may be considered monopolies in the UK.

Monopoly power

REVISED

A firm need not have a pure monopoly in order to exert **monopoly power** and there are many industries dominated by a small number of firms with monopoly power. In such industries, barriers to entry to the market will tend to be high. Firms with monopoly power can restrict their output in order to raise price, which boosts their supernormal profits. Because of barriers to entry, firms are able to maintain these profits because it is unlikely that new firms can easily enter the market to compete the profits away. This is shown in Figure 5.10.

> **Monopoly power**: the power of a firm in a market to act as a price maker.
>
> **Price maker**: a firm with the power to set the ruling market price.

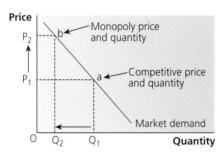

Figure 5.10 A firm with monopoly power restricts output to raise price

Profit maximisation under monopoly

The profit-maximising equilibrium situation for a monopolist is shown in Figure 5.11. As in all market structures, the monopolist maximises profit at the level of output at which MC = MR, i.e. at Q_1. The profit-maximising price is found by plotting the construction line vertically from the equilibrium quantity to the demand curve and then across to the y-axis, i.e. at P_1. The firm makes supernormal profit equal to the rectangular area P_1BDC_1.

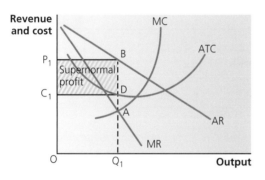

Figure 5.11 Profit maximisation under monopoly

Barriers to entry

Barriers to entry are features of a market that make it difficult for new firms to enter that market and can therefore lead to monopoly power. There are several possible barriers to entry, which include the following.

> **Barrier to entry:** any feature of a market that makes it difficult or impossible for new firms to enter.

Natural barriers to entry

These may include naturally occurring climatic, geographical or geological factors that make the product difficult to replicate elsewhere. For example, it is said that the soil and weather around Reims and Epernay in northern France are ideal for the production of the grape varieties that are combined to make champagne. Therefore other sparkling wines do not have the same exclusivity.

Economies of scale

Economies of scale occur when a firm's average costs of production fall as output increases. These mean that large firms can set their prices below those of any potential new entrant firms to the market, and still make a supernormal profit. For example, a large supermarket such as Tesco will be able to negotiate a much cheaper price per unit when buying dairy products from farmers in terms of a bulk-buying discount, than a much smaller, independent convenience store. This acts as a deterrent for new firms to enter the market.

Legal barriers

These include patents, copyrights and trademarks and essentially give a single firm or individual the right to have a monopoly over a new product, process or other intellectual property either forever or over a given time. For example, the British inventor James Dyson holds many patents over his original designs for a range of household appliances, most notably vacuum cleaners, which cannot legally be copied.

Product differentiation

Existing firms in a market may have spent considerable sums of money over many years on advertising and branding in order to build up a significant consumer loyalty and marketing profile — the process of **product differentiation**. For example, it would be extremely difficult for any new cola manufacturer to take market share from Coca-Cola and PepsiCo. Both firms have spent billions of dollars over many years on advertising, including the sponsorship of major sporting events such as the football World Cup and American Super Bowl.

> **Product differentiation**: using advertising or product design to make a product seem different from those of competitors.

Sunk costs

Sunk costs are the costs that cannot easily be recovered if a firm is unsuccessful in a market and has to exit, i.e. these financial commitments are essentially lost, or 'sunk'. Such costs may include spending on specialist market research or specialist equipment that could not easily be sold to another firm. For example, an oil company may have to spend many millions of pounds on detecting resources of crude oil before it begins to extract any. The threat of losing this money acts as a deterrent to new firms considering entering a market.

> **Sunk costs**: costs that cannot easily be recovered if a firm is unsuccessful in a market and has to exit.

Now test yourself

TESTED

4 Which of the following may create a barrier to entry?
  A two small firms merging in a large industry
  B a government granting exclusive rights to a firm to run a rail franchise on a major route
  C a firm cutting its price in a highly competitive market
  D the setting up of a price comparison website

Answer on p. 227

Concentrated markets

REVISED

Monopolies and oligopolies (close to monopoly on the spectrum of competition) may be considered **concentrated markets**, i.e. markets dominated by a small number of firms. It is possible to calculate the degree of concentration that exists by using the concentration ratio. This is equal to the total market share held by the largest firms in a market.

> **Concentrated market**: a market dominated by a small number of firms.

5 Which of the following would be a consequence of a perfectly competitive market being replaced by a monopoly?
  A   lower price and higher output
  B   higher price and restricted output
  C   lower profit
  D   lower barriers to entry

Answer on p. 227

Advantages and disadvantages of monopoly   REVISED

If perfect competition leads, in theory at least, to desirable outcomes in terms of productive and allocative efficiency, this implies that monopolies are undesirable. Indeed, in theory, there is a range of potential disadvantages of firms holding monopoly power. However, there are many examples of industries dominated by a small number of large firms and so there must also be potential advantages of monopolies to society.

Disadvantages of monopoly

There are some potential disadvantages of monopoly, which the government would take into account when deciding whether or not a large firm is operating in the public's best interests.

Productive and allocative inefficiency

Productive efficiency occurs when firms produce at minimum average total cost, i.e. when minimum inputs are used to produce maximum outputs. It is assumed that monopolies do not have to be competitive to survive, because they do not face the threat of firms taking their market share and so there is little incentive (other than generating profits for shareholders) to cut costs to a minimum. Allocative efficiency occurs when firms produce products that consumers value most highly, in the right quantities. Because monopolies do not have to produce the 'best' goods and services, because there are few, if any, competitors, consumers may have little choice but to buy whatever is produced. This would be allocatively inefficient.

X-inefficiency

X-inefficiency is the lack of willingness of firms with monopoly power to control their costs of production. This means that firms with monopoly power operate with higher costs than necessary.

Productive inefficiency, allocative inefficiency and x-inefficiency under monopoly are shown in Figure 5.12.

> **X-inefficiency:** the lack of willingness of firms with monopoly power to control their costs of production.

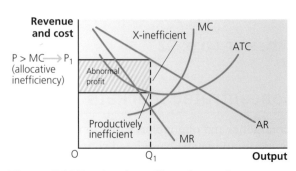

Figure 5.12 **Productive, allocative and x-inefficiency under monopoly**

Diseconomies of scale

Diseconomies of scale exist when a firm's average costs of production begin to increase as it expands its output. Very large firms may suffer from problems of control or communication. In a multinational company that operates across time zones and languages, the company's operations may be so vast that it is difficult to coordinate every employee and product line.

Possible advantages of monopoly

There must be some possible benefits arising from the existence of monopolies, or they would surely be outlawed.

Economies of scale

One of the main advantages of monopoly is a range of potential economies of scale, which means that as a firm increases its output, its average costs of production fall. Such economies of scale could be:
● financial
● technical
● marketing
● managerial

Innovation

Since firms in concentrated markets such as monopolies make supernormal profits, there is arguably more funding available to invest in research and development, leading to **innovation** and better-quality products. This is the argument in favour of granting legal monopolies in the form of patents to large pharmaceutical companies: if they could not make supernormal profits, they might argue, people's quality of life might suffer due to a lack of new medicines and vaccines.

> **Innovation:** new products and production processes that are developed into marketable goods or services.

> ### Now test yourself
> TESTED ☐
>
> 6 Which of the following is a potential benefit to consumers of a monopoly?
>   A   allocative efficiency
>   B   perfect information
>   C   supernormal profit
>   D   innovation
>
> Answer on p. 227

Natural monopoly
REVISED ☐

One special case, which is another argument in favour of concentrated markets, is that of a **natural monopoly**. This is where it is uneconomic for more than one firm to supply a market because a firm enjoys continuous economies of scale.

> **Natural monopoly:** a market where a single firm can benefit from continuous economies of scale.

Examples often used are the utilities markets, such as household gas, electricity and water. Using the language of economists, the supply infrastructure of these markets most closely fits the concept of a natural monopoly. For example, if more than one firm were responsible for supplying gas pipelines to homes and businesses, roads would be constantly dug up when users changed their supplier. As it is, effectively just one firm (currently National Grid) deals with the pipeline aspect of gas supply, but allows other energy billing companies, such as E.ON and npower, to use the pipelines to supply the gas itself to homes and businesses. It is productively efficient for just a single firm to supply the market, as several individual firms could never achieve the low costs of the single firm.

In a natural monopoly, firms experience continuous economies of scale, which means that as they increase their output, their average costs of production continue to fall, as highlighted in Figure 5.13. This implies that if the market were broken into more than one firm, average costs would be higher than for a single firm, meaning that prices might have to be higher.

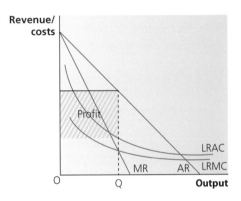

Figure 5.13 Continuously falling long-run average costs under natural monopoly

Price discrimination, consumer and producer surplus

Price discrimination occurs where firms with monopoly power charge different groups of consumers different prices for the same product. Price discrimination allows a firm to increase its producer surplus at the expense of consumer surplus.

> **Price discrimination**: where firms with monopoly power charge different groups of consumers different prices for the same product.

Conditions necessary for price discrimination

REVISED

- Firms must have a degree of monopoly power.
- Different sub-markets of consumers with different elasticities of demand.
- No 'seepage' between markets — those consumers being charged the higher price must not be able to access the cheaper prices.

Consumer and producer surplus

REVISED

Consumer surplus and **producer surplus** are concepts of economic welfare.

> **Consumer surplus**: the difference between what a consumer would be prepared to pay and the price they actually pay for a good or service.
>
> **Producer surplus**: the difference between what a firm would be willing to accept for a good or service and what they actually receive.

Consumer surplus is the difference between what a consumer would be prepared to pay for a good or service and the price they actually pay. In other words, it is the surplus value or satisfaction that consumers enjoy. In Figure 5.14 this is equal to the area given by the triangle P_1EA.

Producer surplus is the difference between what a firm would be willing to sell a good or service for and the price they receive. Therefore it may be regarded as surplus value enjoyed by producers. This is equal to the area given by the triangle P₁AF in Figure 5.14.

Figure 5.15 shows the effects of price discrimination on the profits of a firm with monopoly power.

By selling in separate markets (A and B) with differing elasticities of demand, the monopolist is able to enjoy a level of revenue in the whole market greater than would otherwise be the case.

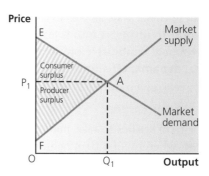

Figure 5.14 Illustrating consumer surplus and producer surplus

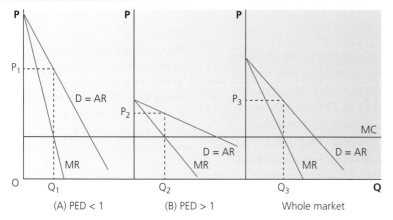

Figure 5.15 The effects of price discrimination on the profits of a firm with monopoly power

Advantages of price discrimination

- Supernormal profits may be re-invested by the price-discriminating firm, leading to a better quality product for consumers, e.g. Virgin Rail's technologically advanced trains.
- It may be that the price discriminator is only using the inelastic market to help generate normal profit overall, 'subsidising' those paying a lower price, e.g. children's and senior citizens' rail travel.
- Those on lower incomes may now be able to access services, e.g. lower-priced off-peak or advance-purchase fares.

Disadvantages of price discrimination

- If a firm with monopoly power is able to earn or increase supernormal profit, then this can be seen as inequitable.
- Increases producer surplus at the expense of consumer surplus.
- May be seen as exploiting those in greatest need who have no choice about using peak-time services.

The competitive market process

How firms in concentrated markets behave

REVISED

Price competition

Firms in concentrated markets are likely to benefit from economies of scale, which reduce their average costs of production such that firms may be able to reduce prices while still making a supernormal profit.

> **Exam tip**
>
> The concepts of consumer and producer surplus are important in an analysis of the impact on economic welfare of price and output changes.

> **Typical mistake**
>
> Do not presume that price discrimination is always bad for consumers and producers. It may be used to cross-subsidise cheaper prices for less well-off members of society, for example.

> **Price competition:** reducing the price of a good or service in order to make it more attractive than those of competitors.

These firms may, as we have seen, also be able to make use of these profits to re-invest into research and development in order to come up with new, innovative products and methods of production. This can lead to a **dynamic efficiency** which leads to a reduction in the firms' costs at every given output level. Again, this can allow firms to reduce prices while still being able to make a supernormal profit.

If a firm wishes to take market share from rivals, it may initiate a **price war**, whereby one firm begins by undercutting others. This will, however, tend to reduce the profits earned by all firms and is therefore often only used as a last resort.

> **Dynamic efficiency**: improvement in productive efficiency over time.
>
> **Price war**: where firms in an industry repeatedly cut prices below those of competitors in order to win market share.

Non-price competition

Firms in highly concentrated markets compete vigorously on the basis of factors other than price. This is because any attempt by one firm to undercut the prices of its rivals may spark extreme price competition — a price war — which can damage the profits of all firms involved. For example, quality of service can attract customers to give a firm repeat business. A number of major car retailers pride themselves on high-quality after-sales service to maintain a strong consumer loyalty. Similarly, the major supermarkets make extensive use of customer loyalty cards. In return for exchanging commercially valuable information with the supermarket, consumers build up points that give special offers.

> **Non-price competition**: competition on the basis of product features other than price, such as quality, advertising or after-sales service.

The dynamics of competition and competitive market processes

REVISED

Firms in concentrated markets may compete on the basis of both price and/or non-price factors. Large firms may use the benefits they obtain from economies of scale to reduce their prices and thus take some market share from rival firms. However, firms often compete using non-price factors such as quality, reliability and strategies to increase consumer loyalty. Over time, a process known as creative destruction means that firms in monopoly use innovation to overcome existing barriers to entry, often in dramatic ways. For example, consider how Amazon and eBay have transformed the market for online shopping. Similarly, Uber has transformed the often monopolistic market for taxis in many cities around the world.

Contestable and non-contestable markets

Contestable markets are those where the barriers to entry and exit can be overcome. It is argued that making markets more contestable leads to incumbent firms behaving in more economically desirable ways with regard to pricing and static efficiency.

> **Contestable market**: a market with freedom of entry and exit.

Features of perfectly contestable markets

REVISED

- Freedom of entry to and exit from the market.
- No sunk costs.
- Perfect information.
- Firms produce where price = marginal cost.

It is argued that making markets more contestable leads to incumbent firms behaving in more economically desirable ways with regard to pricing and static efficiency. This is because of the threat of new entrants taking a share of any supernormal profits that might exist if the incumbent firms did not behave as if they were in a perfectly competitive industry. This would be termed '**hit and run' competition**.

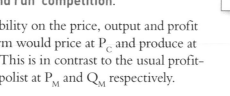

'Hit and run' competition: in contestable markets, where new entrants take a share of the supernormal profits and then exit the industry.

Figure 5.16 shows the effects of contestability on the price, output and profit of a firm with monopoly power. The firm would price at P_C and produce at output Q_C, making only normal profit. This is in contrast to the usual profit-maximising price and output of a monopolist at P_M and Q_M respectively.

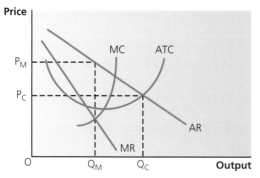

Figure 5.16 The effects of contestability on price, output and profit

Market structure, static efficiency, dynamic efficiency and resource allocation

The performance of different market structures can be judged by the extent to which they are statically efficient or dynamically efficient. Static efficiency is efficiency at a point in time, whereas dynamic efficiency is efficiency over time.

Static efficiency consists of productive efficiency and allocative efficiency. In general, perfect competition performs well in terms of static efficiency but less well in terms of dynamic efficiency.

Static efficiency in perfect competition is shown in Figure 5.17.

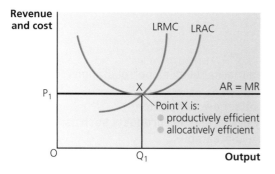

Figure 5.17 Static efficiency in perfect competition

Dynamic efficiency arises from improvements in productive efficiency over time. This may arise from technological development and leads to a

Dynamic efficiency: improvements in productive efficiency over time.

reduction in a firm's costs at every level of output. Larger firms in either oligopoly or monopoly may have easier access to the necessary financial resources to be dynamically efficient, i.e. from supernormal profits. They may also have strong incentives to do so if there are competitive pressures in their industry.

Dynamic efficiency is shown in Figure 5.18, with a reduction in long-run average costs from $LRAC_1$ to $LRAC_2$, leading to a fall in cost at every level of output.

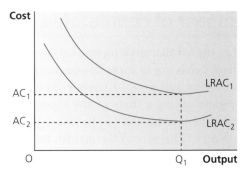

Figure 5.18 Dynamic efficiency

Exam practice

1 Explain two reasons why you think some firms may seek objectives other than profit maximisation. [4]
2 Identify four main features of perfectly competitive markets. [4]
3 With the help of a diagram, explain how price is determined in a competitive market. [9]
4 Using a supply and demand diagram, explain what would happen in the market for wheat following the entry of several new firms. [9]
5 Use a diagram to explain how firms in perfect competition can be both productively and allocatively efficient. [9]
6 Using a diagram, explain the profit-maximising equilibrium for a monopolistically competitive firm (i) in the short run, and (ii) in the long run. [9]
7 Compare and contrast perfect competition with monopoly in terms of resource allocation. [9]
8 Using the following table, calculate the market share of the top five firms in the UK high street banking market in 2014. [2]

Market shares held by selected high street banks in the UK, 2014

Bank	Market share (%)
Lloyds	15.6
Barclays	13.2
NatWest	11.4
HSBC	11.2
Santander	10.1
Halifax	9.1
Nationwide	6.2
Bank of Scotland	4.2
Royal Bank of Scotland	3.8
Co-operative Bank	2.1

Source: GfK/NOP

9 How would you expect existing firms in a highly concentrated market such as petrol stations to behave? [4]
10 How might the existing firms respond to the threat of a potential new competitor? [4]
11 Evaluate the view that the best way to improve the efficiency of markets for products such as telecommunications and other utilities is to make them more contestable. [25]

Answers and quick quiz 5 online

ONLINE

Summary

You should have an understanding of:

- The meaning of market structure.
- The main types of market structure.
- Objectives of firms, such as profit maximisation.
- The profit-maximising rule, MC = MR.
- The reasons for and consequences of a divorce of ownership from control.
- The formal diagrammatic analysis of perfect competition in the short and the long run.
- The main features of perfect competition and their implications for how firms in perfect competition behave and perform.
- The formal diagrammatic analysis of monopolistic competition in the short and the long run and the main characteristics of monopolistically competitive markets.
- The main characteristics of oligopoly and the significance of interdependence and uncertainty.
- Concentration ratios and how to calculate them.
- The difference between collusive and non-collusive oligopoly.
- The kinked demand curve model.
- The reasons for non-price competition, the operation of cartels, price leadership, price agreements, price wars and barriers to entry.
- The advantages and disadvantages of oligopoly.
- The formal diagrammatic analysis of the monopoly model.
- How monopoly power is influenced by factors such as barriers to entry, the number of competitors, advertising and the degree of product differentiation.
- The advantages and disadvantages of monopoly.
- The conditions necessary for price discrimination, real-world examples and diagrammatic analysis.
- The advantages and disadvantages of price discrimination.
- Competitive market processes.
- The significance of market contestability for the performance of an industry, including the concepts of sunk costs and 'hit and run' competition.
- The difference between static efficiency and dynamic efficiency.
- The concepts of consumer and producer surplus.

6 The labour market

The demand for labour

Derived demand REVISED

The demand for factors of production, such as labour, is derived from the demand for the product they are used to make. For example, if demand for foreign holidays increases, the derived demand for airline pilots is likely to increase.

Marginal productivity theory REVISED

The demand for labour is also known as the theory of **marginal revenue productivity (MRP)**. This is because a firm's demand for labour depends on the productivity of additional units of labour, known as **marginal physical product (MPP)** multiplied by the selling price of the product. MRP is the addition to a firm's revenue from employing an additional unit of labour.

The demand curve for labour, usually referred to as the MRP curve, shows the relationship between the wage rate and the number of workers employed. This is equal to MPP in the labour market multiplied by the marginal revenue (MR) obtained in the market for the firm's product. In a perfectly competitive product market, MR is constant and therefore the gradient of the MPP and MRP curves will be the same. This is shown in Figure 6.1.

> **Marginal revenue productivity (MRP):** the addition to a firm's revenue from employing an additional unit of a factor of production, usually labour.
>
> **Marginal physical product (MPP):** the addition to output from employing an additional unit of a factor of production, usually labour.

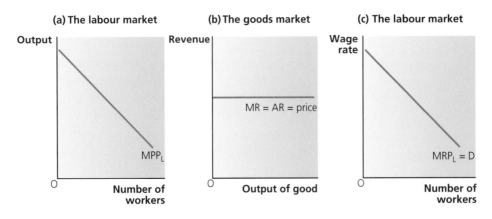

Figure 6.1 MPP × MR = MRP and the demand for labour

Determinants of labour demand

- **Wage rates:** as wages are the price of labour, higher wages will lead to a contractionary movement along the demand curve for labour.
- **Labour productivity:** as the output per worker per hour increases, this makes them more valuable to an employer and will lead to an increase in demand for labour.

- **The price of substitute factors:** if, for example, capital equipment becomes cheaper, this will lead to a reduction in demand for labour, as seen in the market for supermarket checkout assistants.
- **Other labour costs:** these include employers' national insurance and pension contributions. If these increase, the demand for labour will fall.

A change in wage rate will lead to a movement along the demand curve for labour, while a change in the other determinants will lead to a shift of the demand curve for labour.

Now test yourself

TESTED

1 Which of the following would lead to a rightward shift of a firm's demand curve for labour?
   A   a fall in the wage rate
   B   an increase in employers' pension contributions
   C   a fall in the price of capital equipment
   D   an increase in the productivity of employees

Answer on p. 227

Determinants of elasticity of demand for labour

The **elasticity of demand for labour** is a measure of the responsiveness of the quantity of labour demanded following a change in the wage rate.

The formula is:

$$\text{Elasticity of demand for labour} = \frac{\text{percentage change in quantity of labour demanded}}{\text{percentage change in wage rate}}$$

Elasticity of demand for labour: a measure of the responsiveness of the quantity of labour demanded following a change in the wage rate.

The factors determining the elasticity of demand for labour include:
- **Ease of substitution:** the easier it is to substitute labour for other factors of production, such as capital machinery, the more elastic will be the demand for labour.
- **Time:** the longer the time period, the easier it becomes to substitute labour with other factors such as capital, making demand for labour more elastic.
- **Elasticity of demand for the good or service:** since labour has a derived demand, if the elasticity of demand for the good or service that workers produce is inelastic, e.g. brain surgery, as a result of difficulty of substitution, then the demand for labour will also be inelastic.
- **Proportion of labour cost to total cost of production:** the larger the proportion of labour cost to total cost of production, for example in labour-intensive organisations such as schools and colleges, the greater the elasticity of demand for labour.

The difference between elastic and inelastic demand for labour is highlighted in Figure 6.2.

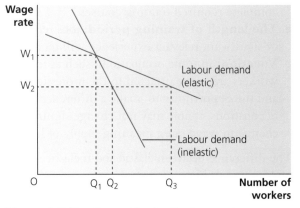

Figure 6.2 Elastic and inelastic demand curves for labour

Influences upon the supply of labour to different markets

The supply of labour to a particular occupation

The supply curve for labour shows the relationship between the wage rate and number of workers willing and able to work in a particular occupation. The supply of labour to a particular occupation is influenced by monetary factors such as the wage rate, and non-monetary factors such as job satisfaction and working conditions.

Determinants of supply of labour

- **Wage rates:** as wages are the reward to labour for working, higher wages will lead to an extension along the supply curve for labour.
- **Size of working population:** if the number of people of working age increases, the potential supply of labour increases.
- **Non-monetary factors:** these include relative satisfaction, job status, promotion prospects, job security, working conditions and holiday allowance.

A change in wage rate will lead to a movement along the supply curve for labour, while a change in the other determinants will lead to a shift of the supply curve for labour.

> **Exam tip**
>
> Workers will take into account the monetary and non-monetary features of a job when deciding to supply their labour, a concept referred to as 'net advantage'. Good non-monetary factors may compensate for relatively poor pay, and vice versa.

Determinants of elasticity of supply of labour

The **elasticity of supply of labour** is a measure of the responsiveness of the quantity of labour supplied following a change in the wage rate.

The formula is:

$$\text{Elasticity of supply of labour} = \frac{\text{percentage change in quantity of labour supplied}}{\text{percentage change in wage rate}}$$

> **Elasticity of supply of labour:** a measure of the responsiveness of the quantity of labour supplied following a change in the wage rate.

The factors determining the elasticity of supply of labour include:

- **Time:** the longer the time period, the more elastic the supply of labour as individual workers are more able to switch occupations and/or complete required training courses.
- **The length of training period:** jobs requiring a long training period or significant relevant experience will tend to have an inelastic supply.
- **Vocation:** in some occupations, such as teaching and nursing, workers are often attracted to the profession by a sense of vocation, and the opportunity to 'make a difference' to people's lives. In such occupations, supply may not change significantly in response to a change in wage rates, meaning supply of labour is relatively inelastic.

The difference between elastic and inelastic supply for labour is highlighted in Figure 6.3.

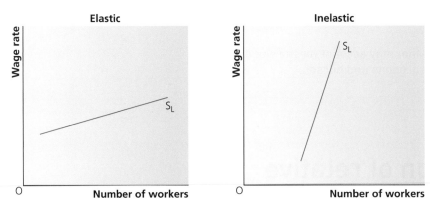

Figure 6.3 Elastic and inelastic supply curves for labour

Now test yourself

TESTED

2 Which of the following will tend to lead to an inelastic supply curve for labour?
   A a relatively long training period in order to qualify
   B a very low skill requirement
   C a large number of currently unemployed people able to perform the job
   D low costs of training

Answer on p. 227

Wage differentials

The factors determining the extent and elasticities of demand and supply for labour examined earlier in this chapter can be put together to explain why some groups of workers earn more or less than others.

There are other factors which explain the relative bargaining power of workers and employers, such as trade unions and the existence of a monopsony, but these are outlined later in this chapter.

Figure 6.4 shows the difference in wages that is likely to arise between surgeons and nurses because of the differing characteristics of demand and supply for each occupation. The surgeon may be considered as being relatively more skilled than the nurse.

> **Exam tip**
>
> It is helpful to be able to use economic theory to explain **wage differentials**.

> **Wage differentials**: differences in wages arising between individuals, occupations, industries and regions.

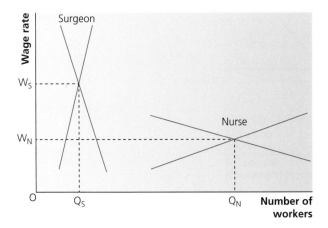

Figure 6.4 The wage differential that may exist between surgeons and nurses

3 Using Figure 6.4, list the factors that may account for the wage differential that exists between surgeons and nurses. `

Answer on p. 227

The determination of relative wage rates and levels of employment in perfectly competitive labour markets

A perfectly competitive labour market has the following characteristics:
- Each unit of labour is homogeneous and unable to influence the wage rate.
- Workers must therefore accept the going wage rate, determined by supply and demand at market level.
- Similarly, individual firms are wage takers, since if they pay a wage below the equilibrium, workers will not accept this and will work for rival firms.
- Individual firms maximise profit by employing the quantity of labour at which $MRP = MC$ (the wage rate).
- Perfect information.
- Freedom of entry to and exit from the industry.

In a perfectly competitive labour market, each individual employer has to accept the ruling market wage, as shown in the right-hand diagram in Figure 6.5. Since each firm can employ all the labour it requires at this rate, it faces a perfectly elastic supply curve at the ruling market wage, shown in the left-hand diagram. Similar to the product market, where firms maximise profit by producing where $MR = MC$, when deciding how many workers to employ firms equate MRP with the marginal cost of employing labour, which is also the wage rate in this case.

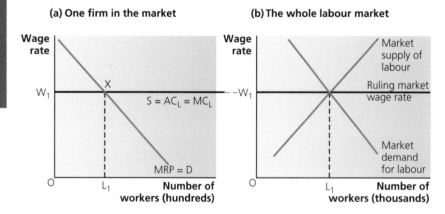

Figure 6.5 Determination of wages and employment levels in a perfectly competitive labour market

The determination of relative wage rates and levels of employment in imperfectly competitive labour markets

All labour markets are imperfect to some extent. Factors such as monopsony power, trade unions and imperfect information are some of the various sources of labour market imperfection.

Monopsony

A **monopsony** labour market is one with a single dominant buyer of workers, such as the government in relation to state school teachers. In a monopsony labour market, the employer can use market power to reduce the wage rate and level of employment below those of a perfectly competitive labour market.

In a monopsony labour market the marginal cost (MC) of employing workers exceeds the average cost (AC). To attract an additional worker the firm has to pay more to this worker as well as to all other employees.

Figure 6.6 shows the equilibrium position in a monopsony labour market.

In order to maximise profit, the monopsonist employs workers where MRP = MC, which results in a wage rate of W_1 and Q_1 of labour employed. The wage rate and level of employment are both below those that would exist in a competitive labour market.

> **Monopsony:** a market with a single dominant buyer, such as the government in relation to state school teachers.

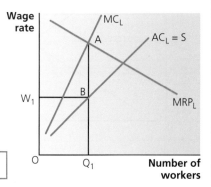

Figure 6.6 The equilibrium position in a monopsony labour market

Now test yourself

TESTED

4 Which of the following distinguishes an imperfectly competitive labour market from a perfectly competitive one?
   A homogeneous units of labour
   B ability of firms to set wage levels
   C perfect information
   D freedom of entry to and exit from the market

Answer on p. 227

The influence of trade unions in determining wages and levels of employment

Trade unions are organisations of workers set up to further the interests of their membership through a process of bargaining collectively with employers. This gives workers power to set wages higher than they would otherwise be.

> **Trade union:** a group of workers that bargains collectively with employers to increase its members' wages.

Trade unions introduced to previously competitive labour markets

REVISED

Economic theory suggests that the introduction of a trade union to a perfectly competitive labour market will increase wages for those who keep their job, but reduce employment levels.

Figure 6.7 illustrates the effects of introducing a trade union to a competitive labour market. The competitive wage rate before the introduction of a trade union is W_1, with Q_1 workers employed. If employees join a trade union they are able to negotiate a higher wage of W_2, with Q_3 workers willing to supply their labour at this wage. However, the firm is willing to demand only Q_2 of labour at this higher wage, leading to an excess supply of workers of $Q_3 - Q_2$, which is effectively unemployment. The introduction of a trade union to a previously competitive labour market has thus resulted in additional unemployment of $Q_1 - Q_2$.

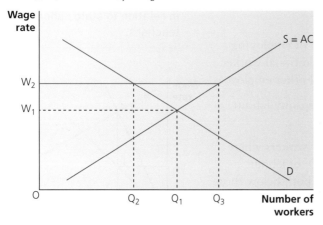

Figure 6.7 The effects of introducing a trade union to a previously competitive labour market

Critics of this analysis argue that it is too simplistic and that trade unions may not reduce employment. Many modern instances of bargaining between trade unions and employers have led to pay rises for workers in return for agreement to adopt more productive working methods, such as using machines or computers or agreeing to retrain. This will increase workers' MRP and hence demand for labour, which may lead to no excess demand arising.

Trade unions in imperfectly competitive labour markets

REVISED

In imperfectly competitive labour markets such as monopsonies, the introduction of a trade union is predicted to increase both the wage rate and the level of employment.

Figure 6.8 illustrates the effects of introducing a trade union to a monopsony labour market, an example of a bilateral monopoly. In our earlier analysis, a monopsony employer would employ Q_1 workers at the wage rate W_1. The introduction of a trade union has the same effect on the labour supply curve as in a competitive market. In Figure 6.8, with the union setting a wage of W_2, the kinked line W_2XS is the labour supply curve and the average cost of labour curve (AC_L). In monopsony, however, W_2XS is not the marginal cost of labour curve. The MC_L curve is W_2XZV which exhibits a double kink. As long as the monopsonist employs a number of workers less than or equal to Q_2, the marginal cost of employing an extra worker equals both the average cost and the wage W_2, as set by the trade union. Beyond Q_2 and point X, the monopsonist has to offer a higher wage in order to attract further workers. Since the firm now has to pay all workers the higher wage, the MC_L curve lies above the AC_L curve, shown by the upward-sloping line ZV. This gives rise to a vertical discontinuity between the horizontal section of the MC_L curve and the upward-sloping section ZV. With the introduction of the trade union setting the wage rate at W_2, employment is at Q_2, compared with Q_1 without a trade union. The trade union has therefore managed to increase the wage rate and the level of employment.

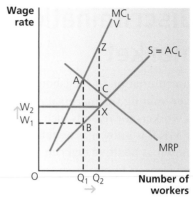

Figure 6.8 The effects of introducing a trade union to a monopsony labour market

Now test yourself

TESTED

5 Which of the following would be a likely effect of introducing a trade union to a monopsony labour market?
   A a higher wage rate and a lower level of employment than previously
   B a lower wage rate and a lower level of employment than previously
   C a higher wage rate and a higher level of employment than previously
   D a lower wage rate and a higher level of employment than previously

Answer on p. 227

The National Minimum Wage

A **National Minimum Wage (NMW)** is one which legally obliges employers to pay their workers at least a certain hourly rate. Depending upon the elasticities of demand and supply for labour, the introduction or raising of the NMW may have significant impacts upon employment levels.

The effects of introducing an NMW are illustrated in Figure 6.9. The free market equilibrium wage and quantity of labour employed are W_1 and Q_1 respectively. A minimum wage introduced above the free market wage, e.g. at W_2, would lead to an excess supply of labour equal to $Q_3 - Q_2$, which would be unemployment.

However, there is little empirical evidence to support this theoretical analysis. One suggestion is that by increasing the incomes of the low-paid, who tend to have a high marginal propensity to consume, extra demand is created in the product market, which increases workers' MRP, and hence the demand for labour actually increases.

National Minimum Wage (NMW): a statutory minimum wage used to increase the earnings of the low-paid.

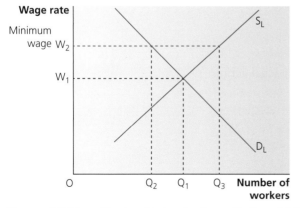

Figure 6.9 The effects of introducing a National Minimum Wage

Exam tip

The diagram in Figure 6.9 is very similar to the analysis of the effects of the introduction of a trade union to a perfectly competitive market.

Discrimination in the labour market

Discrimination in the labour market involves employers under-valuing or over-valuing the marginal revenue productivity (MRP) of certain groups of workers for reasons such as ethnicity, gender or age. Under-valuation of MRP is known as **negative discrimination** while over-valuation is known as **positive discrimination**. Each of these leads to market failure and impacts upon wages and levels of employment.

> **Negative discrimination:** where employers treat a specific group of workers less favourably than others in terms of pay and employment levels.
>
> **Positive discrimination:** where employers treat a specific group of workers more favourably than others in terms of pay and employment levels.

Conditions necessary for wage discrimination

- Firms must have some wage-setting ability, therefore the labour market must be imperfect.
- Distinct/separate labour markets, i.e. workers unable to successfully offer their labour in a different market for a higher wage.
- Lack of legal protection or imperfect information about the discrimination on the part of the government.

Figure 6.10 shows the effects of wage discrimination on labour markets.

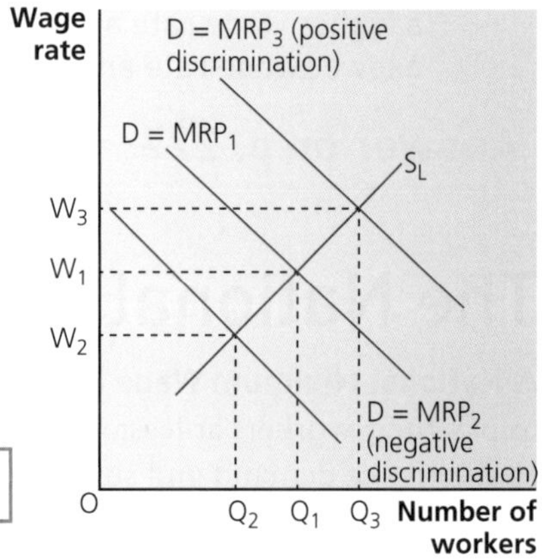

Figure 6.10 The effects of wage discrimination on labour markets

Now test yourself TESTED

6 Which of the following is a predicted effect of negative wage discrimination?
- A higher wage rate, higher level of employment
- B higher wage rate, lower level of employment
- C lower wage rate, higher level of employment
- D lower wage rate, lower level of employment

Answer on p. 227

Economic disadvantages of wage discrimination

- May lead to some groups being underpaid and under-employed, worsening relative poverty.
- Increased government spending on welfare benefits.
- Waste of scarce, valuable resources.
- May lead to increased litigation as workers attempt to take legal action against employers.
- Lack of cultural diversity in the workplace.
- May create social tensions.

Possible economic advantages of wage discrimination

- Firms can reduce their wage bills and therefore be more competitive.
- May be beneficial to some firms if their consumers are racially prejudiced.
- Can be difficult to successfully prove discrimination.
- Positive discrimination, e.g. 'affirmative action', can boost cultural diversity and social justice.

Exam practice

1 Explain the difference between monetary and non-monetary influences on the supply of labour to a particular occupation. [4]
2 Using a diagram, explain the effect on demand for labour of an increase in employee productivity in that industry. [9]
3 Using a diagram, explain how a monopsony employer, such as the government, can influence the wage rate and employment levels in occupations such as the armed forces. [9]
4 Using a diagram, explain the impact of a trade union on a previously perfectly competitive labour market. [9]
5 Evaluate the arguments for and against government intervention to tackle various forms of labour market failure. [25]

Answers and quick quiz 6 online

ONLINE

Summary

You should have an understanding of:
- The demand for labour and marginal productivity theory.
- The causes of shifts in the demand curve for labour.
- The determinants of the elasticity of demand for labour.
- How the supply of labour to a particular occupation is influenced by monetary and non-monetary factors.
- The causes of shifts in the market supply curve for labour.
- The determination of relative wage rates and employment levels in perfectly competitive labour markets.

- The determination of relative wage rates and employment levels in imperfectly competitive labour markets.
- The influence of trade unions in determining wages and levels of employment in perfectly competitive and monopsony labour markets.
- The effects of a National Minimum Wage upon labour markets.
- The advantages and disadvantages of a National Minimum Wage.
- The impact of discrimination in the labour market.

7 The distribution of income and wealth: poverty and inequality

The distribution of income and wealth

The difference between income and wealth

Income is a flow of money to a factor of production, usually labour, and therefore includes wages and welfare benefits. **Wealth** is a stock of valuable assets, such as property, shares and pensions. Both income and wealth tend to be unequally distributed between households in the UK.

> **Income**: a flow of money to a factor of production, usually labour.
>
> **Wealth**: a stock of valuable assets such as property or shares.

Factors leading to an unequal distribution of income

The distribution of income is defined as how income is shared out between the population. The following factors may lead to an unequal distribution of income:
- **Differences in skills, qualifications and work experience.** Individuals with skills, qualifications and work experience that are in high demand will tend to earn more than those lacking in these.
- **Differences in wealth.** Wealthier individuals and households tend to earn more income from their holdings of assets in the form of dividends and interest.
- **Impact of the state.** A free market economic system would provide fewer welfare benefits than a command economic system.

> **Exam tip**
>
> Differences in skills, qualifications and work experience lead to wage differentials, as explained in Chapter 6.

Factors leading to an unequal distribution of wealth

The distribution of wealth is defined as how wealth is shared out among the population. The following factors may lead to an unequal distribution of wealth:
- **Differences in income.** Higher earners are more able to save money and earn interest and so increase their wealth.
- **Inheritance.** Property and other valuable assets can be passed down from one generation of wealthy families to the next.
- **Marriage.** Wealthy people tend to marry other wealthy people, leading to a concentration of wealth among a relatively small number of families.
- **Property.** Wealth can generate wealth for those who own valuable assets such as property if the income earned from rental is saved or used to purchase further valuable assets.

Equality versus equity

Equality means that income and wealth are shared out equally between all members of society whereas equity is the notion of fairness. Under the notion of equity it may be seen by some societies as fair that income and wealth are unequally shared out between different people. This may be justified if some work longer or harder than others, or have sacrificed earnings in order to complete further or higher education, or taken a business risk as an entrepreneur.

> **Typical mistake**
>
> Make sure you understand the difference between equality and equity: they are not the same.

Measuring inequality: the Lorenz Curve and the Gini Coefficient

The Lorenz Curve

One method of measuring and illustrating the extent of income and wealth inequality is using a Lorenz Curve. The further the Lorenz Curve is from the 45 degree line of perfect equality, the greater the inequality, as shown in Figure 7.1.

The Gini Coefficient

The Gini Coefficient is a statistical measure of the degree of inequality. It is the ratio of the area between the 45 degree line and the Lorenz Curve divided by the total area below the 45 degree line. Using Figure 7.1 this is calculated by the formula:

Area $\dfrac{A}{(A + B)}$

- The higher the value, the more inequality exists.
- Perfect equality gives a Gini Coefficient of 0.
- Perfect inequality gives a Gini Coefficient of 1.

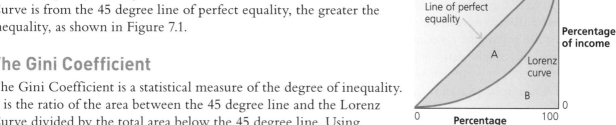

Figure 7.1 A Lorenz Curve

> **Now test yourself**
>
>
> 1 Which one of the following may be used to measure the extent of inequality in the distribution of income or wealth?
>   A   the Claimant Count
>   B   the Gini Coefficient
>   C   the rate of inheritance tax
>   D   the output gap
>
> Answer on p. 227

> **Exam tip**
>
> You should understand that the degree of inequality can be measured but that whether or not a given distribution of income is equitable or fair is a normative matter.

Possible costs of income and wealth inequality

- **Social tensions:** significant inequality in the distribution of income and wealth may fuel social tensions, as poorer members of society come to resent richer members of society. This may lead to friction, crime and rioting.
- **The creation of an 'underclass':** with a relatively low standard of living and little obvious chance of bettering their position via 'social mobility', there may be a significant segment of society that comes to be reliant on welfare benefits.

Possible benefits of income and wealth inequality

REVISED

- **Incentive effects:** the existence of high earners and the 'super rich' suggests the possibility of many people being able to earn high salaries or profits through hard work, innovation or setting up businesses as entrepreneurs. Free market capitalists would argue that these incentive effects help to generate economic growth, making average incomes higher. Without these incentives, economic activity may be lower.
- **'Trickle-down':** free market economists would argue that the economic benefits of having relatively high earners can trickle down to all sectors of society, since high earners and the very wealthy tend to be business owners who therefore create employment opportunities. Furthermore, they may also pay higher taxes, which can be redistributed to raise the living standards of the relatively poor. In addition, their taxes can be used to fund merit goods such as healthcare and education, free at the point of consumption for all members of society.

Trickle-down: a free market view that poorer members of society will benefit from high earners and the relatively wealthy, e.g. through job opportunities and helping to fund merit goods.

Now test yourself

TESTED

2 Which one of the following may be a possible advantage of inequality in the distribution of income or wealth?
   A   increased tax avoidance
   B   increased relative poverty
   C   increased incentives to work
   D   increased social tensions

Answer on p. 227

The problem of poverty

Inequality in the distribution of income and wealth can lead to poverty, which can be either relative or absolute.

The difference between relative and absolute poverty

REVISED

- **Relative poverty** exists when some people in society are worse off than others and is often defined as earning less than 60% of a country's median income.
- **Absolute poverty** exists when some people can't afford the basic necessities to sustain life, such as food, shelter and warmth.

Relative poverty: when some people in society are worse off than others, e.g. earning less than 60% of a country's median income.

Absolute poverty: when some people can't afford the basic necessities to sustain life, e.g. food, shelter and warmth.

Causes of poverty

REVISED

Possible causes of poverty include the following:

- **Relatively low wages:** workers with relatively low skills, with few, if any relevant qualifications, will find themselves either in low-paid jobs or unable to secure work.
- **Unemployment:** individuals who are reliant on unemployment benefits tend to have incomes significantly lower than those in work.
- **Regressive taxation:** increases in the numbers and rates of regressive taxes since the 1980s have placed a higher burden on the poorest members of society.
- **Old age:** welfare benefits and the state pension are still the major sources of income for older members of society, and these have not grown in line with average earnings over the last 20 years.
- **Imperfect information:** some people are unaware of their eligibility to claim certain welfare benefits.

Effects of poverty

REVISED

It is not easy to disentangle all the effects of poverty from one another, with some groups in society suffering multiple effects of deprivation. Possible effects of poverty include:

- **Greater demands on the welfare system:** people in poverty are more likely to be eligible to claim welfare benefits and not earn incomes high enough to pay income tax, so will impose a greater cost on the government than those on higher incomes.
- **Poor educational attainment:** people from poorer backgrounds tend to perform less well at all levels of education, meaning they are less likely to go on to further and higher education. This in turn means that they will have a lower MRP than those with higher levels of attainment, meaning they tend to earn relatively low wages.
- **Poor health:** those in poverty tend to suffer from poorer health, both physical and mental, and more incidence of chronic illness, which may further hamper their ability to maintain paid employment. This puts further strain on the nation's resources.

It is clear that poverty can cause some groups in society to be caught in a vicious circle, unable to break free from deprivation. This makes it very difficult for the government to implement effective policies to alleviate poverty.

Government policies to alleviate poverty and to influence the distribution of income and wealth

Governments may choose from a range of policies to alleviate poverty, including progressive income taxes, welfare benefits, a National Minimum Wage and various merit goods provided 'free' at the point of consumption, such as education and healthcare.

Policies to influence the distribution of income and wealth and to alleviate poverty

REVISED

- **Progressive taxes:** this means making higher earners pay a larger percentage of their income in taxation, such as the introduction of the 45% highest tax rate in the UK in 2013, reduced quickly from 50%. Raising the tax-free threshold, so that the low-paid do not pay tax until they earn a certain amount, e.g. £11,000, is also an example of making income tax more progressive.
- **National Minimum Wage:** this is a legal minimum wage designed to prevent employers from exploiting those in relatively low-skilled occupations by paying low wages.
- **Welfare benefits:** these can be 'means-tested' in order to target those in greatest need, i.e. those on the lowest incomes.
- **Education and training:** raising standards of education and training will help to increase the marginal revenue productivity of the labour force, reducing occupational immobility and enhancing employability.
- **Reducing unemployment:** unemployment can be tackled by specific policies depending upon whether the unemployment is due to a lack of aggregate demand or supply-side problems.
- **Promoting 'trickle-down':** policies to promote economic growth will, in theory, raise average incomes while also creating more opportunities for entrepreneurship. Those members of society who benefit most from these opportunities can contribute to raising the living standards of poorer people by creating jobs and paying higher taxes to fund merit goods such as state education and the NHS.

The economic consequences of policies to alleviate poverty

REVISED

- **Progressive taxes:** critics of highly progressive taxes argue that they can create disincentives to work, leading to voluntary unemployment, slower economic growth and reduced income tax revenues overall for the government. In addition, they may create disincentives to invest and be entrepreneurial if they relate to corporation tax on business profits or income taxes on the self-employed. Furthermore, high taxes may encourage a 'brain drain' as high earners move overseas to relatively low-tax countries.
- **National Minimum Wage:** some critics argue that if the NMW is set too high it could lead to increased unemployment. Also, increasing the NMW will not benefit those already unemployed.
- **Welfare benefits:** increasing benefits may increase the replacement ratio and reduce incentives to work. Means-testing benefits is arguably better than providing universal benefits, but may cost more to check and administer. The government has sought to offer various tax credits as an alternative, increasing the disposable income of low-paid working households.
- **Education and training:** an individual may take a long time to feel the positive impacts of education and training in terms of increased employability. Many courses are expensive — a problem if the individual has to pay for the courses themselves. Furthermore, some courses may not be appropriate for current job vacancies and therefore may not lead to increased employment prospects.

- **Reducing unemployment:** expansionary fiscal and monetary policies have time lags before their full effects are felt and may also lead to demand-pull inflation, depending on the extent of supply-side inflexibilities.
- **Promoting 'trickle-down':** critics of trickle-down argue that while it sounds promising in theory, in reality it doesn't really work. This may be because the highest earners in society can afford the best tax accountants to help them exploit loopholes in the system in order to minimise the tax they pay.

Now test yourself

TESTED

3 Which of the following may be an adverse consequence of government policies to alleviate poverty?
   A a more equitable distribution of income
   B the overseas migration of talented workers
   C reduced unemployment
   D increased educational attainment

Answer on p. 227

Exam practice

1 The table below shows Gini Coefficients of wealth for two countries, A and B.

Country	Gini Coefficient
A	0.3
B	0.5

It can be inferred that:
   A the distribution of income is more unequal in country B than in country A
   B 50% of the people in country B have more than the median income
   C the distribution of wealth is more equal in country A than in country B
   D the distribution of wealth is more equal in country B than in country A [1]
2 Explain three factors that may determine the distribution of income in the UK. [9]
3 Explain how a Lorenz Curve may be used to show income inequality in an economy. [9]
4 Explain one method that could be used to alleviate relative poverty. [9]
5 Using the data and your economic knowledge, evaluate the arguments for and against the government intervening to alter the distribution of income in the UK economy. [25]

Answers and quick quiz 7 online

ONLINE

Summary

You should have an understanding of:
- The difference between income and wealth.
- The various factors which influence the distribution of income and wealth.
- The difference between equality and equity in relation to the distribution of income and wealth.
- The Lorenz Curve and the Gini Coefficient.
- The likely benefits and costs of more equal and more unequal distributions of income and wealth.

- The difference between relative and absolute poverty.
- The causes and effects of poverty.
- The policies available to influence the distribution of income and wealth and to alleviate poverty, and the economic consequences of these policies.

8 The market mechanism, market failure and government intervention in markets

How markets and prices allocate resources

The functions of prices

REVISED

The price mechanism has four key functions in a free market economy:

1 **The rationing function:** as prices rise, excess demand is removed and only those consumers with the ability to pay are able to purchase the good.
2 **The signalling function:** prices provide important market signals to market participants, e.g. to producers to either increase or decrease production.
3 **The incentive function:** increased prices strengthen incentives to firms to produce more in order to make a profit.
4 **The allocative function:** the allocative function acts to divert resources to where they can maximise their returns and away from uses where they do not.

When any of these key functions of prices breaks down, market failure is said to occur.

> **Rationing function:** increasing prices rations demand to those most able to afford a good or service.
>
> **Signalling function:** prices provide important information to market participants.
>
> **Incentive function:** prices create incentives for market participants to change their actions.
>
> **Allocative function:** the function of prices that acts to divert resources to where returns can be maximised.

Now test yourself

TESTED

1 The rationing function of prices means that:
   A changes in prices provide information to producers and consumers about changes in demand and supply
   B an increase in prices will encourage more firms to enter an industry
   C when there is a shortage of a product, prices will rise and put some consumers off buying the product
   D a rise in price will worsen any shortage of a product

Answer on p. 227

The meaning of market failure

Market failure occurs whenever a market leads to a misallocation of resources — in other words, when a market fails to achieve productive efficiency, allocative efficiency or equity.

Market failure can be complete or partial. **Complete market failure** occurs when the free market fails to create a market for a good or service (i.e. a missing market). A prime example would be for so-called 'public goods' such as lighthouses, since everybody would have an incentive to wait for somebody else to provide them. **Partial market failure** arises when a market exists, but does not provide resources in the optimum quantities, i.e. there is either over-production/consumption or under-production/consumption of a good or service.

> **Market failure:** when the free market leads to a misallocation of resources in an economy.
>
> **Complete market failure:** when the free market fails to create a market for a good or service, also referred to as a missing market.
>
> **Partial market failure:** when a market for a good or service exists, but it is consumed or produced in quantities that do not maximise economic welfare.

Now test yourself

TESTED ☐

Exam tip

Make sure you understand the difference between complete and partial market failure.

2 Partial market failure exists when:
  A a product is both non-excludable and non-rival
  B there is excess supply in a market at the current market price
  C a market exists but there is under-production
  D the market can only be competitive with government subsidies

Answer on p. 227

Public goods, private goods and quasi-public goods

Public goods are those that possess two key characteristics: they are **non-excludable** and **non-rival**.

- **Non-excludable** means that non-paying customers cannot be excluded from consuming a good, once it has been produced. For example, once a lighthouse has emitted its beam of light, all ships in the vicinity can use this light to avoid rocks and other hazards at sea.
- **Non-rival** means that one person's enjoyment of the good does not diminish another person's enjoyment of the good. For example, one person listening to a radio broadcast does not diminish the quality of radio signal to any other listener.

Public good: a good that is non-excludable and non-rival in consumption.

Non-excludable: where it is not possible to prevent non-paying customers from consuming a good.

Non-rival: where one person's enjoyment of a good does not diminish another person's enjoyment of the good.

Now test yourself

TESTED ☐

Exam tip

Make sure you understand the two key characteristics of public goods.

3 A good is non-excludable if:
  A its price is zero
  B it is supplied by the government rather than the free market
  C it is not possible to prevent non-paying customers from enjoying it
  D one person's use affects the quantity available for others

Answer on p. 227

The free-rider problem

REVISED ☐

Public goods are an example of complete market failure, as the free market would have no incentive to provide them. For example, in the case of sea defences such as flood protection, coastal homeowners would have an incentive to wait for their neighbours or others in a similar situation to fund the flood protection and thus it will not be provided at all. This is referred to as the free-rider problem, since individual consumers hope to get a 'free ride' without paying for the benefit they enjoy.

Private goods

REVISED ☐

Private goods are the opposite of public goods, i.e. they are both excludable and rival. This means that non-payers can be excluded from consuming a good and consumption by one person diminishes the enjoyment of the good by another. For example, if you eat a slice of pizza, another person cannot also enjoy that slice.

Private good: a good that is rival and excludable in consumption.

Quasi-public goods

Quasi- (or near) **public goods** are those that possess some, but not all, characteristics of a public good. For example, they may be partially excludable, or partially rival. Depending on location and time of day, roads may be considered private goods, quasi-public goods or public goods.

> **Quasi-public good**: a good which exhibits some, but not all, of the characteristics of a public good, i.e. it is partially non-excludable and/or partially non-rival.

Externalities

Externalities are the knock-on effects of economic transactions upon third parties. There are many instances where the actions of individual consumers or producers have consequences that affect others.

> **Externality**: a knock-on effect of an economic transaction upon third parties.

Positive externalities in production

Positive externalities in production occur when the actions of firms have wider benefits to society. For example, when a new airport runway is built there may be positive knock-on effects in terms of increased tourism revenue to UK firms and an increased attractiveness to the UK for foreign investment. In this case, it is said that the **private costs** to the firm are greater than the costs to society, as shown in Figure 8.1.

> **Positive externality**: a positive knock-on effect of an economic transaction upon third parties, also known as an external benefit.
>
> **Private cost**: the cost to an individual producer involved in a market transaction.

Figure 8.1 Positive externalities in production

The private costs in this case are given by supply curve S_1 while **social costs** are given by supply curve S_2. The vertical distance between the two supply curves shows the external benefit from the building of the runway. The free market quantity of runway capacity would be Q_1, at price P_1. The free market would thus lead to underproduction of $Q_2 - Q_1$ as the free market would be unlikely to take into account the full benefits to society.

> **Social cost**: the total of private cost plus external cost of an economic transaction.

Positive externalities in consumption

Positive externalities in consumption occur when the actions of an individual consumer have positive knock-on impacts on others in society, i.e. external benefits arise. An individual who adopts a healthy lifestyle and gets regular medical check-ups may be expected to take fewer days off work through illness and be more productive than somebody who does not. As such, they may require less overall government health spending over the course of their lives and may contribute to a higher standard of living for the nation as a whole. In such cases, **social benefits** exceed **private benefits**, as shown in

> **Social benefit**: the total of private benefit plus external benefit of an economic transaction.
>
> **Private benefit**: the benefit to an individual consumer involved in a market transaction.

Exam practice answers and quick quizzes at **www.hoddereducation.co.uk/myrevisionnotes**

Figure 8.2. In a free market with no government intervention, there will be under-consumption of goods with positive externalities. In other words, demand is too low. There is overlap with the concept of a merit good.

In the diagram, demand curve D_1 reflects the private benefits of exercise and a healthy lifestyle. However, the full benefits to society of all citizens pursuing a healthy lifestyle, shown by demand curve D_2, are not fully appreciated and thus there is under-consumption of $Q_2 - Q_1$.

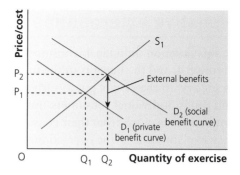

Figure 8.2 Positive externalities in consumption

Negative externalities in production

REVISED ☐

Negative externalities in production may arise if a firm fails to take into account the wider negative impacts of their activities upon society, i.e. there are external costs. A coastal oil refinery not obliged to account for its wider impact may pollute the atmosphere and local beaches with its emissions and waste products. This will clearly have negative consequences for groups beyond the owners of the factory, including health and environmental consequences. In these situations, social costs exceed the private costs of production (such as raw materials and wages). The market failure arises because output is greater than the social optimum and the price is too low to take full account of all costs of production, including external costs, as shown in Figure 8.3.

> **Negative externality:** a negative knock-on effect of an economic transaction upon third parties, also known as an external cost.

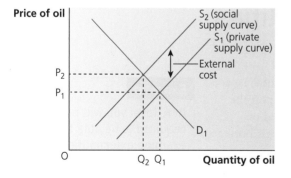

Figure 8.3 Negative externalities in production

Negative externalities in consumption

In this situation individuals consume 'too much' of a product, as shown in Figure 8.4, and the benefits to the individual consumer exceed the benefits to society. In the case of goods such as less-healthy foods, alcohol, tobacco and drugs, individual consumers/users fail to appreciate that society may not benefit as much from their consumption. Indeed, **information failure** may explain some of the over-consumption of such goods if people become intoxicated or addicted and less able to make 'rational' decisions. Thus there is overlap with the concept of demerit goods.

Information failure: a source of market failure where market participants do not have enough information to be able to make effective judgements about the 'correct' levels of consumption or production of a good.

Exam tip

Make sure you can draw accurate diagrams to illustrate positive and negative externalities.

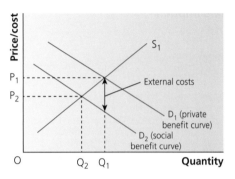

Figure 8.4 Negative externalities in consumption

Now test yourself

5 Which of the products below has a market price which most accounts for negative externalities?

Product	Private cost per unit (£)	External cost per unit (£)	Market price (£)
A	15	5	16
B	20	2	22
C	12	10	13
D	16	7	21

Answer on p. 227

Marginal analysis of externalities for A-level

The concepts of the margin and marginal analysis are fundamental aspects of microeconomic theory. The 'margin' means analysis based upon the last or an additional unit of output of a good or service produced or consumed. You have already come across marginal analysis in this book, for example in relation to marginal utility in Chapter 2, marginal costs and revenues in Chapters 3 and 4, and marginal revenue productivity in Chapter 6.

Exam tip

At A-level you will be required to be able to examine externalities in production and consumption using marginal analysis and show this analysis diagrammatically.

We can extend and refine our explanation of externalities with marginal analysis. Key points of understanding are that:

● marginal private cost (MPC) + marginal external cost (MEC) = marginal social cost (MSC)
● marginal private benefit (MPB) + marginal external benefit (MEB) = marginal social benefit (MSB)
● social welfare is optimised when MSB = MSC

Positive externalities in production

As noted earlier, positive externalities in production occur when the actions of firms have wider benefits to society, such as in the case of building a new airport runway. In a free market situation, the individual firm would take into account only its private costs and benefits and not those of wider society. In the case of positive externalities in production, as shown in Figure 8.5, MPC > MSC, meaning there is a negative marginal external cost, equal to the vertical distance between the MPC and MSC curves at the free market equilibrium quantity, Q_1. As the social optimum quantity occurs where MSB = MSC, i.e. at Q_2, there is under-production of airport capacity equal to $Q_2 - Q_1$, leading to an overall welfare loss equal to the shaded triangle.

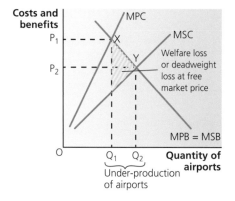

Exam tip

The area of welfare loss shown in externality diagrams is also referred to as the area of deadweight loss.

Figure 8.5 Positive externalities in production

Positive externalities in consumption

Positive externalities in consumption occur when the actions of individual consumers have wider benefits to society, such as in the case of maintaining a healthy lifestyle, e.g. taking regular exercise and eating healthy food. In a free market situation, the individual consumer would take into account only their private costs and benefits and not those of wider society. In the case of positive externalities in consumption, as shown in Figure 8.6, MSB > MPB, meaning there is a marginal external benefit, equal to the vertical distance between the MSB and MPB curves at the free market equilibrium quantity, Q_1. As the social optimum quantity occurs where MSB = MSC, i.e. at Q_2, there is under-consumption of healthy food and exercise equal to $Q_2 - Q_1$, leading to an overall welfare loss equal to the shaded triangle. Note that this analysis can also be used to examine the market failure associated with the under-consumption of merit goods.

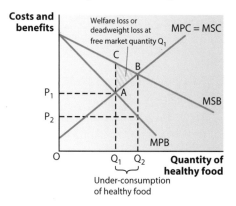

Figure 8.6 Positive externalities in consumption

Negative externalities in production

REVISED

Negative externalities in production occur when the actions of firms have wider costs to society, such as in the case of a coastal oil refinery. In a free market situation, the individual firm would take into account only its private costs and benefits and not those of wider society. In the case of negative externalities in production, as shown in Figure 8.7, MSC > MPC, meaning there is a marginal external cost, equal to the vertical distance between the MSC and MPC curves at the free market equilibrium quantity, Q_1. As the social optimum quantity occurs where MSB = MSC, i.e. at Q_2, there is over-production by the oil refinery equal to $Q_1 - Q_2$, leading to an overall welfare loss equal to the shaded triangle.

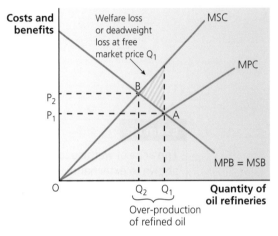

Figure 8.7 Negative externalities in production

Negative externalities in consumption

REVISED

Negative externalities in consumption occur when the perceived benefits of consumption activities to individual consumers exceed the benefits to society, such as in the case of excessive consumption of demerit goods such as alcohol, tobacco and fatty foods. In a free market situation, the individual consumer would take into account only their private costs and benefits and not those of wider society. In the case of negative externalities in consumption, as shown in Figure 8.8, MPB > MSB, meaning there is a negative marginal external benefit, equal to the vertical distance between the MPB and MSB curves at the free market equilibrium quantity, Q_1. As the social optimum quantity occurs where MSB = MSC, i.e. at Q_2, there is over-consumption of demerit goods equal to $Q_2 - Q_1$, leading to an overall welfare loss equal to the shaded triangle.

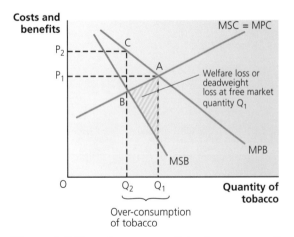

Figure 8.8 Negative externalities in consumption

Exam practice answers and quick quizzes at **www.hoddereducation.co.uk/myrevisionnotes**

Environmental market failure and the tragedy of the commons

Environmental market failure

REVISED

Environmental market failures are essentially negative externalities that lead to some form of environmental damage. These may include over-use of non-renewable resources such as oil, coal and gas, or exploitation of the oceans, forests or atmosphere. Major environmental market failures that are likely to dominate world affairs for the foreseeable future are the related problems of global warming and climate change.

One reason for environmental market failures is a lack of clearly defined **property rights** relating to environmental resources such as the oceans, the forests or the atmosphere. Economic agents such as individual firms or consumers therefore do not suffer any penalty for polluting the atmosphere, dumping waste in the oceans, or excessive deforestation, for example. This leads to over-use of these resources and the rapid depletion of non-renewable resources.

> **Environmental market failure**: negative externalities arising from the over-exploitation of environmental resources.
>
> **Property rights**: the legal rights of ownership or use of an economic resource.

The tragedy of the commons

REVISED

Environmental market failures are related to the concept of the **tragedy of the commons**. This is a relatively old term that relates to the over-grazing of common land by animals, leading to degradation of grassland, with dire consequences for the future. In a modern sense, the term has been extended to mean the over-use of any natural resource, such as the oceans, forests, atmosphere or minerals in the ground.

Environmental market failures and the tragedy of the commons can both be analysed using negative externality diagrams, in production and consumption.

> **Tragedy of the commons**: the over-use or exploitation of resources such as the oceans, the forests or the atmosphere that are not owned by individuals or organisations.

Merit and demerit goods

Sometimes, society judges that some goods or services are either under-consumed or over-consumed. Goods that are under-consumed in a free market are known as **merit goods**, while those that would be over-consumed are known as **demerit goods**. 'Under-consumption' and 'over-consumption' in this sense are normative, subjective terms that involve value judgements being made by the governments of the countries concerned.

> **Merit good**: a good that would be under-consumed in a free market.
>
> **Demerit good**: a good that would be over-consumed in a free market.

Merit goods

REVISED

Classic examples of merit goods include education and healthcare, though several other goods and services may fit the criteria outlined below, including:
- exercise
- car insurance
- healthy foods

There is some overlap between the concepts of a merit good and a positive externality in consumption.

Merit goods would be under-consumed in a free market, for several possible reasons:

- People are not aware of the potential private benefits to themselves from consuming the merit good, especially in the long term. In the case of education, it is very difficult for some individuals to appreciate fully the benefits to themselves from attending school or college for several years; it can be hard to see the relevance of parts of a standard curriculum to their daily lives. This is an example of information failure, which means that one, or both, parties to an economic transaction do not possess all the information they need to make an accurate decision, or they are not aware of how to use the information available. In terms of education, people may not see personal benefits such as increased productivity and employability, leading to higher earnings over the course of their lifetime.
- People may not be able to afford the product. It would cost an individual several thousands of pounds per person per year to fund their own education and many would not be able to afford this.
- People may not take into account the wider benefits to society of their use of merit goods. These wider benefits can be seen as positive externalities and may include, in the case of education, a greater overall standard of living for society as a result of higher output and increased innovation. Individual consumers are not, however, required to take these into account.

Now test yourself

TESTED

6 A merit good, such as education is:
  A non-excludable with positive externalities in production
  B non-rival with positive externalities in consumption
  C rival with positive externalities in production only
  D excludable with positive externalities in consumption

Answer on p. 227

Demerit goods

REVISED

Demerit goods include 'recreational' drugs, such as alcohol and tobacco, and other aspects of an unhealthy lifestyle such as fatty, sugary foods. Demerit goods are those that would be over-consumed in a free market, and often give rise to negative externalities in consumption.

Demerit goods are over-consumed for a number of reasons:

- People may not be aware of the damage to their health arising from consumption. For example, in the case of smoking cigarettes, people are not aware of, or choose to ignore, the various smoking-related illnesses. This is another example of information failure.
- Goods are too cheap and so people can too easily afford them, or they are too accessible. For example, some people are concerned that strong alcohol is too cheap and too easily available, even to the under-aged.
- Individuals do not take account of the wider external costs associated with their consumption. For example, cigarette smoking by one person may inflict health damage on others in the vicinity. Similarly, excessive drinking by certain groups may lead to antisocial behaviour, which may create noise or other disturbance to others outside the group.

> **Typical mistake**
>
> Note that not all products that result in positive or negative externalities in consumption are either merit or demerit goods.

Market imperfections

Economists often make use of theoretical 'perfect' markets in order to make comparisons with markets in reality. Perfect markets have the following features:

- perfect information
- no barriers to entry and exit
- homogeneous products and factors of production
- large numbers of buyers and sellers
- perfect mobility of factors of production

These features are clearly unrealistic and real-life markets tend to have a range of imperfections as outlined below.

Imperfect and asymmetric information

REVISED

Imperfect information exists when economic agents (consumers, employees, producers or government) do not know everything they need to know in order to make a fully informed decision. Individual consumers may not be fully aware of the positive and negative consequences of their use of certain goods, especially in the long term. As a result they may consume insufficient or excessive amounts in terms of maximising the overall welfare of society.

Asymmetric information is a similar concept but implies that one economic agent knows more than another, giving that agent more power in the decision-making process. A good example of this is in the market for second-hand cars, where the seller often knows whether or not the car is in full working order. Unless the buyer knows what he or she is looking for, the only signal they may have as to the quality of the car is the price. Being aware of this, the seller will price good and bad examples of the same car at similar prices, making it even more difficult for uninformed buyers to make favourable decisions. Unscrupulous producers may thus exploit consumers. Appropriate government intervention here may be designed to improve the quality and reliability of information held by economic agents, and to redress the imbalance in the case of asymmetric information.

> **Imperfect information**: when economic agents do not know everything they need to know in order to make a fully informed decision.
>
> **Asymmetric information**: a source of information failure where one economic agent knows more than another, giving them more power in a market transaction.

Monopoly

REVISED

Monopoly is an extreme example of a market structure that, in its pure form, means that only one firm supplies a market. In a free market without government intervention, a monopoly producer has no incentive to be economically efficient, since there are no rival firms to take its market share. This is because of significant barriers to entry to the market, such as product differentiation and large economies of scale. This means that consumers will not benefit from the lowest prices, or have a choice of products. Thus the market failure leads to productive and allocative inefficiency and possibly reduced choice for consumers, an equity issue.

Now test yourself

TESTED

7 A highly competitive market is taken over by a monopoly producer. This may result in:
   A lower costs
   B lower prices
   C lower profits
   D lower research and development

Answer on p. 227

Immobility of factors of production

REVISED

Factors of production, especially labour, are unlikely to be perfectly mobile between different uses or occupations. For example, a former steel worker may not find it easy to switch quickly to working as an IT consultant, since he or she may lack the specific skills and qualifications required. This is referred to as **occupational immobility**.

In addition, individuals may not be aware of, or easily able to move to, where jobs exist. For example, an IT consultant currently living and working in the north of England may not be able to afford accommodation in London or the southeast of the country, and so may not be able to obtain a promotion in their field of work. It is also possible that they have dependent relatives in their current location and so may not wish to leave their home city. This would lead to **geographical immobility**.

> **Occupational immobility**: a source of factor immobility that means workers find it difficult to move between occupations for reasons of lack of desirable skills.
>
> **Geographical immobility**: a source of factor immobility that means workers have difficulty in moving to locations where jobs are available for reasons such as a lack of affordable housing or family commitments.

Now test yourself

TESTED

8 Which one of the following is most likely to lead to immobility of labour?
   A   government subsidising training courses
   B   regional differences in house prices
   C   improved information about job availability
   D   government subsidising public transport

Answer on p. 227

An inequitable distribution of income and wealth

Equity is the notion of fairness in the allocation of economic resources. In a market economy, with no government intervention, those individuals with the greatest ability to pay, i.e. the highest incomes, will tend to have access to the greatest share of resources.

Different economies around the world and over time have taken a range of views about what level of inequality is acceptable. Free market capitalists would argue that inequality creates useful incentives among economic agents that positively influence overall national income and can 'trickle down' to poorer members of society, raising overall living standards. Critics of free market capitalism might say that inequality creates social tensions between the relatively rich and poor, leading to reduced living standards.

> **Equity**: the notion of fairness in society.
>
> **Inequitable distribution of income and wealth**: when the way in which income and wealth are distributed in society is considered unfair.

Government intervention in markets

Reasons for government intervention

REVISED

The free market often fails to achieve an efficient or equitable allocation of resources. Cases such as over-consumption of certain demerit goods and the potential hiking of prices by monopoly firms provide justification for some form or forms of intervention.

However, reasons for government intervention are not solely microeconomic. The government has important wider macroeconomic objectives that are focused on improving the overall performance of the UK economy and living standards for the population as a whole.

So the main reasons for government intervention are to:
● correct any market failure
● achieve a fairer (or more equitable) distribution of income and wealth
● achieve the government's macroeconomic objectives for the economy

Indirect taxation

Governments can use **indirect taxes** to alter the supply of certain goods or services. Indirect taxes have the effect of increasing the costs of firms, which means they lead to the supply curve shifting leftwards.

> **Indirect tax**: a tax on spending, sometimes used to reduce consumption of demerit goods.

The government can use two different types of indirect taxation:
1 **Specific, or unit taxes** — these involve a fixed amount being added per unit of a good or service, such as that on bottles of alcohol.
2 *Ad valorem* **taxes** — these involve adding a percentage of the price of a good or service: for example, VAT at 20% would add 20p to a product costing £1, but £20 to a product costing £100.

The impacts of the two different types of indirect tax are shown in Figure 8.9.

Advantages of using indirect taxation

● Indirect taxes are often placed on goods that have inelastic demand. This means that strong tax revenues can be gained for governments, which can then be assigned to specific areas of spending, such as healthcare.
● Use of the price mechanism leaves it up to consumers and producers to decide how to adjust their behaviour.
● Assuming governments have applied the correct rate of taxation, the tax helps to internalise an external cost, i.e. to reflect more accurately the impact of a negative externality on price and quantity.

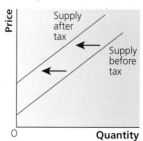

Figure 8.9 Indirect taxation shifting a supply curve

Disadvantages of using indirect taxation

● Because indirect taxes are often placed on inelastic goods, the quantity demanded may not fall very much unless the tax is very large, which reduces the impact of the tax.
● In practice, it can be extremely difficult to place an accurate monetary value on external costs, which makes it almost impossible to correctly 'internalise' a negative externality.
● Indirect taxes tend to be regressive in nature, which means they take a larger percentage of a poorer person's income. This may be seen as unfair.
● UK firms may be concerned that their international competitiveness may be reduced by the imposition of indirect taxes, which increase their production costs relative to those of foreign competitors.

Subsidies

REVISED

Subsidies are government grants paid to producers to encourage increased production of certain goods or services, such as merit goods. By reducing the price of specific goods or services, the government is also attempting to increase their consumption. Subsidies can also be used to promote the use of products which reduce external costs, such as public transport. Granting a government subsidy has the effect of shifting the supply curve to the right.

The impact of a subsidy is shown in Figure 8.10.

Subsidy: a payment made to producers to encourage increased production of a good or service.

Advantages of using subsidies

- Subsidies on merit goods can increase their consumption, bringing the equilibrium quantity closer to the social optimum, helping to internalise the external benefit.
- Subsidies reduce the price of a good, making it more affordable for those on lower incomes, so reducing the effects of relative poverty.

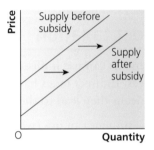

Figure 8.10 **A subsidy shifting a supply curve**

Disadvantages of using subsidies

- As in the case of taxing negative externalities, it is extremely difficult in practice to place an accurate monetary value on the size of external benefits.
- Funding for subsidies carries an opportunity cost, i.e. the money could have been spent on other things such as building new hospitals or roads.
- Firms receiving subsidies may become reliant on them, encouraging productive inefficiency and laziness, and reducing international competitiveness in the long run.
- Subsidies for UK firms may be viewed by foreign governments as a form of artificial trade protection, encouraging them to retaliate by erecting their own forms of protection.
- If subsidies are placed on goods or services with inelastic demand, they may reduce price but not significantly increase consumption.

Now test yourself

TESTED

9 A government subsidy:
   A   leads to a rise in the equilibrium price of goods
   B   shifts the supply curve of a good leftwards
   C   leads to an increase in the equilibrium output of goods
   D   reduces the price elasticity of demand of goods

Answer on p. 227

Minimum prices

REVISED

Minimum prices are price floors that establish a legal level below which prices are not allowed to fall. Examples of this intervention include the setting of a National Minimum Wage and guaranteed minimum prices paid to farmers for their agricultural products, such as with the European Union's Common Agricultural Policy (CAP).

Minimum price: a price floor placed above the free market equilibrium price.

The impact of a minimum price is shown in Figure 8.11. A minimum price (P_1) set above the free market price (P^*) for a good will create excess supply, equal to $Q_S - Q_D$, as shown in the diagram.

Advantages of minimum prices

- They give producers a guaranteed minimum price and income, which helps to generate a reasonable standard of living, such as in the case of farmers in less developed countries.
- They encourage production of essential products, such as the foodstuffs produced by EU farmers covered by the CAP.
- Excess supplies may be bought up and stored, to be released in times of future shortage.

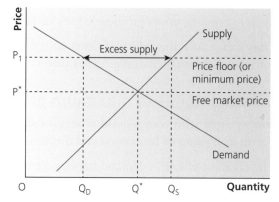

Figure 8.11 The effect of a minimum price

Disadvantages of minimum prices

- Consumers must pay a higher price, reducing their disposable income.
- They can encourage over-production, especially in the case of the CAP, which is an inefficient use of resources. This excess supply may need to be put into storage, which generates further costs.
- If governments or other authorities have to purchase excess supplies, this leads to opportunity costs, i.e. these funds could have been used elsewhere.
- They may reduce international competitiveness if the price is raised above those of foreign competitors.
- In the case of interventions to reduce the affordability of demerit goods, such as hard drugs or alcohol, they may encourage people to seek cheaper, potentially more harmful alternatives, leading to government failure.

Maximum prices

A **maximum price** is an upper limit, or price ceiling, above which prices are not permitted to rise. The justification for their use is usually that the free market equilibrium price would be too high for many consumers, leading to problems of reduced affordability. Examples include rent controls in densely populated cities, and limits on the ability of utility companies to raise their price above the rate of inflation.

> **Maximum price:** a price ceiling above which prices are not permitted to rise.

The impact of a maximum price is shown in Figure 8.12. A maximum price (P_1) set below the free market price (P^*) for a good will create excess demand, equal to $Q_2 - Q_1$, as shown in the diagram.

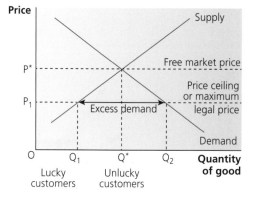

Figure 8.12 The effect of a maximum price

> **Exam tip**
>
> Practise drawing accurate minimum and maximum price diagrams and illustrating how they may lead to excess supply and excess demand respectively.

Advantages of maximum prices

Without a maximum price, some people would not be able to afford certain goods and services, for example some prescription medications. Thus maximum prices promote equity or fairness.

They can reduce the ability of firms with monopoly power to exploit consumers through charging higher prices.

Disadvantages of maximum prices

Some people who want a good or service will simply not be able to obtain it, leading to frustration and dissatisfaction.

The creation of excess demand implies queues, shortages and waiting lists, which, in the case of markets such as healthcare in the UK, can have serious implications.

Maximum prices may lead to the establishment of black markets for goods and services, such as secondary markets for music and sporting event tickets.

> **Typical mistake**
>
> Getting maximum price and minimum price the wrong way round. Remember that a maximum price is intended to stop prices rising too high and a minimum price is intended to stop prices falling too low. This distinction is often tested in multiple-choice questions.

Direct provision

REVISED

Sometimes a government might take the view that provision of a good or service cannot be left to the free market at all, since it may be provided in insufficient or excessive quantities (in the case of merit and demerit goods) or not at all (in the case of public goods). Typically, the government will organise provision of the product in question, then raise the necessary funds out of tax revenue. The government itself need not produce the good or service; it may pay a private sector firm to do this, wholly or partially. For example, it may pay a construction firm to build a new school.

Generally, these goods or services may be free or nearly free, 'at the point of consumption', so individuals do not have to worry about making a payment every time they attend state school or require medical treatment.

Regulation

REVISED

Regulations are rules or laws used to control or restrict the actions of economic agents in order to reduce market failure.

Examples of regulations used to tackle market failures include:
- banning smoking in public places
- a minimum legal age to drink alcohol
- maximum emissions levels on new cars
- noise thresholds on aeroplanes as they take off in urban areas
- establishing green-belt land around major cities
- setting up regulatory bodies (such as OFGEM) to restrict the activities of dominant firms

> **Regulation**: rules or laws used to control or restrict the actions of economic agents in order to reduce market failure.

If firms or consumers do not adhere to the rules and laws they may be punished, for example with fines, limitations on trading activities, or even imprisonment.

Correcting information failure

REVISED

Governments may attempt to intervene in markets where they believe that consumers consume either too many or too few goods or services

Exam practice answers and quick quizzes at **www.hoddereducation.co.uk/myrevisionnotes**

because of a lack of information about the effects of consumption and production.

Goods which qualify as merit goods would be under-consumed in a free market because consumers lack knowledge, or are unable to make rational decisions, about the benefits of consumption, especially in the long run. Conversely, demerit goods would be over-consumed in a free market, again because of a lack of knowledge or ability to make rational choices about the problems arising from consumption.

Governments may use a range of methods to remedy information failure, all of which will affect the demand for the good or service in question, which, if done successfully, will bring the quantity demanded closer to the social optimum. Examples of attempts to correct information failure include:

- compulsory labelling on food, along with 'traffic-lighting' levels of fat, salt, etc.
- strong health warnings on packs of cigarettes
- TV advertising campaigns discouraging excessive alcohol consumption
- the publication of local and national league tables for schools and hospitals

There are several drawbacks of government attempts to correct information failure in these ways, however. For example, government advertising campaigns often have a high cost and their effectiveness is questioned, particularly their ability in the long term to cause people to change their behaviour amidst the volume of information with which consumers are regularly bombarded. Indeed, the marketing power and skill of the world's leading soft drinks companies such as Coca-Cola may be greater than those of individual governments attempting to counter them.

Extending property rights and the use of pollution permits

In the case of environmental market failure, as outlined earlier in this chapter, a key reason recognised for the over-exploitation of natural resources such as oceans, forests and the atmosphere is a lack of clearly defined property rights or ownership of these resources.

Economists suggest that defining or extending property rights over environmental resources in such cases can be a powerful market-based approach in reducing over-exploitation and encouraging firms and consumers to value the environment more highly, reducing environmental damage and resource depletion.

One example of extending property rights and creating a market for pollution is the use of **pollution permits.** These are legal rights to use or exploit economic resources to a specific degree and include fishing permits, deforestation permits and CO_2 pollution permits.

> **Pollution permit:** the right to use or exploit an economic resource to a specific degree, e.g. a fishing permit or permits to release CO_2 into the atmosphere.

Pollution permits can be presented and analysed using a diagram, as in Figure 8.13. A regulating organisation such as a government will set a fixed supply of permits, such as S_{2016}, deciding how many permits to release in the year 2016, based on the perceived social optimum level of output. This leads to a perfectly inelastic supply of permits at Q_{2016}. Demand by CO_2-emitting firms in 2016 is given by the demand curve D_{2016}. An equilibrium price is thus set at P_{2016}. The use of the market mechanism can provide powerful incentives to firms to reduce their carbon emissions as they now have to pay a price to generate these emissions. Firms that improve their carbon efficiency can sell any spare permits in the carbon market, increasing their profit.

However, firms that do not manage to reduce their carbon emissions have to buy additional permits in the carbon market, which reduces their profit. In both cases, firms should be incentivised to reduce their CO_2 emissions, perhaps by investing in so-called 'green' technologies.

If the organisation overseeing the carbon market wishes to speed up the rate at which industrial emissions are reduced, it can reduce the supply of permits, e.g. to S_{2020}, such as the EU has done with its 20-20-20 policy, aiming to reduce EU CO_2 emissions by 20% compared with 1990 levels by the year 2020.

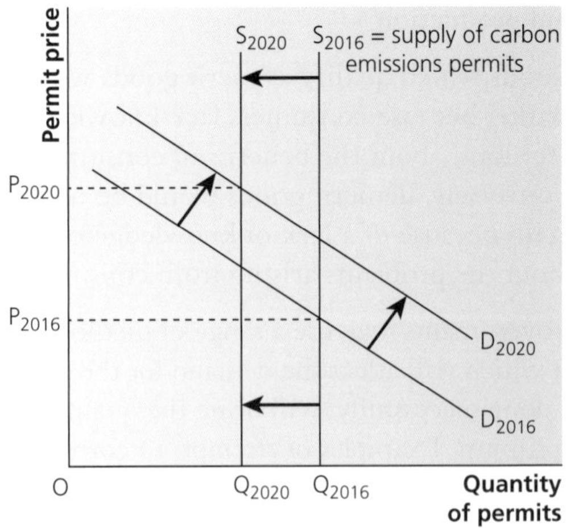

Advantages of pollution permits

● The method uses the market mechanism, which can provide powerful incentives for firms to reduce their carbon emissions.
● Revenues raised from selling permits can be used to fund 'green' technologies and other environmental schemes.

Disadvantages of pollution permits

● Governments are likely to suffer from imperfect information about the full social costs of CO_2 emissions, which may lead to government failure in deciding the quantity of permits to set.
● If the price of permits is set too low, firms will not be sufficiently incentivised to cut their CO_2 emissions.

Figure 8.13 **Using pollution permits to tackle environmental market failure**

Competition policy

UK competition policy involves measures to enhance competition between firms in order to improve economic outcomes for society. Measures include legislation, privatisation, deregulation, prevention of mergers and various actions to prevent restrictive trade practices and abuse of monopoly power. UK competition policy is currently overseen by the Competition and Markets Authority (CMA).

Principles of UK competition policy

Competition policy is government policy which aims to make markets more competitive. In the UK, the CMA is the government agency responsible for overseeing competition policy. The main theoretical principles underpinning UK competition policy include the following:
● Ignoring economies of scale, perfect competition is more likely to be productively and allocatively efficient than monopoly.
● Monopolists restrict output to raise price and gain supernormal profit. This results in a net loss of welfare as consumer surplus is reduced and producer surplus is increased.

But:
● If economies of scale are present, monopolies may produce output at a lower average total cost than firms in perfect competition.
● Monopoly firms making supernormal profit can be more innovative and dynamically efficient than firms in perfect competition.
● In general, each case is judged on its own merits.

> **Exam tip**
>
> Detailed knowledge of UK and EU competition law is *not* required.

REVISED

> **Competition policy:** government policy which aims to make markets more competitive.

Competition policy in the UK is focused on four areas:
- monopolies
- mergers
- restrictive trading practices
- promoting competition

Monopolies

Since there are few, if any, examples of actual monopolies, competition policy is focused on concentrated markets, which may be more correctly described as oligopolies. The CMA uses a structure, conduct and performance approach to judging the relative merits of each investigation it makes. Possible approaches to tackling monopolies include:
- **Compulsory break-up:** free market economists who believe that efficiency and consumer sovereignty are maximised when competition is encouraged would advocate the breaking-up of monopolies in all industries.
- **Windfall taxes on 'excess' or supernormal profits.**
- **Price controls:** e.g. maximum prices may be used to limit excessive profits.
- **Public ownership (nationalisation):** publicly owned monopolies are assumed by some economists to be more likely to operate in the best interests of society, e.g. by targeting an allocatively efficient output rather than one that maximises profit.
- **Privatisation:** an opposing view, held by the Conservative government of the 1980s for example, is that selling formerly state-owned monopolies to private owners is more likely to lead to efficient, consumer-focused businesses. The supernormal profits that privately run monopolies may earn can arguably lead to greater dynamic efficiency in terms of innovation. In addition, subjecting monopolies to a 'stock market discipline', being answerable to shareholders, may be a powerful driver of productive efficiency in order to maximise profits.
- **Deregulation:** removing barriers to entry may make monopolies more contestable and so more likely to operate in society's best interests. The theory of contestable markets is covered in Chapter 5.

Mergers

A **merger** occurs when two or more firms willingly join together. Competition policy concerning mergers considers whether mergers and **takeovers** might create a new monopoly and therefore present the anti-competitive dangers associated with dominant firms. Mergers and takeovers may thus be prohibited if they are predicted to be against the public interest by substantially reducing competition in a market.

> **Merger:** when two or more firms willingly join together.
>
> **Takeover:** when two or more firms unwillingly join together.

Restrictive trading practices

Restrictive trading practices include:
- forming a cartel to fix the price of a good or service
- refusal to supply a specific retailer
- 'full-line forcing' — obliging a retailer to stock all products in the firm's current range
- charging discriminatory prices, e.g. discounts for bulk orders

Upon investigation and gathering of evidence to establish a restrictive trade practice, the CMA will usually require the firm(s) involved to stop the practice under threat of prosecution.

Public ownership, privatisation, regulation and deregulation of markets

Economists and politicians argue about the best ways to improve the economic performance of firms and markets in the UK. Those favouring the free market would encourage greater privatisation and deregulation, while others would recommend increased state ownership and tighter regulation.

Public ownership

REVISED

Public ownership means that firms, industries or other assets are owned by government. Advantages of public ownership include:

- **Taking account of externalities:** nationalised monopolies are arguably more likely to take account of externalities since they are not responsible to shareholders who seek profit maximisation.
- **Social welfare:** state-run monopolies are more likely to produce at an allocatively efficient output rather than restrict output in order to maximise profits. This may mean, for example, that in the area of transport, loss-making routes such as rural bus services, which a profit-seeking private firm might not offer, would still be provided.
- **Strategic importance:** historically, key industries such as rail, energy, steel and water were regarded as the 'commanding heights' of the UK economy and too important to be run by private organisations which might cut corners to maximise profits. The 'too big to fail' argument was used to support the partial **nationalisation** of several UK banks following the financial crisis of 2008.

Disadvantages of public ownership include:

- **Lack of dynamic efficiency:** the ability of governments to 'subsidise' organisations from tax revenue and a lack of pressure to maximise profits may be argued to lead to a lack of dynamic efficiency. Critics of public ownership might point to many years of under-investment in the UK's transport network. The absence of competition may also be a reason for inefficiency.
- **Lack of expertise:** some economists argue that the best managers and leaders are to be found in the private sector, where financial rewards may also be significantly higher, rather than the public sector.

> **Public ownership**: government ownership of firms, industries or other assets.
>
> **Nationalisation**: the transfer of assets from the private sector to public ownership.

Privatisation

REVISED

Advantages of **privatisation** include:

- **Raising extra revenue for the government:** the sale of state-owned assets to the private sector can generate significant short-term revenue. At the height of the 'privatisation era' in the 1980s, several billion pounds a year were generated.
- **Promoting competition:** in theory, selling state-owned firms to the private sector exposes them to potential competition, whereas previously they were protected by government monopoly.
- **Promoting efficiency:** free market supporters would argue that incentives created by the profit motive lead firms to cut production costs to remain competitive.
- **Popular capitalism:** encouraging greater share ownership by the general public may lead to greater pressure on firms to act in the public interest.

> **Privatisation**: the sale of government-owned assets to the private sector.

Disadvantages of privatisation include:

- **Exploitation of monopoly power:** critics would argue that privatised monopolies may lead to a worse allocation of resources since, as explained in Chapter 5, profit-maximising monopolies restrict output below productively and allocatively efficient levels in order to generate supernormal profits. This would lead to a loss of economic welfare compared with a state-run monopoly.
- **Short-termism:** pressure from shareholders who demand annual dividends may mean a focus on cost-cutting to maximise short-term profits rather than on longer-term investment projects. This may also include the closure of any sections of a business that are making losses, e.g. railway branch lines or countryside bus routes.
- **Ignoring externalities**: private firms may ignore the negative as well as the positive externalities associated with their activities because it would not be profitable to take into account the spillover effects of their actions, again leading to a loss of economic welfare compared with a state-run monopoly.

Regulation

REVISED

Regulation involves the imposition of rules and laws which restrict market freedom. Regulation comes in two forms: external regulation and self-regulation. The first involves external agencies such as the CMA imposing rules and restrictions. The latter involves organisations in particular industries voluntarily regulating themselves, e.g. via membership of a professional governing body such as the Institute of Chartered Accountants in England and Wales or the Law Society.

While regulation may impose additional costs on businesses, which may reduce their profit and potentially compromise innovation and dynamic efficiency, it is felt to be justified in protecting consumers from abuse of monopoly power and external costs. However, regulation may lead to the problem of **regulatory capture**.

> **Regulation**: the imposition of rules and laws which restrict market freedom.
>
> **Regulatory capture**: when the regulatory bodies (such as OFGEM in the case of gas and electricity suppliers) set up to oversee the behaviour of privatised monopolies come to be unduly influenced by the firms they have been set up to monitor.

Deregulation

REVISED

Deregulation involves the removal of rules and regulations in order to increase the efficiency of markets. Examples include the deregulation of various utilities markets such as domestic energy, water and telecommunications in order to promote competition and market contestability.

> **Deregulation**: the removal of rules and regulations in order to increase the efficiency of markets.

The removal of so-called 'red tape' or excessive bureaucracy is one benefit of deregulation, which may be argued to reduce firms' costs of production, meaning consumers may benefit from lower prices. The promotion of competition may also lead to a more contestable market by removing artificial barriers to entry. Deregulation is also felt to help avoid the problem of regulatory capture.

Now test yourself

TESTED

10 List three competition policy measures that could be used to enhance competition between firms in the UK.

Answer on p. 227

8 The market mechanism, market failure and government intervention in markets

Government failure

Government failure is said to occur when government intervention in a market leads to a misallocation of resources. There are a number of reasons for government failure, and several causes may exist at the same time.

> **Government failure:** when government intervention in a market reduces overall economic welfare.

Reasons for government failure

REVISED

Inadequate information

As noted earlier, governments often act with very imperfect information. For example, it is exteremely difficult in practice to place an accurate monetary value on external costs and benefits. For this reason, the subsequent indirect tax or subsidy used to deal with the issue is unlikely to internalise completely these externalities and lead to the social optimum, or allocatively efficient, quantity being produced and consumed.

Unintended consequences

A government seeking to reduce the consumption of demerit goods such as alcohol may impose a minimum price per unit of alcohol. However, this may lead to arguably more harmful intoxicants such as hard drugs becoming relatively cheap, encouraging greater consumption, with associated impacts upon health services and policing. Reduced consumption of alcohol may also lead to increased unemployment of people working in the drinks industry. These consequences may have been unforeseen by the government and so would be considered to be unintended.

Market distortions

Attempts by governments to correct market failure may lead to inefficiencies, surpluses and shortages. For example, a maximum price on aspects of healthcare such as prescriptions may lead to excess demand, while a minimum wage may lead to an excess supply of workers in some low-paid occupations.

Administrative costs

It is possible that the costs of researching and implementing any intervention may outweigh the benefit of the policy itself, leading to a worsening of the allocation of resources. For example, the cost of recruiting and paying a staff of inspectors to ensure firms and individuals adhere to specific regulations may exceed the size of the external cost arising from the market failure.

Regulatory capture

This is said to occur when the regulatory bodies (such as OFGEM in the case of gas and electricity suppliers) set up to oversee the behaviour of privatised monopolies come to be unduly influenced by the firms they have been set up to monitor. This is because, to an extent, the regulators depend upon the existence of dominant firms in such industries for their existence, and so may be more easily swayed.

Now test yourself

11 Which one of the following is an example of government failure?
   A   state provision of national defence
   B   all subsidies given to firms
   C   the government allowing the free market to raise the price of petrol
   D   the government overproducing a merit good

Answer on p. 227

Exam practice

1 Market failure arises whenever firms:
   A   make workers redundant
   B   increase prices
   C   create negative externalities
   D   make a loss   [1]
2 The following table shows the marginal private and external benefits and the marginal private and external costs of a product provided by the free market.

Benefits/costs	£
Marginal private benefit	15
Marginal external benefit	12
Marginal private cost	15
Marginal external cost	0

Government intervention in this market may improve economic welfare because the product is likely to be:
   A   an inferior good
   B   a public good
   C   a demerit good
   D   a merit good   [1]
3 Market failure may be corrected if a government:
   A   provides public goods
   B   subsidises all private sector firms
   C   places an indirect tax on merit goods
   D   places a maximum price on demerit goods   [1]
4 Market failure may best be reduced by:
   A   the existence of merit goods
   B   reduced mobility of factors of production
   C   increasing economies of scale
   D   improving the availability of information to consumers   [1]
5 Using marginal analysis, explain the possible externalities that may arise due to the construction of a new high-speed rail link across England.   [9]
6 With the aid of a diagram, explain why individuals may consume too much unhealthy food.   [9]
7 Using a diagram, explain how a government subsidy may be used to correct the market failure associated with merit goods.   [9]
8 Explain how the concept of the tragedy of the commons might be applied to waste disposal by households and firms.   [9]
9 Explain how pollution permits may be used to deal with environmental market failure.   [9]
10 Evaluate the arguments for and against the privatisation and deregulation of previously state-owned organisations.   [25]
11 Evaluate methods that the government could use to control the activities of monopolies.   [25]

Answers and quick quiz 8 online

ONLINE ☐

Summary

You should have an understanding of:

- The four key functions of prices.
- The advantages and disadvantages of the price mechanism and of extending its use into new areas of activity.
- The meaning of market failure.
- The distinction between complete market failure and partial market failure.
- The key characteristics of a public good.
- The differences between a public good, a private good and a quasi-public good.
- The tragedy of the commons.
- The concept of an externality.
- Diagrams showing positive and negative externalities, using marginal private and social cost and benefit curves.
- How positive and negative externalities lead to market failure.
- How an absence of property rights can lead to externalities.
- The difference between a merit good and a demerit good.
- How the under-consumption of merit goods and over-consumption of demerit goods may lead to market failure.
- The concept of information failure.
- How monopoly may lead to market failure and a misallocation of resources.
- How the immobility of factors of production can lead to market failure.
- The general principles of UK competition policy and some awareness of EU competition policy.
- The costs and benefits of competition policy.
- The arguments for and against the public ownership and private ownership of firms and industries.
- The arguments for and against regulation and deregulation of markets.
- The problem of regulatory capture.
- How governments may intervene in markets in order to correct cases of market failure.
- Government failure: meaning and causes.

Exam practice answers and quick quizzes at **www.hoddereducation.co.uk/myrevisionnotes**

9 The measurement of macroeconomic performance

The objectives of government economic policy

Any government will aim to influence how the **macroeconomy** performs over time and will have **macroeconomic objectives**. These objectives are goals or aims that they wish to achieve. Macroeconomic objectives are the goals a government wants to achieve for the whole economy.

The tools and methods that are used to influence the macroeconomy are referred to as **economic policies**. Therefore the objectives of government economic policy are the goals a government would like to achieve through the manipulation of the various tools it has available to use.

The main objectives of government macroeconomic policy are outlined below.

> **Macroeconomics**: refers to the economy as a whole, i.e. on a national scale.
>
> **Macroeconomic objective**: a goal a government would like to achieve for the macroeconomy.
>
> **Economic policy**: the economic tools and instruments available for a government to use to influence economic performance.

Economic growth

REVISED

Economic growth measures how much the value of output produced in an economy (known as national income) has grown over a period of time, usually over one year. It is calculated as the percentage change in national income over a period of time.

> **Economic growth**: the change in national income measured over a period of time.

Price stability

REVISED

This is concerned with how fast the average level of prices of a range of goods and services rises over a period of one year.

Minimising unemployment

REVISED

This involves minimising the numbers of those of working age who are looking for work but are unable to find a job.

Stable balance of payments on current account

REVISED

The **balance of payments** measures the difference between the value of goods and services sold abroad and the value of goods and services bought from abroad.

> **Balance of payments**: the record of financial transactions between the UK and the rest of the world.

Balancing the budget

REVISED

The government would like the value of government expenditure and the value of taxation to be the same as each other so that the **government's budget** is balanced.

> **Government's budget**: refers to the value of government spending compared with the money earned by the government through taxation over a period of time.

Achieving an equitable distribution of income

REVISED

Incomes are not shared out equally across households in the economy. Achieving an equitable **distribution of income** means the government would like to ensure that the gap between the richest and poorest does not become excessively wide.

> **Distribution of income**: how evenly incomes are shared between individuals and households across the economy.

Now test yourself

TESTED

1 If national income in one year was £800 billion and rose in the following year to £820 billion, what was the rate of economic growth over this time period?

Answer on p. 228

> **Typical mistake**
>
> The level of national income is important but most people are more interested in the change in the level of national income — i.e. its rate of growth. Be careful to make it clear which one you are talking about.

Conflicts in achieving these objectives

REVISED

Achieving different economic objectives simultaneously is difficult. This is because there is the possibility of conflict arising in attempts to achieve different objectives at the same time.

A **policy conflict** that has occurred frequently concerns the conflict between minimising unemployment and achieving price stability. Success in reducing the level of unemployment has often come at the expense of prices rising at a faster rate, and vice versa.

The conflicts that exist are often said to exist only in the short term. It is suggested that in the long term, it is possible to achieve all the objectives at the same time, with no policy conflict. Some would argue that there is no conflict even in the short term. This is open to debate.

> **Policy conflict**: attempts to achieve one economic objective move us further away from another economic objective.

> **Typical mistake**
>
> Do not assume that being unable to achieve an objective means it is not worth trying to achieve it. Getting as close as possible may be seen as good enough. Economics is about making the best use of scarce resources or getting as close as possible to the best use.

> **Exam tip**
>
> The concept of a trade-off in achieving multiple objectives is a good way of developing extended answers — and a way of evaluating the success of a policy.

Importance of economic objectives

REVISED

The following are generally seen as the main priorities among the government's economic objectives:

- economic growth
- price stability
- minimising unemployment

Governments do not view all their economic objectives as equally important. They have priorities for their objectives and these priorities change as circumstances change. For example, after winning the 2015 general election, George Osborne, the Chancellor of the Exchequer at that time, decided to make eliminating the budget deficit less of a priority than it had been in the previous parliament.

> **Exam tip**
>
> The conflict between objectives in the short term may not exist in the long term.

Similarly, some objectives have become less important over time. For example, achieving a stable balance of payments on current account is no longer considered as important as it was up until the 1970s.

Macroeconomic indicators

In order to assess how close we are to achieving economic objectives we have to examine the data from a range of macroeconomic indicators. These indicators each focus on an economic variable that measures economic performance. The main economic indicators are outlined below.

Real gross domestic product (GDP)

Gross domestic product (GDP) is a measure of the **national income** of an economy. It is based on the value of all incomes earned in an economy over a period of time (data are produced every quarter, though the yearly figure is the one that attracts most attention).

Real GDP measures the value of GDP after removing the effect of price changes from its value. This ensures that an increase in GDP from one year to the next represents increased output of goods and services rather than just increases in prices.

Although there is no actual target for growth in real GDP, the government would like to achieve a positive rate — usually growth of between 2% and 3% per year.

> **Gross domestic product**: the term used widely to represent the national income of an economy.
>
> **National income**: the total income generated within an economy over a period of time.

Now test yourself

2 If economic growth in 2015 was 2% but then fell in 2016 to 1%, what has happened to the level of GDP?

Answer on p. 228

Real GDP per capita

Real GDP is often used to make comparisons between countries in terms of the standard of living enjoyed by the population.

To make comparisons more meaningful, average income per person is often used. This is known as real GDP **per capita** and it is calculated as follows:

$$\text{Real GDP per capita (measured in monetary units, e.g. £s)} = \frac{\text{real GDP (total) (£)}}{\text{population level}}$$

> **Real gross domestic product**: real variables are those adjusted for changes in the level of prices, adjusting real GDP national income for changes in average prices.
>
> **Per capita**: a variable adjusted to give an average amount per person.

Now test yourself

3 Calculate the GDP per capita of the UK and Norway based on the following estimates:

	GDP 2014 (US$ billions)	Population (estimate) (millions)
UK	2945	64
Norway	500	5.2

4 Explain why a government wants to achieve economic growth as one of its objectives.

Answers on p. 228

Exam tip

Real GDP per capita is very useful in telling us about the standard of living in a country but it doesn't take into account how that income is shared out — this depends on the distribution of income.

Typical mistake

When dealing with large numbers ensure you don't confuse millions and billions — always check to see if your answer makes sense.

Consumer price index (CPI) and retail price index (RPI)

One government objective is to achieve price stability. This is where the average level of prices is reasonably stable. An increase in the **price level** over time is referred to as **inflation**.

High and unstable inflation is something governments wish to avoid. As a result the government has a target **rate of inflation** that it wishes to achieve of 2%. This means that the government wishes to see the average level of prices rising by no more than 2% annually (actually the target allows a margin of error of 1%, which means inflation can still be on target as long as it is no lower than 1% and no higher than 3%).

In the UK, two main measures of the price level are used to record the rate of inflation:
- consumer price index (CPI)
- retail price index (RPI)

Both measures include the prices of goods and services typically bought by households in the UK.

Although the CPI measure is the 'official' measure used to calculate inflation, the RPI is still used by the government. For example, the prices of tickets set by rail companies are regulated by the government and can rise no faster than the inflation rate based on the RPI.

It is the job of the Bank of England (the UK's central bank) to achieve this inflation target.

Price level: the average level of prices of a range of goods and services at a point in time (measured monthly).

Inflation: an increase in the average level of prices measured over a period of time.

Inflation rate: the percentage change in the price level measured over the period of 1 year.

Typical mistake

Falling inflation does not mean falling prices — just that the rate of price increases is lower.

Now test yourself

5 If the rate of inflation falls from 3% to 2%, explain what is happening to average prices in this economy?

Answer on p. 228

Measures of unemployment

There are plenty of people who are not working in the economy (children, the elderly, those raising families), but people only count as part of the **unemployment** statistics if they are part of the **labour force** (i.e. those in work or actively seeking work).

In the UK there are two main measures of unemployment:
- **The claimant count** — includes the number of people receiving welfare benefits for being unemployed. The usual benefit received by those unemployed is jobseeker's allowance (JSA).
- **The Labour Force Survey (LFS)** — based on a monthly sample of people, it records those who report they are looking work but cannot find it, regardless of whether they receive benefits or not. This information is used to produce an estimate of the national unemployment level.

In the UK, the LFS measure is normally higher than the claimant count measure as it includes all those receiving benefits as well as those who do not qualify for (or do not wish to claim) benefits.

Although the level of unemployment (expressed as a number) is published, it is the rate of unemployment which will often be seen as more significant. The **unemployment rate** is calculated as:

$$\text{Unemployment rate (\%)} = \frac{\text{number of people unemployed}}{\text{size of labour force}} \times 100$$

> **Unemployment:** those of working age who are currently out of work but are actively seeking work.
>
> **Labour force:** those of working age who are either in work or actively seeking work.
>
> **Claimant count:** the measure of unemployment in the UK that counts those who are receiving unemployment benefits.
>
> **Unemployment rate:** the number of unemployed people expressed as a percentage of the current labour force.

Now test yourself

TESTED

6 Explain why the claimant count rate may be lower than the LFS measure of unemployment.

Answer on p. 228

> **Typical mistake**
>
> Many people lose or choose to leave their jobs, but the vast majority find work almost immediately.

Productivity

Productivity measures how much output is being produced by each unit of labour (such as per worker, or per hour worked). **Labour productivity** measures the output of workers, whereas **capital productivity** looks at the efficiency of machinery and equipment.

Economic growth in the long run mainly comes from improvements in productivity (i.e. getting more output from existing resources).

Improvements in productivity will come from making workers more efficient (either faster or better) in producing output and also improving the efficiency of the economy's capital equipment (machines etc.)

> **Productivity:** a measure of efficiency comparing the level of output with the level of inputs.
>
> **Labour productivity:** the output of the workforce compared with the amount of labour (either in people or in hours) used to produce the output.
>
> **Capital productivity:** the output per item of capital equipment measured over a period of time.

Now test yourself

TESTED

7 Explain two reasons why labour productivity may not grow as fast as the government wishes.

Answer on p. 228

> **Exam tip**
>
> Be careful to distinguish between short-run and long-run growth when writing about economic growth.

Current account on the balance of payments

The balance of payments is divided into three sections: the **current account**, the capital account and the financial account. However, at AS level we are concerned only with the current account.

The main section of the current account relates to foreign trade, i.e.:

- exports of goods and services (produced in the UK but sold to foreigners)
- imports of goods and services (produced overseas but purchased by the UK)

The difference between these two values (exports minus imports) is referred to as the **balance of trade**.

> **Value of exports > value of imports = trade surplus**
>
> **Value of exports < value of imports = trade deficit**

Although the current account includes other components (which are explored in Chapter 14), it is foreign trade which largely determines the current account balance.

The UK normally has a surplus on the balance of trade for services but a deficit on the balance of trade for goods.

Overall, the UK normally experiences a **current account deficit**. The government would like to see this balance move closer towards a current account surplus.

> **Current account**: part of the balance of payments which looks at the net income flows earned through either trade in goods and services or the reward from investments located overseas.

> **Current account deficit**: where the flows of money from trade and other incomes out of the country are greater than the equivalent flows into the country.

> **Typical mistake**
>
> Many people — including many TV broadcasters — will talk about the balance of payments when they mean the current account of the balance of payments.

> **Exam tip**
>
> The balance of payments should always balance; it is the individual components of the balance of payments that may be in surplus or deficit.

Uses of index numbers

Index numbers are frequently used to illustrate economic variables when data are presented.

Index numbers are useful when making comparisons over periods of time. They are particularly useful when it is the size of changes in variables that need to be highlighted (rather than the actual values of the variables themselves).

Index numbers will start off with a value of 100 and this value is known as the **base year** value. The change in the index number will show how far the variable has moved away from its starting value.

For example, an index number of 120 would indicate that the variable's value had increased by 20% since the base year starting value. Presenting these index numbers as a line graph increases the ease with which the changes in values can be understood and interpreted.

> **Index number**: a number designed to be used to show the size of changes in a variable over time.

> **Exam tip**
>
> If two variables are translated into index numbers, even if they both start at 100, this does not mean they have the same value in reality — the index number is used to make comparisons and contrasts as the variables change.

Example

UK production indices

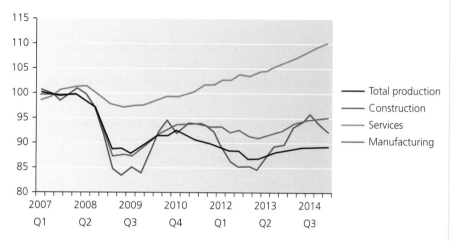

Figure 9.1 **Level of output in the production, manufacturing, construction and services industries (base year: 2007 = 100)**

Source: Office for National Statistics

This diagram shows the index of output for each of the main contributors to GDP: construction, services and manufacturing, along with total production.

We don't know the actual output level of each of these sectors but by using these as index numbers we can quickly see how each sector has performed in relation to the others. Key points would include:
- the output of all sectors fell in the recession of 2008–09
- recovery in all sectors started in 2009
- the services sector has grown quickly compared to other sectors

Although all sectors start with an index of 100, this does not mean their output was all at the same level — it is how the levels change over time that concerns us.

Now test yourself

TESTED ☐

8 Explain why index numbers may be used to show changes in the price of a commodity over time.

Answer on p. 228

Consumer price index (CPI)

Controlling inflation is a major macroeconomic objective. In the UK, the inflation rate is measured through the annual percentage change in the CPI — an index number measuring the average level of prices for the UK.

The CPI is calculated by combining price data for the UK as a whole for a variety of different products bought by an imaginary 'typical' family. This means the CPI is meant to represent the spending patterns of a typical, average UK household.

The range of goods and services included in the calculation is often referred to as a **basket of goods and services**. This inflation 'basket' includes over 700 items and the prices of these are checked in thousands of shops across the UK each month.

The basket of goods and services is updated annually as new products emerge and old ones decline in popularity. For example, in 2015, E-cigarettes were added to this inflation 'basket' whereas frozen pizza was removed (we still like eating pizza, but largely prefer chilled ones!).

The CPI is a **weighted price index**. 'Weights' are attached to items in the CPI according to their relative importance to an average family in their spending patterns. For example, a doubling of the price of light bulbs will

> **Price index**: an average level of prices based on a selection of goods bought by the typical household.
>
> **Basket of goods and services**: the selection of products to be included within the price index based on typical household purchases.
>
> **Weighted price index**: an average level of prices adjusted so that price changes in popular items affect the price index more than price changes in seldom-bought items.

have less impact on the CPI number than a doubling of the price of cars, or holidays, or restaurant meals because light bulbs are a less significant item in our average spending plans.

Issues with the CPI

As it is based on an 'imaginary' typical family, the CPI never really reflects anyone's exact spending patterns — how representative it is depends on how close an individual's spending patterns are to those on which the CPI is based.

The inflation 'basket' has to include many goods and services that not everyone buys: for example, most people don't smoke but cigarettes are still included within the basket to account for those who do.

Regular updates to the basket mean we are not always comparing like with like (i.e. the 2016 basket will differ from the 2015 basket), though the updated items are small in number.

No account is taken of the quality of the items included. A computer may cost slightly more in 2016 than in 2009 but it will be much better in terms of capability — does this mean it really has become more 'expensive'?

> **Typical mistake**
>
> House prices and mortgages are not in the CPI basket, so rapid house price increases or cuts in mortgage repayments will not show up in the CPI.

> **Exam tip**
>
> An inflation rate of zero means that on average prices are stable. In reality, even with a zero rate, some prices are rising and some are falling at the same time.

> **Revision activity**
>
> Make an A4 sheet with brief details on how each of the government's main objectives is measured in the UK.

Now test yourself

TESTED

9 Give two reasons why inflation may not be a reliable indicator of price changes.
10 This table shows the weights used (expressed as percentages) within the CPI basket of goods and services used to calculate the UK inflation rate.

CPI (consumer price index)	Weight 2015 (%)	Weight 2014 (%)
Food and non-alcoholic beverages	11.0	11.2
Alcoholic beverages and tobacco	4.3	4.5
Clothing and footwear	7.0	7.2
Housing, water, electricity, gas and other fuels	12.8	12.9
Furniture, household equipment and maintenance	5.9	6.0
Health	2.5	2.4
Transport	14.9	15.2
Communication	3.1	3.2
Recreation and culture	14.7	14.4
Education	2.6	2.2
Restaurants and hotels	12.1	12.0
Miscellaneous goods and services	9.1	8.8

Source: Office for National Statistics

(a) Explain why the largest weightings are attached to housing, transport, and recreation and culture.
(b) Explain why you think the weights used in the CPI are updated and, if necessary, changed each year.

Answers on p. 228

Uses of national income data

Real GDP shows what GDP can 'buy' after adjusting for changes in prices over time. This measure of GDP is frequently used to assess the standard of living enjoyed by a country's population. The standard of living refers to the quality of life typically experienced by people within that country. To use GDP to measure living standards it would be appropriate to use GDP per capita for an economy to see how 'well off' individuals are.

A higher GDP per capita typically means individuals are able to buy more goods and services, which increases the population's standard of living compared with that of a population with a lower real GDP per capita. Some of the main uses of national income data are:
- to determine economic growth
- to estimate likely tax revenues
- to estimate likely welfare expenditure (such as unemployment benefits)
- to assess inflationary pressure (if national income is found to be rising rapidly)

Exam tip

Make sure you are comparing per capita measures of GDP if making judgements about living standards.

Limitations of national income data

REVISED

There are further considerations to be made if we are to use real GDP per capita as an indicator of living standards. These considerations include the following.

Distribution of income

How income is shared out will matter. A country with high income inequality, i.e. a greater gap between the incomes of the rich and the poor, will have more people with incomes significantly below the average GDP per capita compared with a country with a more equal distribution of income. This means greater income inequality makes GDP per capita less reliable in measuring the country's living standards.

Composition of GDP

How national income is generated matters. In some countries, military expenditure is a very important contributor to GDP. It will create some jobs and will contribute to GDP, but military expenditure does not add much to the general living standards of the population, which could have been improved if the money had been spent on, say, health or education.

Shadow economy

The **shadow economy** refers to income generated from unrecorded transactions (also known as the black or underground economy). These may include:
- income from transactions that are legal but unrecorded (often to avoid tax charges), or
- transactions which are both illegal and unrecorded (trade in drugs being an obvious example)

Unrecorded transactions add to the living standards of the population but do not show in the official GDP data. This means that official GDP generally understates living standards. Estimates suggest that the UK's shadow economy is worth around 10% of actual GDP.

Shadow economy: the value of transactions which are not recorded in the official national income data (often so as to avoid tax or for a transaction which otherwise would be illegal, e.g. drug trade).

Now test yourself

TESTED

11 Explain two ways in which estimates could be made for the size of the UK's shadow economy.

Answer on p. 228

Non-marketed output

Plenty of goods and services add to people's wellbeing and their standard of living but do not show up in official GDP data. Services such as DIY and childcare can be obtained as paid-for services but are often conducted by families for free as normal parts of household life. These will add to the family's welfare without ever showing up in the official data.

> **Non-marketed output:** transactions which occur without a monetary payment being made in exchange for a good or service.

Negative externalities

Additions to GDP often generate negative externalities which reduce the standard of living of those who suffer the externalities generated. Pollution and traffic congestion usually arise out of increased activity but reduce people's quality of life. Therefore increases in GDP often exaggerate the improvements to people's standard of living by ignoring the negative aspects of these increases.

Non-financial factors

The standard of living may be derived primarily from income, but there are plenty of other factors which add to people's general quality of life. These include:

- the quality of health provision (and whether or not it is made available freely for the population)
- education provision (how many years' schooling does the average person typically receive? Is the quality of the provision of a high standard?)
- individual freedoms (of speech, of travel and so on)
- the amount of leisure time enjoyed on average (are there paid-for holidays? Limits on working hours?)

All of the above factors (and there may be others) contribute to living standards but do not directly appear in the GDP data.

> **Typical mistake**
>
> Just because there are weaknesses in using GDP per capita to determine living standards, the statistic is still a useful guide and should not be dismissed.

Purchasing power parity (PPP)

REVISED

Making comparisons of living standards between countries means we need to convert GDP into a common exchange rate.

If exchange rates are volatile then it becomes harder to make meaningful comparisons between countries once converted into the same currency. A currency may remain 'over-valued' or 'under-valued' for a long period of time, which may give us misleading information once converted into a common currency. The purchasing power parity exchange rate is a way of avoiding the problem of using inappropriate exchange rates.

> **Purchasing power parity:** the exchange rate which would equalise the price of goods and services in different countries once converted into the same currency.

The PPP exchange rate is the rate where goods and services in different countries would appear as the same price once converted into common currencies. For example, a basket of goods and services priced at £1,000 in the UK but priced at $1,500 in the USA gives us a PPP exchange rate of £1 = $1.50 ($1,500/£1,000) — where the price of the basket of goods is the same in each country once converted into a common currency.

A problem with this approach is that it assumes the goods being compared in prices are identical — which is unlikely to be the case. For many years, *The Economist* magazine has published a comparison of current exchange rates and the calculated PPP exchange rates based on the current prices in different countries of a McDonald's Big Mac — this is known as the 'Big Mac index'.

Now test yourself

TESTED ☐

12 If the price of a Big Mac in the UK was £3 and in the USA was $4, what would be the PPP exchange rate based on this product alone?

Answer on p. 228

> **Typical mistake**
>
> The factors determining the exchange rate are complex, meaning it is unlikely to always settle at its PPP rate.

Evaluation of GDP data in determining living standards

GDP per capita is not a perfect measure of living standards but remains the most commonly used statistic. Adjustments can be made (such as adding on the estimates for the shadow economy and correcting for wider income inequality), but GDP remains an easy to understand, widely used measure. Other measurements, such as the Human Development Index (HDI), can be used but are not widely understood or accepted.

> **Exam tip**
>
> Remember when writing about the usefulness of national income statistics in representing living standards, that just because there are problems with the data, this does not mean it lacks use — just use the data with care and caution.

Now test yourself

TESTED ☐

13 Explain three reasons why, although the USA has the world's largest total GDP, the standard of living enjoyed by its population may not be as high as that enjoyed by the population of Canada, which has a much lower total GDP.

Answer on p. 228

Exam practice

	GDP ($) 2013 estimates	Population (millions) 2013
USA	16 720	304
China	13 390	1330
India	4990	1150
Germany	3227	82

Source: CIA World Factbook

1 Based on the data above:
   (a) Calculate the GDP per capita for 2013 for each country. [4]
   (b) Which of the countries has the (i) largest and (ii) lowest GDP per capita? [2]
   (c) Explain two limitations of using GDP per capita when making judgements about living standards in different countries. [8]

Answers and quick quiz 9 online

ONLINE

Summary

You should have an understanding of:
● What the government's main economic objectives are and how these are measured through indicators in the UK.
● How there may be policy conflicts in attempting to achieve multiple objectives.
● How index numbers are used to show changes in economic variables.

● What is meant by a price index and how this is used in the UK.
● The uses and limitations of GDP.
● The uses and limitations of GDP in reflecting living standards in a country.
● How purchasing power parity (PPP) exchange rates can be used for making comparisons in GDP in different countries.

10 How the macroeconomy works

The circular flow of income

National income

We know that national income refers to the income of an economy (a country) earned by all workers and businesses over a period of time. Income is a flow variable that is measured over time. A stock variable, such as household wealth, is measured at a point in time.

National income can be calculated in three ways:
1 expenditure method
2 income method
3 output method

Expenditure method

This involves adding up all the spending over a period of time:
- **Consumption** (C)
- **Investment** (I)
- **Government expenditure** (G) (not including welfare benefits paid out)
- **Net exports** (X − M)

Income method

This involves adding up all incomes earned over a period of time:
- wages and salaries earned by those in work
- rent earned by those who allow their land and property to be used by others
- interest earned by those who invest capital in financial assets
- profits earned by companies trading goods and services

Output method

This involves totalling the value of all output produced in the economy for a period of time for each sector of the economy. Steps need to be taken to avoid double counting: for example, the output of the steel industry may be used in the production of cars and this should appear only once.

For the non-traded sectors, such as state education and the NHS, a value of their output is based on the cost of their provision, i.e. how much the government spends on these sectors over a period of time.

Comparison of the three methods

All three methods should give the same value as they include all the same economics transactions for a period of time, but each method views the transaction from a different perspective, i.e. one person's spending is another person's income. In reality, the totals for the three methods will often differ by a small amount, which is mainly due to mistakes and unrecorded transactions.

Bear in mind that:

national income = national expenditure = national output

> **Consumption**: spending by households on goods and services.
>
> **Investment**: spending by businesses on additions to the capital stock, such as new premises or equipment, or the building up of inventory (stock) levels.
>
> **Government expenditure**: spending by the government at both national and local levels within the economy.
>
> **Net exports**: the value of exports less the value of imports in an economy over a period of time.

> **Exam tip**
>
> Although you will not be directly tested on the construction of the national income accounts, it is useful to see the three methods and how they are related.

Now test yourself

TESTED

1 Explain why total expenditure in an economy should equal total income.

Answer on p. 228

Real national income versus nominal national income

REVISED

Real national income measures national income after removing the effect of price changes from its value. This means that any increase in real income refers to increases in output (or income) and does not merely represent higher prices charged for the same amount of production.

National income that is unadjusted for changes in prices is known as **nominal national income** or money national income.

> **Nominal national income:** national income unadjusted for changes in prices (also known as money income).

How to calculate real national income is shown in the following example.

Example

If nominal national income rose from £1300 billion in 2015 to £1400 billion in 2016, then the nominal increase of £100 billion would represent a percentage increase of 7.7% between 2015 and 2016. However, if we are told that the price index rose from 100 to 104 over this period then part of the rise in national income is explained by price increases rather than increases in output.

Real national income (NI) would be calculated as follows:

$$\text{Real NI} = \text{nominal NI} \times \left(\frac{\text{price level in previous year}}{\text{price level in current year}}\right)$$

Real GDP for 2016 is calculated as follows:

$$\text{Real NI} = £1400\,\text{bn} \times \left(\frac{100}{104}\right) = £1346.15\,\text{bn}$$

Economic growth would be measured by the percentage change in real national income over the period of one year. For example, using the data from the previous question, economic growth could be calculated as follows:

$$\text{Economic growth for 2016} = \left(\frac{£1346.15\,\text{bn} - £1300\,\text{bn}}{£1300\,\text{bn}}\right) \times 100 = 3.6\%$$

Now test yourself

TESTED

2 From the data here, calculate:
   (a) real GDP for 2016
   (b) economic growth for 2016 (in real terms)

Year	Nominal GDP (€) (billions)	Price level
2015	800	150
2016	980	175

Answer on p. 228

GDP and real national income

Real national income is one of the most used macroeconomic variables. It is often referred to as gross domestic product (GDP). Technically, real national income and real GDP are not the same variable, as some UK national income comes from incomes earned outside the UK but still belonging to UK citizens.

Gross national income (real GNI) includes incomes from overseas assets. However, the difference between GDP and GNI is small and these terms are often used interchangeably.

Uses of real national income

Real national income provides useful information:
● It is a measure of how successful the economy is — countries are often ranked in importance by the size of their national incomes.
● It shows how well off the population is — through measuring national income per person.
● It allows a government to estimate how much can be collected in taxation (most taxes are placed on incomes and expenditure — both measures of national income).

Now test yourself

3 State three ways in which real national income per capita does not provide a good indicator of living standards within a country.

Answer on p. 228

The circular flow of income model

A simple circular flow of income

The connection between national income, output and expenditure can be incorporated into a simple model of the macroeconomy known as the **circular flow of income**. This shows how money flows around the economy as a result of the transactions taking place.

> **Circular flow of income**: a model of the economy where income and spending flow between households and firms.

In a simple two-sector economy (consisting of just the business and the household sector), businesses employ factors of production supplied by households to produce goods and services.

In return, as Figure 10.1 shows, households supply their labour (and other factors) and earn incomes from firms, which households then spend as consumption on goods and services.

The level of national income will remain constant as money flows from households to businesses and back again; although obviously this is not how the actual UK economy behaves.

The modified model of the circular flow shown in Figure 10.2 allows for **injections** (in the form of investment by businesses) and **withdrawals** (in the form of household savings). If injections are greater than withdrawals, more is being added to the circular flow and income overall will rise. The opposite is also true; a greater quantity of withdrawals than injections will lead to falling income.

> **Injections**: extra money placed into the circular flow of income.
>
> **Withdrawals**: money taken out of the circular flow of income.

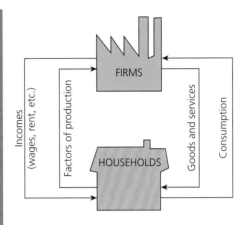

Figure 10.1 The simple circular flow of income

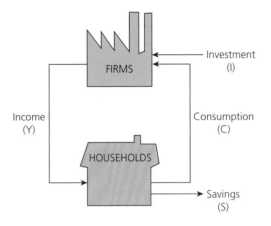

Figure 10.2 The two-sector model of the circular flow of income, with money withdrawn in the form of savings and injected back into the flow in the form of investment

A more complex circular flow of income

Adding the government sector and the foreign sector to the model gives the representation of the circular flow of income shown in Figure 10.3.

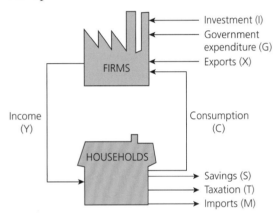

Figure 10.3 The circular flow of income with the addition of the government sector and foreign trade sector

There are now three injections into the circular flow:
- investment (I)
- government expenditure (G)
- exports (X)

There are now also three withdrawals from the circular flow:
- savings (S)
- taxation (T)
- imports (M)

Equilibrium in the circular flow of income

Macroeconomic equilibrium is reached in the circular flow of income model if there is no pressure on national income to rise or to fall.

In the circular flow model the economy will remain in equilibrium as long as the total of planned injections is equal to the total of planned withdrawals. This can be stated as:

$$I + G + X = S + T + M$$

> **Macroeconomic equilibrium:** the level of national income where there is no tendency for the level to change.

If the total injections are higher than total withdrawals, then national income will increase until a new equilibrium level of national income is reached when injections are again equal to withdrawals. Likewise, if withdrawals are greater than injections, then national income will fall until a new equilibrium is reached at a lower level of national income.

To summarise:
- injections = withdrawals: macroeconomic equilibrium
- injections > withdrawals: national income increases
- withdrawals > injections: national income falls

If a government wishes to increase national income in the economy then it could increase government spending. As long as nothing else changes, this should lead to an increase in the level of national income.

> **Exam tip**
>
> It does not matter whether imports are equal to exports, or whether government spending matches taxation, it is the total of injections and withdrawals that matters. As long as they are equal, then the national income for the economy will remain constant.

Now test yourself

TESTED

4 Using the table of data here, state whether the economy is in equilibrium. Back this up with numerical justification. Explain what is likely to happen to national income.

	£ billion
Investment	120
Exports	80
Imports	140
Government expenditure	600
Taxation	550
Savings	75

Answer on p. 228

Aggregate demand and aggregate supply

Aggregate demand

REVISED

Another model for looking at macroeconomic equilibrium is **aggregate demand** (AD) and aggregate supply (AS) analysis.

This considers the equilibrium position of the macroeconomy in terms of the level of real national income (or real GDP) and also the price level at that equilibrium position.

It is more useful than the circular flow of income model as it is possible to see the potential inflationary and deflationary impacts of changes in government policy, as well as the effect on national income.

Aggregate demand consists of:
- consumption (C)
- investment (I)
- government expenditure (G)
- net exports (exports − imports) (X − M)

$$AD = C + I + G + X - M$$

> **Aggregate demand:** total planned spending in an economy over a period of time at any given price level. It is calculated as $C + I + G + X - M$.

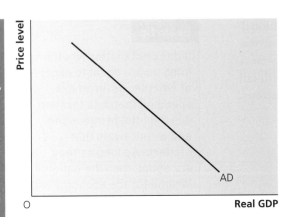

Figure 10.4 Aggregate demand (AD) showing the amounts of planned expenditure that would occur at different price levels

The AD curve appears as downward sloping from left to right (see Figure 10.4). This is because:

- At a lower price level, the value of any assets such as property and shares will increase in real terms. This may lead to a **wealth effect** — making consumers feel as though they have greater **wealth**, leading to higher consumption levels.
- A lower price level will make UK exports more price competitive (compared to foreign substitutes), thus leading to a higher level of exports sold abroad. It will also make domestic goods relatively cheaper than imported goods, which should reduce the level of imports.

Wealth effect: increases in the value of a household's assets cause people to feel wealthier and encourage them to spend more of their current income (or to borrow more to finance the increases in spending).

Wealth: wealth refers to the value of the assets held by households. Most wealth will be held in the value of property (or equity) owned by the household.

Factors determining aggregate demand

REVISED

Higher levels of national income will mean there is more money to spend. However, even with a constant level of national income there will be changes to the level of aggregate demand if one of its components changes. These will shift the AD curve left or right as shown in Figure 10.5.

Consumption

Consumption is the largest competent of aggregate demand, comprising around 70% of overall AD. Households do not spend all of their income on consumption, as they will make decisions on whether or not to save. Factors affecting consumption include the following.

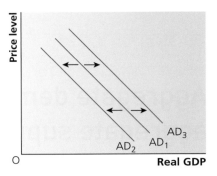

Figure 10.5 Shifts in the AD curve

Interest rates

Interest rates affect consumption in three ways:

- If interest rates rise then those who have variable-rate mortgages will find that their monthly payments increase, which means less money is available for households to spend on consumption.
- Higher interest rates reduce the desire of households to engage in credit-financed consumption (i.e. consumption financed by borrowing).
- Higher interest rates increase the reward for savings which, by definition, reduces the level of consumption.

Interest rate: the cost of borrowing money expressed as a percentage of the amount borrowed.

Exam tip

Although interest rates affect consumption in three ways, the incentive to save 'effect' is not significant.

Consumer confidence

Households will have varying degrees of confidence about the future. If they feel that their incomes are likely to fall or that their jobs are less secure, they are more likely to reduce their current consumption

Exam practice answers and quick quizzes at **www.hoddereducation.co.uk/myrevisionnotes**

in preparation for these times. The converse is also true. Therefore, consumption will rise and fall in line with consumer confidence.

Taxation

Changes in taxation will affect how much households have to spend. Increases in taxes, especially income taxes, will reduce the disposable income of households, leading to reduced overall consumption.

Wealth

If household wealth increases then this will have a positive 'wealth effect' on households, which means they will probably spend more on consumer goods and services (even if financed by borrowing).

Unemployment

If more people are unemployed and relying on welfare benefits, then the level of consumption is likely to be lower.

Investment

The main determinants of investment are described below.

Interest rates

Increases in interest rates raise the cost of borrowing and will reduce the profitability of any investment project. Even if investment is not financed by borrowing, higher interest rates will raise the opportunity cost of using money for investment purposes.

Business confidence

If businesses expect that sales will increase in the future then they will be more likely to spend money on investment goods, so as to increase their productive capacity to satisfy increased future demand for their goods and services.

Tax

Companies are taxed on their profits (in the UK this is called corporation tax) and if this tax is lowered, businesses will have more of their profits available to spend. This is likely to lead to higher investment.

Technology

New technologies should increase efficiency of production, which should lead to firms investing more in new technology in order to increase their profitability.

Introduction of new technologies will generate new markets for firms and will lead to firms investing more as a way of exploiting the new opportunities that technology brings.

Accelerator theory

The **accelerator theory** of investment states that increases and decreases in the rate of growth of national income will lead to even larger increases in the level of investment.

> **Accelerator theory**: where increases in national income lead to firms spending more on investment, in order to expand their capacity to exploit the rising income.

If growth in national income increases, then firms will need a larger productive capacity in order to produce a higher level of output to meet the higher level of spending in the economy.

Similarly, if the growth rate of national income falls then firms will not need as a large a productive capacity and therefore investment in maintaining capacity can fall.

Typical mistake

Investment should not be confused with savings. The two are often used interchangeably in everyday usage but in economics they are distinct. In economics, 'savings' refers to household income that is not spent on consumer products. 'Investment' refers to spending by businesses on additions to overall **capital stock**.

Capital stock: the value of the existing level of investment products in an economy at a point in time (i.e. the value of machinery, equipment, premises, etc.)

Government expenditure

Governments will spend money on a number of areas within the economy, including:

- **public services** — such as health, education, transport and defence
- **local government services** — such as libraries and other council services
- **welfare expenditure** — pensions, care allowances, tax credits and benefits
- **interest on debt** — payments on outstanding government debt accumulated over time

Government expenditure is financed through taxation. However, it is very likely that the two totals of government spending and tax revenue collected will not be equal. The difference is known as the **budget balance**. It is highly likely that the budget will be in **deficit** (or less likely, in **surplus** or **balanced**).

Budget balance: the difference between government spending and the taxation revenue collected.

Budget deficit: government expenditure > taxation.

Budget surplus: government expenditure < taxation.

Balanced budget: government expenditure = taxation.

Net exports (exports – imports)

Exports and imports are affected by the following:

- **exchange rates**
- foreign growth
- UK growth
- relative inflation

All these factors are explored in Chapter 14. It might be worth reading ahead if you need a reminder.

Exchange rate: the price of one currency expressed in terms of another currency.

Now test yourself

TESTED ☐

5 Draw an aggregate demand curve and show any shifts in the curve that may result from each of the following:
  (a) an increase in house prices boosting consumer confidence
  (b) a rise in interest rates
  (c) an increase in tuition fees
  (d) a rise in inflation rates amongst EU states

Answer on p. 228

Revision activity

Make a mind map showing all the factors that will affect the level of consumption in an economy.

The multiplier process

Any change in a component of AD will shift the AD curve. Changes in AD will also be affected by the **multiplier process**.

This multiplier effect occurs because any extra spending creates income for another person or business. This extra income will in turn be spent again, thus creating income elsewhere for another group, and so on.

The further increases in income will not continue for ever and will decrease in size as extra income is taxed, saved or spent on imports, meaning less is 'passed on' in the circular flow with each extra transaction.

The size of the multiplier process can be determined by comparing the size of the overall change in national income with the size of the initial change in aggregate demand.

> **Multiplier process**: how a change in aggregate demand leads to a proportionately larger change in overall national income.

Example

A government decides to spend an extra £400 million on a new bypass. It is estimated that national income, as a result, eventually rose by £1000 million. What was the size of the multiplier?

$$\text{Size of the multiplier} = \frac{\text{change in national income}}{\text{initial change in AD}} = \frac{£1000m}{£400m} = 2.5$$

Negative multiplier

Although the multiplier process might sound a very useful way for a government to boost national income with a smaller increase in government spending, the multiplier can also work in the opposite direction. A fall in any of the components of aggregate demand will lead to a proportionately larger fall in overall national income. This effect is sometimes referred to as the 'negative' or 'backwards' multiplier effect.

> **Exam tip**
>
> In reality, the size of the multiplier is likely to be quite small; not much bigger than 1.

Now test yourself

6 Explain why an initial rise in aggregate demand does not lead to continual rises in national income as spending and incomes are passed on around the economy.

Answer on p. 228

The multiplier and the marginal propensity to consume (MPC)

The proportion of any additional income received by an individual or household that is spent is referred to as the **marginal propensity to consume**. This will be a number between 0 and 1.

An MPC of 1 would mean that all of any addition to income is spent, whereas an MPC of 0.5 means that half of any additional income received is spent.

The MPC will determine the size of the multiplier as the size of the multiplier depends on any money received being passed on around the economy as extra expenditure.

The size of the multiplier is calculated as follows:

$$\text{Size of multiplier} = \frac{1}{1 - \text{MPC}}$$

> **Marginal propensity to consume**: refers to the proportion of any additional income that is spent and passed on around the circular flow of income.

For example, if in an economy the MPC was 0.8, then the size of the multiplier would be $1/(1 − 0.8) = 5$.

In this case, any increase in aggregate demand would lead to an overall increase in national income five times greater than the original rise in AD.

If the MPC fell to 0.6 then the size of the multiplier would fall to $1/(1 − 0.6) = 2.5$.

A higher MPC means more of any additional income received is 'passed on' around the economy, leading to further rises in national income. As a result, the higher the MPC, the greater the size of the multiplier effect. Remember, of course, that the multiplier effect can work in both a positive and a negative manner.

> **Typical mistake**
>
> Do not confuse the MPC referring to how much of additional income is spent on consumption with the MPC which looks at setting UK interest rates.

Now test yourself

TESTED

7 For each of the following MPC estimates, calculate the size of the economic multiplier.

	MPC
(a)	0.75
(b)	0.8
(c)	2/3
(d)	0.6

8 For each of the following changes to aggregate demand, based on the size of the multiplier, calculate the eventual change to national income.

	Change in AD	MPC
(a)	Increase by £100 m	0.5
(b)	Increase by £20 m	0.75
(c)	Decrease by £120 m	0.4

9 Explain why a higher MPC increases the effectiveness (i.e. the size) of the multiplier.

Answers on p.229

> **Typical mistake**
>
> When calculating the multiplier based on an MPC expressed in fractions, be careful that your answer does not contain unnecessary decimal places, e.g. an MPC of 2/3 would give a multiplier of 3 — which might appear as something like 3.0003 if you work in decimals rather than fractions.

Aggregate supply

REVISED

The level of **aggregate supply** is based on the various costs incurred by a firm when producing output. We distinguish between **short-run aggregate supply** (SRAS) and **long-run aggregate supply** (LRAS).

> **Aggregate supply:** the total quantity of output that all the firms in the economy are willing to produce at a given price level.
>
> **Short-run aggregate supply:** how much firms will produce at a given price level in the short term.
>
> **Long-run aggregate supply:** how much firms will produce in the long run. This will be where an economy is producing its maximum potential output level and will be independent of the price level.

Determinants of short-run aggregate supply (SRAS)

The short-run refers to the period of time during which the prices of factors of production are constant.

In the short run, the aggregate supply curve slopes upwards — there is a positive relationship between the price level and the quantity of output firms are willing to produce and supply (see Figure 10.6).

If any of the production costs change due to changes in the external environment, then the SRAS curve will shift to the left or right, as shown in Figure 10.7. These changes include:

- **Money wage rates** — if wage rates paid to workers increase, then firms will be less willing to supply output as it is less profitable to do so. Therefore there will be a leftward shift in the SRAS.
- **Changes in the cost of raw materials** — if the cost of materials increases, this will reduce the profitability of production, leading to firms being less willing to supply output. Higher costs will shift the SRAS to the left.
- **Business taxation** — businesses will incur certain taxes as part of their operations. Changes in indirect taxes, such as value added tax (VAT), will influence the profitability of production. Higher indirect taxes will lead to a leftward shift in SRAS as firms reduce the amount they are willing to produce.
- **Productivity** — if productivity increases, then firms will find it more profitable to supply greater quantities of output and therefore the SRAS curve will shift to the right.
- **Exchange rate changes** — a change in the exchange rate will alter the price a business pays for imported materials. A fall in the exchange rate will mean imports are more expensive and this will increase production costs for firms that import, shifting the SRAS leftward.

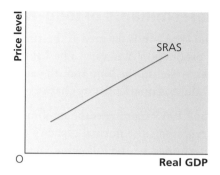

Figure 10.6 The SRAS curve, showing that as the price level increases, firms will be willing to supply more

> **Typical mistake**
>
> Be careful: a rise in the price level moves us along the SRAS curve — it does not shift the curve.

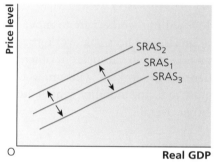

Figure 10.7 Shifts in the SRAS curve

Now test yourself

TESTED

10 Draw a short-run aggregate supply (SRAS) curve and show shifts in the curve based on the following changes:

(a) a fall in the price of imports
(b) workers becoming more efficient in production
(c) the oil price falling
(d) a higher rate of VAT introduced

Answer on p. 229

> **Exam tip**
>
> The gradient of the SRAS is open to debate. Many economists believe that the SRAS in reality is not a straight, upward-sloping line but rather a curve which starts off with a fairly shallow gradient and then sharply curves upwards, becoming almost vertical the closer the economy gets to capacity. However, all the variants of the AS curve that appear here can be used in the exam.

Determinants of long-run aggregate supply (LRAS)

The long run is defined as the time period when the costs of the factors of production may vary. The LRAS curve is assumed to be vertical. This means that in the long run, the amount of output firms are willing to produce is unaffected by changes in the price level.

The LRAS represents the maximum amount an economy can produce — it represents the normal capacity output level for the economy and is determined by the following factors.

Technology

Advances in technology increase the amount firms can produce with the same resources available. This will therefore shift the LRAS curve to the right in Figure 10.8, increasing the capacity of the economy.

Productivity

As workers become more skilled, they are likely to become more productive, meaning that more can be produced in the same of amount of time (or with the same quantity of workers). This will increase the capacity level of an economy and therefore the LRAS curve shifts rightward with increases in productivity.

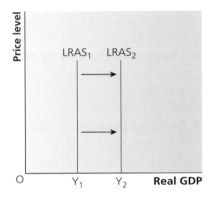

Figure 10.8 Shifts in a vertical LRAS curve

Factor mobility

How willing workers are to move around the country to fill job vacancies, and how able workers are to retrain themselves so they can take up job vacancies in other industries, will affect the LRAS. Increases in workers' willingness to swap locations and types of job will improve factor mobility, which means an economy can produce more output overall.

Enterprise

Encouraging more people to become entrepreneurs and set up their own businesses will increase the capacity of an economy and will shift the LRAS curve rightward. Governments therefore often adopt measures to make it easier for people to set up and run their own businesses.

Economic incentives and attitudes

Government policy can shift the position of the LRAS curve. For example, incentives in taxes and benefits, as well as changes in legislation, can affect how willing people are to work in the first place and how long, and how hard, they will work within their jobs. These economic incentives and how attitudes to work can be influenced are covered in the section on supply-side policies (see Chapter 13).

Figure 10.8 shows LRAS as vertical. This implies that in the long run the economy will operate at its maximum potential level, and this can be increased only through factors affecting the long-run aggregate supply curve.

The institutional structure of the economy

The ability to increase aggregate supply also comes from the **institutional structure** of the economy. This includes how effective the financial sector is in channelling funds from savers to borrowers, as this determines the availability of business funds for investment — which in turn can add to the productive capacity of the economy.

For example, after the 2008 financial crisis, the government took steps (which are covered in Chapter 12) to ensure that funds were more likely to be available for businesses looking to borrow.

The institutional structure of the economy also includes how the legal systems in place make it easy (or hard) for businesses to operate and run efficiently. Increases in the LRAS can be achieved if steps are taken to make it easier for businesses to start up, to comply with laws, and to sort out their financial affairs (such as paying their annual tax bill).

Now test yourself

TESTED

11 Explain two changes in laws or regulations a government could implement which would make it easier for businesses to start up or operate.

12 Explain how cutting subsidies for childcare can lead to a leftward shift in the LRAS.

Answers on p. 229

The Keynesian AS curve

REVISED

An alternative way to present the AS curve is known as the Keynesian AS curve. This is based on the assumptions of those who believe that the macroeconomy works as described originally by the British economist John Maynard Keynes.

Keynesian economists do not make a distinction between the short-run and the long-run time periods. As a result, they assume there is a need for only one type of AS curve — the Keynesian AS curve, which is shown in Figure 10.9.

As we can see in Figure 10.9 there are three parts to the Keynesian AS curve:

- At low levels of real GDP (where unemployment is assumed to be high) it is relatively easy for firms to find workers, to bring into account idle machinery and capacity, and to increase output — without there being any upward pressure on wages. This is why the AS curve is relatively elastic here, i.e. it is horizontal.
- As we get closer to the maximum output level for real GDP, it becomes more difficult to find workers to employ and to find spare capacity without there being upward pressure on wages and prices. As a result, the AS curve will start to curve upwards as factors of production become scarce.
- Eventually, the Keynesian AS curve becomes perfectly inelastic (i.e. vertical) as we reach the full employment level of real GDP. Here, real GDP cannot be increased any more as we have reached the maximum potential level.

The Keynesian AS curve is particularly useful when writing extended answers, as it allows a number of possible economic scenarios to be shown on the same diagram. For example, an increase in AD can be shown to increase real GDP with both a minimal increase in prices and a significant inflationary impact.

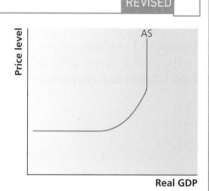

Figure 10.9 The Keynesian AS curve

Now test yourself

TESTED

13 Show on an AD/AS diagram how an increase in aggregate demand can have a number of different effects on the output level and price level depending on where the AD curve is positioned — you will need to use a Keynesian AS curve.

Answer on p. 229

Exam tip

The best AS curve to use in your written answers is the one which allows you the most flexibility in terms of what you are attempting to show. The Keynesian AS curve often givens you the most options to show variations in economic performance.

Aggregate demand and aggregate supply analysis

Short-run macroeconomic equilibrium

REVISED

The interaction between AD and SRAS will give us the macroeconomic equilibrium position for an economy. Unless either AD or AS changes (i.e. shifts), this equilibrium position will be maintained.

Figure 10.10 shows that an increase in AD will lead to a movement along the SRAS curve, which gives both a higher real output level and a higher price level.

Figure 10.11 indicates that a decrease in SRAS (shown as a leftward shift in the SRAS curve) leads to movement along the AD curve, resulting in both a lower real output level and a higher price level.

Typical mistake

Remember that shifts in one curve will cause movements along the other curve.

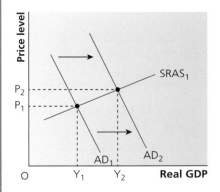

Figure 10.10 The effect of an increase in AD

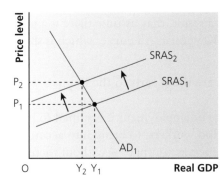

Figure 11.11 The effect of a decrease in SRAS

Now test yourself

TESTED

14 On this diagram, the equilibrium position is A. State which will be the new equilibrium positions when the following changes take place:
(a) a fall in the cost of raw materials and a cut in income tax
(b) an increase in labour productivity
(c) an increase in exports

Answer on p. 229

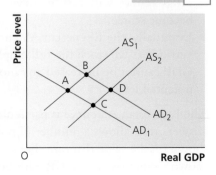

AD/AS analysis and government economic objectives

REVISED

The equilibrium position gives information about how the economy is performing. It shows the real level of national income and the price level. From this information, further assessments can be made about progress towards the government's economic objectives.

- **Economic growth:** This is measured as the change in real national income. It is possible to see if this objective is being achieved: for instance, falling output may indicate that a recession is occurring.
- **Employment:** Jobs depend partly on spending, so moving rightward on the horizontal axis (to a higher level of national income) will lead to a greater demand for workers, so output can increase in response to higher spending. Similarly, a fall in the level of national income is likely to lead to higher unemployment as fewer workers will be needed once output and spending levels have reduced.
- **Inflation:** Changes in the price level reveal whether the economy is experiencing inflation (in the case of a rise in the price level) or deflation (where the price level falls).

Remember, any change in AD is likely to have a greater overall effect on national income due to the multiplier process. This means that it may be difficult to position the AD curve exactly, given the uncertainty over the size of the multiplier.

Long-run macroeconomic equilibrium

REVISED

The long-run equilibrium position occurs where aggregate demand (AD) intersects with the long-run aggregate supply (LRAS) curve (see Figure 10.12). This always occurs at the maximum output level for an economy.

Given that the LRAS curve is vertical, this represents the normal capacity of real output in the economy. Increases in AD mean the equilibrium position moves upwards along the LRAS curve with no increase in real output. The only effect of higher AD in the long run is a higher price level, i.e. it has only inflationary consequences.

A rightward shift in the LRAS curve can be thought of as an outward shift of the production possibility curve (PPC), as it enables more output to be produced with the existing stock of resources. This is referred to as long-run growth.

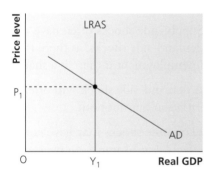

Figure 10.12 Long-run equilibrium

> **Typical mistake**
>
> Even if the economy is operating on the vertical section of the aggregate supply curve, do not assume this means zero unemployment. Operating at this position would mean no unemployment caused by lack of demand (see Chapter 11).

> **Revision activity**
>
> Produce a set of clear AD/AS diagrams for each type of movement and shift.

Now test yourself

TESTED

15 Using an AD/AS diagram, explain how investment in education may lead to a reduction in unemployment.

Answer on p. 229

Economic shocks

Economic shocks can be favourable, but most are unfavourable and are likely to have a significant impact on the ability of the government to meet its economic objectives.

There are two types of economic shocks: demand-side shocks and supply-side shocks.

Demand-side shocks

A **demand-side shock** will affect the level of national income, unemployment and inflation.

Examples of demand-side shocks include:
- the banking crisis of 2008, which affected both business and consumer confidence significantly
- an unexpectedly large change in the exchange rate or in interest rates

Supply-side shocks

A **supply-side shock** will have a knock-on effect on the willingness of firms to produce output and will lead to large changes in the level of aggregate supply.

Examples of supply-side shocks include:
- changes in commodity prices (e.g. the large oil price increases of the 1970s)
- a significant crop failure in an important product (e.g. wheat)
- a conflict in a country that produces a staple product (e.g. conflict between oil-producing countries), which limits the commodity's availability

Supply-side shocks often have more negative consequences than demand-side shocks, as there is likely to be both inflation and higher unemployment if there is a sharp reduction in aggregate supply.

A demand-side shock will often only affect either unemployment or inflation but not both.

Economic shocks may have combined demand-side and supply-side effects. For example, an overseas war may have a supply-side impact on commodity prices but may also affect consumers' confidence, which has a demand-side impact.

> **Economic shocks**: sudden, unexpected events that affect the macroeconomy, especially the growth rate.
>
> **Demand-side shocks**: unexpected and significant changes in the level of aggregate demand.
>
> **Supply-side shocks**: unexpected and significant changes in the price of factors of production or the availability of factors of production.

Now test yourself

TESTED

16 Using an AD/AS diagram, explain the effects of an economic shock caused by a collapse in share prices in an economy.

Answer on p. 229

Exam practice

A recently published report estimated that government support for the UK's screen industry adds more than £6 billion to the UK economy. This industry contains the UK's film, high-end TV, computer games and animation sectors and is seen as one of the UK's modern success stories. It is believed that each pound of support the government gives the industry actually benefits the whole UK economy significantly more. Spill-over benefits have been identified as including increased tourism and merchandising opportunities for UK toy manufacturers.

The UK film industry contributes nearly 40 000 jobs directly to the UK economy but also helps to generate jobs in other industries, such as the set-design, camera and lighting technology industries. It is estimated that another 60 000 jobs are indirectly created as a result of the continued success of the film industry.

A spokesperson for the industry stated that 'We welcome the financial support the British government gives the industry. As the report highlights, there are significant multiplier benefits for the UK as a whole from this help. The report estimates that the UK is £6 billion better off, which is commendable, especially when other sectors are struggling.'

1 Define the term 'multiplier'. [3]
2 It is estimated that the UK economy is £6 billion larger as a result of the government support described in the extract. If the government support totalled £1.5 billion, how big is the economic multiplier? [4]
3 Using an AD/AS diagram, analyse the effect of this government investment on the UK's economic performance. [8]
4 Explain three other policies a government could adopt to encourage further private sector investment into industries like the one mentioned in the extract. [10]

Answers and quick quiz 10 online

ONLINE

Summary

You should have an understanding of:
- The basic and more complex models of the circular flow of income and how an economy reaches macroeconomic equilibrium.
- What determines the level of aggregate demand, what factors would shift this curve and what would move us along the curve.
- The determinants of both the short-run and long-run aggregate supply curves and how changes in these factors will shift both curves.

- What is meant by macroeconomic equilibrium in the AD/AS model and how to show this diagrammatically.
- How the Keynesian AS curve varies from the model of short-run and long-run aggregate supply curves.
- What is meant by economic shocks and how these can be demand-side, supply-side or both.

Economic growth

Short-run and long-run economic growth

Short-run economic growth arises out of increased use of previously unemployed resources (workers or capital stock) resulting in increased overall output. This will appear as a movement from a point within an economy's production possibility curve (PPC) to a place either on or closer to the actual PPC boundary.

Long-run economic growth arises out of increases in long-run aggregate supply. This can be shown as either a rightward shift in the long-run aggregate supply (LRAS) curve or a shift outwards of the PPC.

As Figure 11.1 shows, short-run growth involves utilising previously unemployed factors within an economy (e.g. moving from point A to point B). Long-run growth involves expanding the capacity of the economy – shifting the PPC further out (point B to point C).

> **Short-run economic growth**: growth based on increased utilisation of unemployed resources.
>
> **Long-run economic growth**: growth based on increasing the potential output level of the economy.

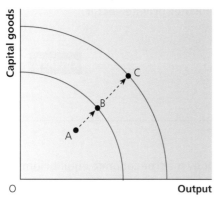

Figure 11.1 Short-run and long-run economic growth

Determinants of short-run growth

Short-run growth can be caused by an increase in either (or both) of the following:
- increases in aggregate demand (AD)
- increases in short-run aggregate supply (SRAS)

In most cases, it is increases in AD that provide the stimulus for short-run growth. An alternative name for short-run growth is **actual growth**. This is the type of growth that features more prominently in news stories and is measured by the percentage change in GDP.

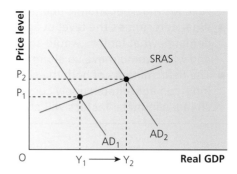

Figure 11.2 Increases in AD will produce short-run growth in the economy

Determinants of long-run growth

Long-run growth comes from increases in the productive capacity of the economy. These increases arise from improvements on the 'supply side' of the economy, which result from improvements in the quantity and quality of the factors of production available to an economy. Long-run growth is normally shown by a rightward shift of the LRAS curve, from $LRAS_1$ to $LRAS_2$ in Figure 11.3.

Factors which would increase long-run growth include those listed below.

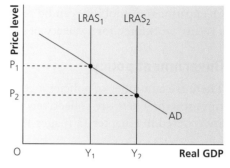

Figure 11.3 Shifts in the LRAS curve generate long-run growth

Increases in the labour force (labour supply)

Population size limits the labour supply but this can be increased through allowing more immigration into an economy.

Increasing the retirement age or encouraging people who are currently **economically inactive** to enter the workforce will also increase the labour supply.

Making it financially less attractive to remain out of work will increase the labour supply. This can be achieved either by paying less generous unemployment benefits, or by increasing incentives for the unemployed to take work (such as through cutting income tax paid, or allowing tax credits to those on low incomes).

> **Economically inactive**: those of working age who are not in work and not looking for work.

Improvements in labour productivity

An increase in the skills level of the workforce should lead to an increase in the amount that can be produced. Therefore increases in training undertaken by workers should boost long-run growth.

Capital investment

Investment contributes both to short-run growth (through increased AD) and to long-run growth (through increases to LRAS).

More investment in capital stock (premises, equipment, machinery, etc.) will enable businesses to produce more goods and services.

Governments can encourage businesses to invest by creating a more stable macroeconomic climate, which means they can plan investment with greater confidence.

Tax incentives can also be used to encourage investment.

New technology

Advances in technology will usually lead to productivity improvements for capital equipment. For example, much design and manufacturing work can now take place more efficiently through robotic and computer technology.

Technology improvements therefore raise the ability of an economy to produce more output with a given capital stock.

Education

Improvements to education within schools, colleges and universities should lead to improvements in worker productivity.

Occupational immobility can be reduced by ensuring education prepares a future workforce for a variety of occupations.

Government policy

There are a number of policies a government can use to encourage long-run growth. These are collectively referred to as 'supply-side' policies and are covered in Chapter 15 (pages 194–200).

Long-run growth is often referred to as **trend growth**. It is estimated to be somewhere between 2% and 2.5% a year in the UK.

Although the actual short-run rate of economic growth can rise beyond the long-run trend growth rate for short periods of time, it is long-run trend growth that represents the overall long-term limit to economic growth.

Attempts to encourage short-run growth in excess of long-run growth for a prolonged period of time are likely to lead to inflationary pressures.

> **Trend growth**: the rate of growth in LRAS over time, representing the maximum potential capacity of the UK economy.

> **Exam tips**
> ● An excellent contrasting point is that policies to promote long-run growth will take many years to be fully effective but will require large amounts of money to be spent in the short run (e.g. a high-speed railway).
> ● It is worth noting that some of the factors contributing to long-run growth will not arise from government policy and may just be the result of other factors, such as breakthroughs in technology.

> **Typical mistake**
> Although policies to prompt long-run growth may be desirable, do not forget that most will carry an opportunity cost in that they will cost money.

Now test yourself

TESTED

1 Which two of the following will lead to an increase in LRAS?
   A   higher exports
   B   reduced imports
   C   advances in technology
   D   policies designed to increase the attractiveness of remaining unemployed
   E   more spending on transport infrastructure
2 Using an AD/AS diagram, explain why increases in business investment are encouraged by most governments.

Answers on p. 229

Costs and benefits of economic growth

REVISED

Economic growth is one of the government's macroeconomic objectives. There are benefits attached to achieving economic growth but there are also costs associated with economic growth. The costs and benefits can be considered in terms of:
● effects on individuals
● effects on economies
● effects on the environment

Benefits of economic growth

● Higher living standards for the population (which may increase the government's popularity)
● Easier to find employment for people — as long as growth is not low
● Improved social indicators for the population — such as less crime (though this link is not definite)

- Increased tax revenue
- Less need for welfare expenditure — which could be spent elsewhere or used to fund tax cuts
- Lower absolute poverty
- Greater international status for the government

TESTED ☐

3 Explain how the government benefits from economic growth.

Answer on p. 229

Costs of economic growth

The costs to economic growth include the following:

- increased negative externalities (e.g. congestion, pollution — both arising out of increased output)
- potential for greater inequality if growth is unevenly shared out
- higher inflation if growth is of a short-term nature
- depletion of natural resources

TESTED ☐

4 Explain two possible drawbacks of economic growth for individuals within a country.

Answer on p. 229

> **Exam tip**
>
> When considering the benefits of growth it is worth making it clear which group(s) actually benefits.

Sustainability of growth

Given the recent higher profile given to environmental issues, some argue that governments should aim only for economic growth that is sustainable.

Sustainable growth is that which can be maintained into the long run and does not rely on the use of non-renewable resources to generate the growth (which clearly can be used to contribute to growth only once).

Governments have been encouraged to intervene so as to shift production towards utilising more sustainable and renewable resources (e.g. subsidies for 'greener' forms of production).

This view is not universally shared as some feel market forces will ensure growth is sustainable. As a resource, such as oil, is depleted, its scarcity will force up the price, which will 'ration' out its use — in other words, prices will adjust so as to allocate the resource efficiently. However, this assumes market and price adjustments happen with few or no barriers.

> **Sustainable growth:** economic growth that does not compromise the economy's ability to grow in the future.

TESTED ☐

5 Explain two ways in which a government can promote sustainable economic growth.

Answer on p. 229

The economic cycle

Although short-run growth varies across the seasons of the year, the **economic cycle** is focused on repeated patterns that occur over a number of years.

> **Economic cycle**: the economic cycle refers to the repeated pattern of fluctuations in short-run economic growth and how it differs from the trend growth of an economy.

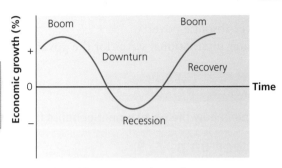

Figure 11.4 The economic cycle

The repeated phases of this cycle (also known as the business cycle or the trade cycle) can be categorised and share common characteristics in terms of macroeconomic indicators.

Boom

- A boom is where short-run economic growth is above the trend growth rate (usually 3% or more).
- Consumer confidence will be high with consumer spending rising quickly and consumers more willing to finance consumption through borrowed money (consumer credit).
- Business confidence is high — business investment is likely to be above average.
- Government finances will move either towards or further into a budget surplus.
- The current account on the balance of payments will move into, or more deeply into, deficit.
- Unemployment is low and falling, though firms may experience difficulties in finding skilled labour.
- Inflation may be rising — often referred to as a sign of an 'overheating' economy.

Downturn

- The rate of short-run growth will start to fall but may still be positive (it is likely to fall below the trend growth rate).
- Business confidence will fall and investment may fall as a result.
- Consumers are likely to reduce the amounts borrowed to finance consumption, and growth in consumer spending is likely to slow.
- Inflation may still be above average but is likely to stop rising due to the falling demand in the economy.
- Tax revenue may begin to fall due to reduced economic activity and the government's budget will move towards, or more deeply into, deficit.
- Spending on imports is likely to fall and the current account balance is likely to move towards a smaller deficit or into surplus.
- Unemployment will stop falling though it may not rise significantly due to firms hoarding labour in case the downturn is short-lived.

Recession

- Growth in the economy will be negative.
- Business confidence will be low and investment will be low as a result.

> **Boom**: period of above average short-run economic growth.
>
> **Downturn**: period where short-run economic growth falls from above average to below average.
>
> **Recession**: two successive quarters of a year where short-run economic growth is negative.
>
> **Recovery**: when short-run economic growth starts to increase after a recession.

- Consumer spending is likely to fall due to falling incomes across the economy and rising unemployment.
- Unemployment will rise and may reach high levels due to the lack of demand for output.
- Inflation should fall (though it depends on the cause of inflation).
- The budget deficit is likely to be at its largest due to higher welfare expenditure (e.g. on unemployment benefits) and lower tax revenue being collected.
- The current account balance is likely to narrow and may move into surplus due to low demand for imports.

Recovery

- Short-term growth will resume and will be positive but is likely to be below the trend growth rate.
- Confidence among consumers and businesses is likely to return — interest rates are likely to be low to encourage both consumption and investment.
- Inflation is likely to remain low.
- Unemployment is likely to remain high but will stop rising (or at least increases may slow).
- The budget deficit should stop increasing (or the rate of increase will slow) as tax revenue may begin to rise.
- The balance on the current account is likely to stop moving closer to a surplus.

Although these are common characteristics of each stage or phase of the economic cycle, it is worth noting that each stage is likely to be different. Unemployment in the most recent recovery period (2010 onwards) fell far earlier and to a far lower level than might have been expected.

Now test yourself

TESTED

6 State which objectives a government is likely to achieve and which it is less likely to achieve in the boom stage of the economic cycle.

Answer on p. 230

Output gaps

REVISED

Trend growth refers to the growth in the productive capacity of the economy. Short-run growth — or actual growth — will rarely be in perfect synchronisation with the trend growth rate. These differences are **output gaps**.

Output gap: the difference between actual growth and trend growth.

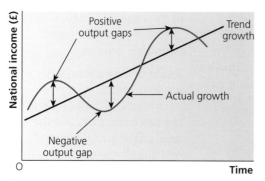

Figure 11.5 Output gaps exist when short-run growth deviates from long-run or trend growth

Output gaps can be either positive or negative:
- A positive output gap exists where actual growth is higher than trend growth.
- A negative output gap exists where actual growth is below trend growth.

Unemployment is likely to rise when the output gap is negative as the economy could produce more; therefore unemployed factors (workers and capital) will exist in the economy.

When the output gap is positive, there is greater demand for goods and services than the productive capacity of the economy allows. This is likely to lead to increases in the price level due to excess demand (i.e. inflation).

> **Exam tip**
>
> It is useful to note that no-one can be entirely sure what the trend growth rate is. It is based on estimates that attempt to calculate productivity improvements, increases in the labour supply and the level of productivity of new investment — none of which is easy to measure.

> **Revision activity**
>
> Produce a table showing how close a government is to achieving each of its objectives at each stage of the economic cycle.

Explanations of the economic cycle

REVISED

Although the cyclical pattern of economic growth may appear natural, a number of explanations have been put forward that attempt to explain why the economic cycle occurs.

Multiplier–accelerator model

Some believe the economic cycle is caused by the combined workings of both the multiplier and the effects of the accelerator. These two effects may combine and 'feed off' each other — a rise in investment has multiplier effects on national income which, in turn, will generate more investment, leading to a further multiplier effect on national income and so on. This process can also work in the opposite direction.

The result is that small fluctuations in GDP can be magnified due to the workings of the **multiplier–accelerator model**.

The inventory cycle

During economic downturns or recessions, falls in the demand for output mean businesses allow inventory levels (stocks of goods and materials) to fall rather than producing more. This means that production of output falls faster than the fall in sales, thus exaggerating the effects of falling output on the economic cycle.

Likewise, in the recovery or boom stage, firms build up inventory again in anticipation of future sales. Thus production levels may exceed actual sales levels as businesses restore inventory levels. Hence the adjustment to inventory levels can affect the rate of production by businesses.

Asset price bubbles

An **asset price bubble** (also known as a speculative bubble) occurs when asset prices (typically, houses, commodities and share prices) rise rapidly beyond what normal demand and supply conditions would predict. Demand may significantly increase, for instance, when people buy the asset hoping to sell later for a profit.

> **Multiplier–accelerator model**: an explanation of the trade cycle where multiplier and accelerator effects combine to magnify cyclical fluctuations in economic growth.
>
> **Inventory cycle**: how changes in inventory levels held by businesses may lead to exaggerated increases or decreases in industrial output — contributing to economic growth.
>
> **Asset price bubble**: where a rise in an asset's price becomes self-fulfilling and the price rises beyond the level that normal demand and supply conditions would generate. This eventually leads to sharp falls in its price when the bubble is burst.

Rising asset prices have wealth effects on consumption and magnify the effects on economic growth. If the asset in question does not feature in the retail price indices monitored as part of the economy's inflation rate, the central bank will not attempt to stop the bubble developing.

Eventually people realise the rapid price rises of the asset bubble do not reflect normal conditions and they will attempt to sell their assets to make a profit. This leads to the price falling and thus to further waves of selling as people attempt to sell before the price collapses. The bubble being 'burst' with rapidly falling prices has a strong downward wealth effect and knock-on effects on consumption, thus magnifying the downturn stage of the economic cycle.

Animal spirits

Animal spirits (as described by Keynes) refers to the collective expectations of businesses and consumers. It is often used to describe how both investment and consumption will be determined by the confidence felt by these groups. If confidence is low, then even with low interest rates the economy may remain in the recession phase as simply the result of it being expected to be there — i.e. it becomes self-fulfilling. Hence, animal spirits will influence which phase of the economic cycle an economy remains in, or moves to.

Herding

Recent studies in behavioural economics (covered earlier in this book) have linked some asset price bubbles to the concept of herding. **Herding** occurs where people imitate other people's behaviour in the same way that animals often act together as a 'herd'. This behaviour can create speculative bubbles where people feel the need to imitate others — say, by buying shares or by investing in property. If people do act together as a herd then these independent but collective decisions will have the power to influence the level of spending in an economy and thus the actual phase of the economic cycle.

> **Animal spirits:** the collective feeling of consumer and business confidence which can affect economic decisions, such as those affecting consumption and investment.
>
> **Herding:** consumer and investor behaviour often moves in similar directions at the same time — in the same way as herd behaviour in groups of animals.

Excessive growth in credit

Households can borrow to finance consumption beyond their income levels, which increases economic growth. However, any slight downturn in economic growth can lead to sharply falling spending due to high proportions of household income being used to pay off debt and interest — with only small amounts of discretionary income left over. Therefore excessive credit levels may mean sharp rises and sharp falls in consumer spending — magnifying the economic cycle.

Economic shocks

Economic shocks can explain movements from one phase to another of the economic cycle. These were covered in the previous chapter.

Now test yourself

TESTED ☐

7 Do any of the explanations of the economic cycle manage to explain why the UK went into such a deep recession in 2008?

Answer on p. 230

Employment and unemployment

In Chapter 9 we saw that being unemployed is more than just looking at who in an economy is without a job. We also saw that there are two ways of measuring unemployment: the claimant count and the labour force survey measures.

Governments want to minimise the level of unemployment. This objective was sometimes referred to as achieving **full employment**. Achieving full employment would not mean that there is a zero level of unemployment (and some economists would argue that even an unemployment rate of 3% might represent the achievement of full employment).

> **Full employment:** the level of employment where those who are economically active (either in work or seeking work — the same concept as the working population) can find work if they are willing to accept jobs at the going wage rate.

> **Typical mistake**
>
> Full employment does not mean zero unemployment.

Types of unemployment

REVISED

Solving the problem of high unemployment requires appropriate economic policies.

To make the job of reducing unemployment easier, it makes sense first to classify why unemployment exists. Economists have classified unemployment into types, or causes, of unemployment.

Cyclical unemployment

Cyclical unemployment is shown on an AD/AS diagram in Figure 11.6. It occurs when AD is below the level needed to produce output at the full employment level (shown here as Y_F). It is referred to as cyclical unemployment due to the periods in the economic cycle where spending falls below the amount needed to generate full employment.

If spending on output is low then this means that workers who would have been producing that output will not be required and unemployment will rise. This type of unemployment is also called **demand-deficient unemployment** or **Keynesian unemployment**.

Cyclical unemployment is linked closely to the existence of a negative output gap within an economy. If economic growth is below the trend rate, the level of demand in the economy will not be high enough to ensure that all workers looking for jobs can find employment. Even if growth is positive, cyclical unemployment might rise.

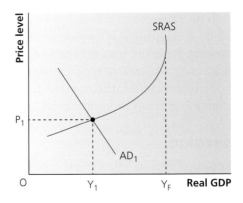

Figure 11.6 **Cyclical unemployment**

> **Cyclical unemployment:** unemployment caused by insufficient aggregate demand within the economy.

Frictional unemployment

Most **frictional unemployment** is short term but it can be lengthened due to lack of information, insufficient retraining opportunities or welfare benefits which are 'too generous' to provide sufficient incentive for people to take jobs sooner.

This type of unemployment can be reduced by improvements in helping people find out, on both a local and a national basis, what job vacancies exist. It is sometimes referred to as **search unemployment** due to the issue of people taking time to find the jobs that do exist.

> **Frictional unemployment:** unemployment resulting from 'friction' due to movements into and out of the job market, i.e. it occurs when people are between jobs.

> **Typical mistake**
>
> Just because there is unemployment, do not assume that there are no job vacancies. In mid-2015, there were over 700000 vacancies for jobs.

Structural unemployment

Structural employment is due to long-term changes in the labour market which mean that certain industries are declining whilst others are growing.

Workers becoming unemployed from one industry may be unable to switch to another industry due to their not having adequate skills for the new, rising industries.

This type of unemployment is associated with occupational immobility but it is more closely connected with long-term trends in industry growth and decline.

Advances in technology may also lead to structural unemployment as workers are replaced by automated production. This type of unemployment is sometimes referred to as technological unemployment.

Structural unemployment can also result from failure to encourage people to move from one region to another, as well as the failure of regions to attract new businesses. This is also known as 'regional unemployment'.

> **Structural unemployment**: unemployment resulting from mismatches between the labour supply available and the labour demand for differently skilled labour.

> **Typical mistake**
>
> Improvements in technology cannot be blamed for rises in unemployment — they do destroy some jobs but they create more jobs than they destroy overall.

Structural unemployment and global factors

Structural unemployment can also be increased by global factors. Many emerging industrial nations (e.g. China and India) are able to produce goods for lower costs than in the UK. This makes these foreign goods much more price competitive.

As a result, there has been a decline in employment in UK manufacturing industries. It is likely that workers from these industries who become unemployed will remain unemployed unless they can fill vacancies in other industries in which the UK has an advantage.

Now test yourself

TESTED

8 Classify each of the following situations into the correct type of unemployment:
   (a) an unemployed steel worker who cannot find work in computer programming
   (b) an accountant in Sheffield, unemployed due to high interest rates and government cuts
   (c) an unemployed shop assistant unwilling to move from a rural area to a larger city
   (d) a person leaving one job but unaware that there are plenty of similar jobs in a nearby town

Answer on p. 230

Demand-side and supply-side factors

REVISED

The types of unemployment can also be categorised by whether they are caused by demand-side or supply-side factors.

Demand-side factors

Cyclical unemployment is caused by demand-side factors — that is, a lack of aggregate demand.

Supply-side factors

Frictional and structural unemployment are caused by issues with the productive potential of the economy, connected with the long-term aggregate supply of an economy. They are therefore caused by supply-side factors.

In order to minimise unemployment, it is likely that governments will use a combination of policies relating to both aggregate demand and aggregate supply (see Chapters 12 and 13).

Now test yourself

9 Explain why unemployment falls when the economy experiences a positive output gap.

Answer on p. 230

Other types of unemployment

REVISED

Voluntary and involuntary unemployment

Another way of distinguishing the types of unemployment is to make the distinction between **voluntary** and **involuntary unemployment**.

- Voluntary unemployment exists when workers could find work at the going wage rate but choose not to accept employment. Frictional unemployment may count in this category if a worker remains unemployed longer due to welfare benefits providing support.
- Involuntary unemployment exists when workers cannot find employment at the current market wage. Cyclical unemployment would count as involuntary unemployment as there are insufficient vacancies due to the derived nature of labour demand.

> **Voluntary unemployment:** where people are unwilling to accept a job at the going wage rate despite there being jobs available.
>
> **Involuntary unemployment:** where people are unable to find employment at the current market wage rate.

Now test yourself

TESTED

10 How would you classify structural unemployment: voluntary unemployment or involuntary unemployment? Explain your answer.

Answer on p. 230

> **Exam tip**
>
> The terms 'voluntary' and 'involuntary unemployment' are probably value judgements as it is very hard to say whether someone is really 'choosing' to remain unemployed.

Real wage unemployment

Real wage unemployment occurs when the real wage paid is above the level needed to bring the labour market into equilibrium. For example, a high minimum wage may mean that workers who are looking for jobs cannot find employment as there is a lower quantity of labour demanded at that wage.

> **Real wage unemployment:** unemployment that exists when the real wage is not allowed to fall to the market clearing level where labour demand equals labour supply.

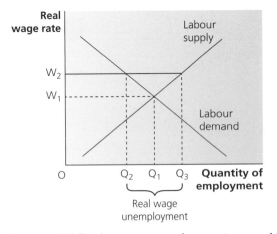

Figure 11.7 Real wage unemployment caused by the failure of the labour market to 'clear'

Figure 11.7 shows that when the real wage is W_1, labour demand equals labour supply at Q_1. However, at a real wage of W_2 there is an excess supply of workers wanting employment compared with the level of labour demand and this leads to a real wage unemployment of $Q_3 - Q_2$ (sometimes known as 'classical unemployment').

Now test yourself

TESTED

11 Explain two effects for the economy of a significant increase in the minimum wage.

Answer on p. 230

The natural rate of unemployment

REVISED

Even when the labour market is in equilibrium, there will still be unemployment present. This unemployment will consist of voluntary unemployment, frictional unemployment and structural unemployment. This may be caused by the following factors.

> **Natural rate of unemployment**: the rate of unemployment that consists of all voluntary, structural and frictional unemployment.

Frictional (or voluntary) factors

● The natural rate of unemployment may increase if the replacement ratio is too high. This is calculated as follows:

$$\text{Replacement ratio} = \frac{\text{disposable income out of work}}{\text{disposable income in work}}$$

● A ratio of close to 1 (or above) would mean that a person could 'earn' in benefits at least as much as they could do in employment. This is highly likely to reduce any incentive to work. Reducing the ratio well below 1 should reduce the incentive to remain 'frictionally' unemployed. The ratio can be reduced through any of the following:
   ○ less generous benefits for the unemployed
   ○ minimum wage increases
   ○ tax credits (which allow people in lower-paid jobs to keep some of their benefits)
   ○ lower income tax or a higher 'tax-free' allowance
● These frictional factors can add to the level of voluntary unemployment.

Structural factors

● Regional unemployment may exist due to the unemployed being unwilling to move to where job vacancies are. This could be due to lack of knowledge of job vacancies in other cities, barriers to moving, such as high house prices, or a move being impractical due to family ties. The harder it is to relocate, the higher will be regional unemployment.
● Unemployed workers may lack the appropriate skills for the job vacancies that exist. For example, the decline of 'heavy industries', such as mining, steel working and shipbuilding, has created a large number of unemployed who are unable to simply move into jobs created in rising industries, such as ICT. This can be solved through better training of these structural unemployed workers.

The natural rate of unemployment will exist even if aggregate demand is high — i.e. cyclical unemployment has largely been eliminated. The policies to reduce the natural rate of unemployment are connected with reforms to the 'supply side' of the economy.

The natural rate of unemployment and aggregate supply

REVISED

The terms 'full employment' and the 'natural rate of unemployment' — where there is no cyclical unemployment — are often used interchangeably. Another way of thinking about the natural rate of unemployment is that it can be represented by the unemployment that exists when the economy is operating on the long-run aggregate supply curve (or the vertical portion of the Keynesian AS curve). Any attempt to reduce unemployment through demand-side policies will only fuel inflation. Supply-side policies will be required to reduce unemployment further.

Inflation and deflation

Inflation was a very common problem in the UK during the twentieth century. However, since the recession of the early 1990s, it has been less so. In recent years, in both the UK and the rest of Europe, governments have increasingly begun to worry about **deflation**. Both inflation and deflation are problematic but for different reasons.

- **Inflation** refers to the annual increase in the general level of prices. The price level in the UK is measured by the consumer price index (CPI).
- **Deflation** refers to the situation where the general level of prices is falling over time. The UK briefly experienced deflation (as measured by the CPI) in 2015. This means that the 'inflation basket' of goods and services was actually cheaper to buy for a period in 2015 than it would have been one year earlier in 2014.
- **Disinflation** refers to the concept of a falling rate of inflation (e.g. where inflation falls from 5% to 2%).

> **Deflation**: a fall in the average level of prices over time.
>
> **Disinflation**: where the rate of inflation is falling but is still positive.

> **Typical mistake**
>
> Falling inflation does not mean that goods and services are getting cheaper — there is still inflation. What it means is that the rate at which prices are increasing is slowing down — a situation known as disinflation.

Now test yourself

TESTED

12 Explain the difference between deflation and low inflation.

Answer on p. 230

Causes of inflation

REVISED

In economic theory, there are two main causes of inflation:
- **demand-pull inflation**
- **cost-push inflation**

Demand-pull inflation

High levels of spending give signals to firms to increase output, but as we get closer to the capacity level of the economy (as dictated by the vertical LRAS curve), the higher spending will lead to firms increasing their prices as they incur higher costs in producing more output. Eventually, in the long run, when the economy is operating on the LRAS, any increase in AD will lead only to inflation, rather than to increases in output.

> **Demand-pull inflation**: inflation caused by excessively high levels of aggregate demand beyond that needed to generate full employment.
>
> **Cost-push inflation**: inflation that occurs due to rises in the costs of production incurred by firms.

In Figure 11.8, growth in AD from AD_1 to AD_4 increases output but eventually leads to demand-pull inflation, shown here by increasingly large rises in the price level from P_1 to P_4.

The solution to reducing demand-pull inflation is to reduce the level of aggregate demand by reducing any of the components of aggregate demand, as this would ease upward pressure on prices.

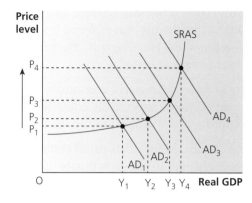

Figure 11.8 Growth in AD and its impact on demand-pull inflation

Cost-push inflation

If any of the costs of production increase, then the rise in costs will reduce a firm's profit margin unless it increases the selling price, thus leading to higher prices. (If firms accepted a lower profit margin when faced with rising costs, cost-push inflation might not occur.)

A fall in the exchange rate will lead to higher costs for imported materials and therefore this can lead to cost-push inflation. (Inflation caused by a falling exchange rate is sometimes referred to as 'imported inflation'.)

As Figure 11.9 shows, a leftward shift in the SRAS curve from $SRAS_1$ to $SRAS_2$ will lead to higher prices caused by cost-push factors. It will also lead to a lower equilibrium output level.

In this way, cost-push inflation leads not only to higher prices but also to falling output (and likely rises in unemployment at the same time). This combination of problems is referred to as 'stagflation' – stagnant growth in national output and inflation occurring together.

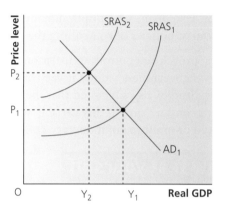

Figure 11.9 The impact of a leftward shift in SRAS

Now test yourself

TESTED ☐

13 Using AS/AD diagrams, explain how deflation can be caused by changes in both aggregate demand and aggregate supply.

Answer on p. 230

The quantity theory of money

REVISED ☐

The **quantity theory of money** provides an alternative explanation of inflation. This is based on the Fisher equation (after the economist Irving Fisher), which is also known as the equation of exchange. The Fisher exchange is a mathematical identity, which states the following (note that this is an identity, which means that each side is equivalent to the other):

$$M \times V \equiv P \times Q$$

where:
- M is the money supply
- V is the **velocity of circulation** (how fast money circulates around the economy, i.e. how many times a unit of currency would be used in a year to make purchases)
- P is the average price level (in the same way as we have indices such as the CPI to represent the price level)
- Q is the real value of national output (sometimes expressed as either Y — real national income — or even T — the number of transactions over a period of time)

> **Quantity theory of money:** an alternative explanation for inflation which states that the only cause of inflation is excessive growth in the money supply.
>
> **Velocity of circulation:** the rate at which money circulates around the economy — i.e. how many times the same banknote is used over a period of time.

Monetarist economists refined this into the quantity theory of money, where the identity was replaced by an equation and a causal relationship was proposed, running from the left-hand side to the right-hand side of the equation.

In addition, Monetarist economists argued that the velocity of circulation in an economy was usually constant, and that the growth of real national output was constant at around the trend growth of national output.

As a result, Monetarists stated that increases in the price level resulted from changes in the growth rate of the money supply. This became a central belief of the Monetarist school of economic thought, that inflation was not caused by demand-pull or cost-push factors but only by excessive growth in the money supply.

This explanation was championed by the Nobel Prize-winning economist Milton Friedman, who inspired many governments in the 1980s to follow Monetarist policies of controlling the money supply.

This approach to controlling inflation was largely abandoned in the late 1980s as governments found it very hard to actually control the money supply. Studies also suggested that the velocity of circulation would remain constant only if this variable was not being used as part of a targeted programme of monetary control.

Now test yourself

TESTED

14 If the monetarist explanation of inflation is correct, what would be the appropriate policy to control the rate of inflation in an economy?

Answer on p. 230

> **Exam tip**
>
> The quantity theory of money does not provide a third separate cause of inflation — those who believe it works would claim that it is the *only* explanation of inflation.

Expectations and changes in the price level

REVISED

When workers negotiate for wages they are likely to build into their claims some form of expectations of what they think will happen to prices over time. For example, if inflation is expected to rise to 10%, workers will probably want to see their nominal wages rise by at least 10% so as to maintain their real incomes and ensure the purchasing power of their income does not fall.

Expectations of inflation and actual inflation are connected. If workers think inflation will rise, they will be more likely to push up wages. Given wages are a major cost for most firms, higher wage costs are likely to feed through to higher selling prices set by firms.

As a result, governments are keen to monitor inflationary expectations. This is one reason why the government has an inflation target — so as to encourage workers to moderate their wage claims (assuming, of course, that the government manages to keep inflation close to its target).

How expectations are formed is a matter of debate. Some think that people are rational and normally can accurately guess what inflation will be; others think that workers can adjust to changes in inflation, but this may take time. This matters, as we will see in the work on the Phillips Curve.

> **Exam tip**
>
> There is a good link to be made between expectations of inflation and consumer behaviour covered in Chapter 2.

Consequences of inflation

Until the 1990s, the UK economy suffered from periods of high inflation. Certainly in the 1970s and 1980s, governments set the reduction of inflation as their main economic objective. Problems of higher inflation include the following.

Uncompetitive exports

If UK inflation is high then UK products which are exported will become less price competitive and may fall in sales volume. Strictly speaking, this problem depends on 'relative inflation', i.e. UK inflation relative to foreign inflation levels.

Menu costs

When prices are rising quickly, firms will update menus, price lists, catalogues and so on much more frequently. This imposes a cost on business which could be avoided if inflation was kept at a low rate. Advances in technology (e.g. use of online catalogues) have minimised this cost.

Search costs

With rising prices individuals will have to spend time having to compare prices offered by different firms. Traditionally, this was referred to as **shoe leather costs** as an individual would have to visit multiple businesses to check prices. Search costs have been lowered by the use of the internet to research prices.

> **Menu costs:** the costs associated with updating for changes in prices over time.
>
> **Search costs:** the costs associated with researching information needed for economic transactions, e.g. who offers the lowest price.
>
> **Shoe leather costs:** the costs in time and money involved in making price comparisons.
>
> **Fiscal drag:** taxpayers pulled into a higher tax band despite incomes not rising in real terms.

Fiscal drag

Even though the real value of someone's income remains unchanged, the rise in nominal income (in order to compensate for inflation) may push ('drag') them into a higher income tax band and consequently the person ends up worse off. This can be avoided if the government 'indexes' its tax bands (i.e. increases the bands on which tax is payable in line with inflation).

Uncertainty

Inflation creates uncertainty. Businesses will find it hard to budget for expenditure and this makes it more likely that a business will be more cautious in its production or expansion plans, which means GDP may not rise as quickly as it would if inflation was under control (though if the inflation that exists is demand–pull, it is likely that economic activity is already high and this may not matter).

Policy response

Governments globally are committed to achieving low inflation. This means they will implement deflationary policies if inflation rises — usually through higher interest rates. Deflationary policies are not good for individuals, especially if they have borrowed substantial amounts of money.

Deflation

A falling level of prices is quite rare in the UK. During 2015, there were brief periods of deflation. However, both the Governor of the Bank of England and the Chancellor were not too concerned with this deflation. There are two types of deflation.

Benign/good deflation

This is caused by increases in aggregate supply. As shown in Figure 11.10, an increase in aggregate supply (either in the short run or in the long run) will lead to a lower price level but also a higher level of real GDP. Typically, this sort of deflation is caused by falls in commodity prices or technological advances, meaning firms experience falling costs of production.

Oil prices fell significantly in 2014–15, which was a major contributor to the deflation experienced in the UK, i.e. it was 'good' deflation.

Malevolent/malign/bad deflation

This is caused by falling aggregate demand. As we can see in Figure 11.11, a fall in aggregate demand leads to falling prices and also falling real GDP (with rising cyclical unemployment). There will be a downward multiplier effect and if this is related to falling confidence, policies designed to boost spending may be less effective.

> **Benign deflation:** a fall in the price level due to increases in aggregate supply (usually due to falling costs of production).
>
> **Malevolent deflation:** a fall in the price level due to a fall in aggregate demand.

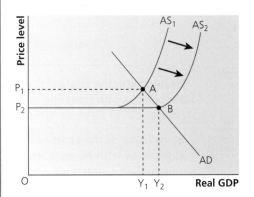

Figure 11.10 Benign deflation — caused by increases in AS

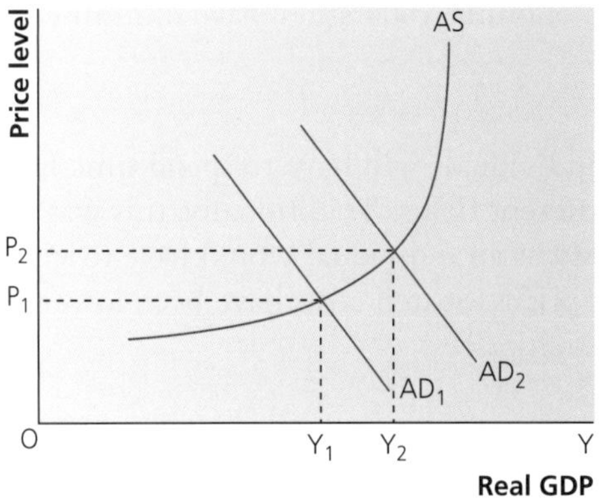

Figure 11.11 Malevolent deflation — caused by falls in AD

Even 'good' deflation is not always welcome for a prolonged period of time as it may eventually become 'bad' deflation.

Consequences of deflation

REVISED ☐

The UK government's inflation target is symmetrical. This means inflation below the target of 2% is viewed as being as equally undesirable as inflation above the target. The negative consequences of deflation include the following.

Delays in consumption

With deflation present, people are more likely to delay purchases until goods are cheaper. This can become self-fulfilling, where the delay prompts businesses to cut prices further to encourage purchases, leading to even further delays in purchases. In reality, this is likely to affect only sales of luxury or high-value items.

Rising real value of debt

Deflation is likely to lead to falls in prices and falls in incomes. However, the value of debt remains constant in nominal terms and will rise in real terms if prices are falling. This will impose difficulties on households and firms which have borrowed substantial amounts.

Wage rigidity

When prices are falling, we would expect to see incomes fall so as to maintain real incomes. However, money wages are often 'sticky' in a downwards direction. This means that although money wages normally rise in periods of inflation to maintain real wages, in periods of deflation, money wages do not normally fall. Sticky wages when there is deflation present may lead to real wage unemployment as wages are too high for the labour market to 'clear'.

> **Wage rigidity:** the situation where wages are sticky and do not fall in line with falling prices.

Now test yourself

TESTED

15 Explain two reasons why wages may be 'sticky downwards'.

Answer on p. 230

Commodity prices and inflation

REVISED

Commodity prices are volatile and as a result **commodities** are often traded for the purposes of making profits through speculation on future price changes.

Oil prices have a significant effect on the inflation rate due to oil's importance as an input to industrial production (it is used not only to transport goods and workers, but also to make goods such as plastics).

Oil-producing nations often coordinate production decisions so as to restrict the quantity of oil being produced and this reduction in supply leads to large increases in oil prices (due to demand being very price inelastic). This can result in sharp rises in inflation, as happened in the UK on more than one occasion in the 1970s (peaking at around 25% inflation in 1975).

> **Commodity:** a homogeneous product (all output of the product is identical) that is often used as a basic input into production. Common examples are oil, copper, minerals, cotton and basic foodstuffs (e.g. wheat and cocoa).

Impact of other economies on UK inflation

REVISED

The UK is a fairly **open economy**. This means that changes in other economies can affect inflation in the UK in a number of ways:

- Growth in foreign economies will increase the demand for UK exports. This in theory could lead to demand-pull inflation (though most demand-pull inflation is caused by excessive growth in consumption rather than exports).
- Similarly, recessions in our major trading partners will ease demand-pull pressure due to reduced spending on UK exports.
- Increased growth in overseas economies will lead to more demand for commodities and other basic production materials. This increased demand will push up prices of these goods and the UK may experience cost-push inflation as a result.
- Changes in the exchange rate between different currencies will also affect inflation. Falls in the exchange rate will lead to cost-push pressure as import prices rise.

> **Open economy:** an economy in which foreign trade accounts for a significant proportion of GDP.

Possible conflicts between macroeconomic policy objectives

As stated in Chapter 9, the UK government has a number of macroeconomic policy objectives. The key objectives are:

- economic growth (positive but stable growth in GDP)
- price stability (an inflation target of 2%)
- minimising unemployment
- stable balance of payments on current account (mainly between exports and imports)
- balancing the budget (between government spending and taxation)

Output gaps

REVISED

An output gap occurs when the actual (short-run) growth rate differs from the trend (long-run) growth rate. These can be negative output gaps or positive output gaps (see Figure 11.5 on p. 145).

Negative output gaps

These occur when actual growth is below trend growth.

If there is a negative output gap then cyclical unemployment is likely to increase.

As growth is below the productive capacity of the economy, there will be resources (workers and capital) which are not required for production. This means that workers will become unemployed.

Unemployment can rise in this way even if actual growth is positive; if the trend growth for the economy is 2% and actual growth is only 1% then this means that fewer workers are needed given that each worker, on average, can produce 2% more each year — and only a 1% increase in output is needed.

The negative output gap can also be shown on an AD/AS diagram (see Figure 11.12). This type of unemployment can best be solved by increasing the level of aggregate demand.

Positive output gaps

These occur when actual growth is above trend growth. A positive output gap will eventually lead to rising prices, i.e. higher inflation.

With a positive output gap, although output is temporarily higher than its trend rate, this cannot be maintained in the long run. In order to keep output at this higher level, firms will find costs increasing (such as paying higher wages to attract workers) and this will lead to inflationary pressures.

The positive output gap can be shown on an AD/AS diagram (see Figure 11.13). This type of inflation can best be solved by decreasing the level of aggregate demand.

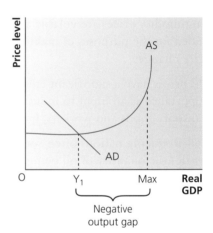

Figure 11.12 A negative output gap is caused here by insufficient AD

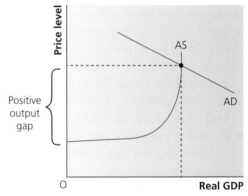

Figure 11.13 A positive output gap here generates inflationary pressure in the economy

Now test yourself

TESTED

16 What are the characteristics of a negative output gap and a positive output gap?

Answer on p. 230

The Phillips Curve

Economist A.W. Phillips discovered a negative correlation between the rate of wage growth and the level of unemployment in the UK economy covering almost 100 years of data. This suggested that there may be a trade-off between inflation and unemployment.

Now test yourself

TESTED ☐

17 Explain how changes in wage rates may be linked to changes in the rate of inflation.

Answer on p. 230

The short-run Phillips Curve

The Phillips Curve shows that when unemployment falls, inflation will rise, and vice versa. The reason for this trade-off is that as unemployment falls to low levels, trade unions and workers will feel more confident in claiming higher wages given that, with labour shortages emerging, they will be unlikely to lose their jobs. These higher wages as a cost of production will lead to higher inflation as firms raise selling prices to cover higher wage costs.

Likewise, when unemployment is high, wage claims are likely to be low due to the lack of job security. This means that inflation will also be low.

The trade-off shown on the Phillips Curve (Figure 11.14) is similar to the trade-off between higher GDP and a higher price level shown on both the SRAS and the Keynesian AS curves.

> **Short-run Phillips Curve:** the apparent trade-off between achieving low inflation but with high unemployment, or vice versa.
>
> **Long-run Phillips Curve:** how in the long run the economy will move towards the non-accelerating inflation rate of unemployment (NAIRU) regardless of the rate of inflation.

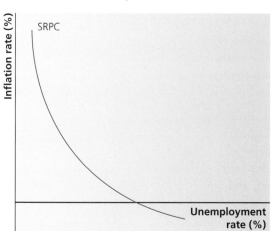

Figure 11.14 The short-run Phillips Curve — showing the trade-off between unemployment and inflation

The trade-off allowed the government to 'position' the economy where it wanted in terms of the unemployment rate and the corresponding inflation rate. However, the apparent relationship between inflation and unemployment appeared to disappear from the late 1960s onwards as unemployment and inflation rose together, which should not have been possible based on the original Phillips Curve.

The long-run Phillips Curve

Milton Friedman, a Monetarist economist, put forward an explanation which attempted to explain why the trade-off had disappeared.

In the short run, workers experience **money illusion** where any rise in inflation is not initially recognised by workers as having reduced their real wages. Workers have **adaptive expectations** with regards to the inflation rate, which means that in the long run workers will base their expected future inflation rate on whatever the current rate of inflation is. This can be shown diagrammatically, as in Figure 11.15.

> **Money illusion:** where workers in the short run confuse nominal wages and real wages.
>
> **Adaptive expectations:** where workers take time to adjust their expectations of the inflation rate to match the actual inflation rate.

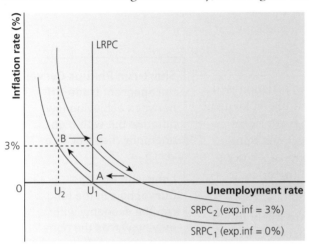

Figure 11.15 The long-run Phillips Curve is vertical — at the natural rate of unemployment

Imagine the economy was in equilibrium at the natural rate of unemployment (shown by U_1) with no inflation. This is shown by point A in Figure 11.15.

If a government increases AD in order to reduce unemployment, we move along the short-run Phillips Curve ($SRPC_1$) as expected — with inflation rising to 3% and unemployment falling to U_2 — shown here as the move from point A to point B.

Initially workers do not realise their real wage has decreased because they suffer from money illusion. However, eventually workers' inflationary expectations adapt, they see the rise in inflation has reduced their real incomes and they will demand higher wages to compensate. This will increase costs for firms, leading to an increase in unemployment, and we move from point B to point C.

We are now back on the long-run Phillips Curve and also on a new short-run Phillips Curve ($SRPC_2$). The new short-run Phillips Curve is based on workers now assuming inflation will remain at 3%.

If the government attempts to reduce unemployment again as it did before, workers will now build the current level of inflation into their wage claims, i.e. the workers will ask for even higher wages as they need to ensure their real wages don't fall.

The lesson for governments is that there are two types of Phillips Curves in operation:
- a short-run Phillips Curve (SRPC) allowing the trade-off only until workers adapt their expectations to higher inflation and push up wage claims (in fact there is a range of SRPCs, each one based on a different level of inflationary expectations)

- a long-run Phillips Curve (LRPC), which is vertical and remains at the level where the labour market is in equilibrium and there is no upward or downward pressure on inflation. This level of unemployment is sometimes referred to as the natural rate of unemployment (NRU or Yn)

Implications for policy makers

- In the short run, there may be a trade-off, which means that unemployment can be lowered by increasing aggregate demand, but only at the cost of increasing inflation.
- Reductions in unemployment may only be temporary — until workers adapt their expectations and claim for higher wages (which then moves unemployment back to the natural rate).
- The speed of the adjustment process for inflationary expectations is not clear. It may take a long period of time for adaptive expectations to adjust — meaning unemployment could be kept below the natural rate for a prolonged period.
- Some economists believe that the adjustment process is quick and any reductions in unemployment through higher aggregate demand will be short-lived.
- A small number of economists deny that there is a trade-off. They believe that workers have rational expectations, which means they know that any attempt to reduce unemployment through higher aggregate demand will lead to higher inflation and will immediately claim for higher wages.
- Unemployment can be reduced below this natural rate in the long term but only through other types of policies (supply-side policies).

The non-accelerating inflation rate of unemployment (NAIRU)

REVISED

The NAIRU and the 'natural rate of unemployment' are often used interchangeably. The NAIRU refers to the rate of unemployment consistent with a constant rate of inflation. As long as unemployment remains at this level, there will be no upward or downward pressure on the inflation rate. The inflation rate may be low or high but will not change if unemployment remains at its NAIRU.

Actual unemployment rate < NAIRU then inflation will rise.

Actual unemployment rate > NAIRU then inflation will fall.

The NAIRU is determined, as is the natural rate, by structural and frictional issues within the economy and can be affected by changes in policy.

Policy conflicts

REVISED

As we can see, two of the main macroeconomic objectives (inflation and unemployment) require different solutions — one requires more and one requires less aggregate demand. This is described as a policy conflict.

A policy conflict exists when attempts to solve one economic problem lead away from solving another problem. We can examine potential conflicts by looking at how certain objectives might be achieved.

Policy objectives needing increased aggregate demand:
- short-run economic growth (spending and income are closely connected)
- reducing cyclical unemployment (jobs depend on the level of spending)

- eliminating a budget deficit (this is easier with higher spending, which means more taxes are collected)

Policy objectives needing lower aggregate demand:
- reducing demand-pull inflation (this inflation is caused by there being too much AD)
- improving the current account balance (this will occur if imports are lower, which follows if spending falls)
- eliminating a budget deficit (this may require lower government spending, though some would dispute this)

Therefore, conflicts will arise between objectives that need higher AD and those that need lower AD. Common conflicts arise between:
- minimising unemployment and keeping inflation low and stable
- increasing economic growth and achieving balance on the current account
- reducing the budget deficit through cuts in government spending, and achieving economic growth and minimising unemployment

Remember, these conflicts can be made worse by multiplier effects. For example, a reduction in government spending in order to close the gap on a budget deficit may lead to a significantly larger fall in national income as a result.

As Figure 11.16 shows, if we rely only on policies that affect AD, then we will face a conflict between experiencing unemployment (with AD_1) or inflation (with AD_2).

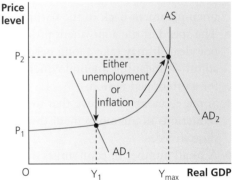

Figure 11.16 The conflict resulting from relying on policies that affect AD only

Policy conflicts in the long run

Most economists agree that there are policy conflicts in the short run at least. However, some would argue that these conflicts do not have to occur in the long run.

Different policies can be used to address different problems, which may minimise the conflict that exists. In the long run, the economy should be operating on the LRAS, meaning that there is no cyclical unemployment in the long run. If there is no cyclical unemployment, then there is no need for higher AD.

Supply-side policies may be the solution to the trade-off that exists between inflation and unemployment in the short run — these are explored in Chapter 13.

There are other conflicts that exist in trying to ensure an equitable distribution of income. Some economists argue that higher growth can be achieved if governments do not worry about unequal distribution of income, and that by cutting taxes for high earners, higher growth can be achieved. This point is open to debate, though.

Another argument is that cutting welfare benefits will reduce unemployment and will improve long-run growth. Again, this would conflict with the objective of an equitable distribution of income.

> **Revision activity**
>
> Draw AD/AS diagrams to illustrate the issues of cyclical unemployment and both types of inflation, and add notes on the effect of these on the achievement of other government objectives.

Now test yourself

TESTED ☐

18 Explain why there may be a conflict between inflation and unemployment.

Answer on p. 230

Exam practice

In 2011, UK inflation was close to 5%. This is significantly above its target level. However, despite this, the Bank of England chose not to raise interest rates. The reason given for not raising rates was that the high inflation was caused by the fall in the pound's value, a recent rise in commodity prices and a recent rise in VAT. The governor of the Bank of England believed that without these factors, inflation would have been below its target level of 2%.

1 Define the term 'disinflation'. [3]
2 Briefly explain how inflation is calculated in the UK. [6]
3 Explain how two factors mentioned in the extract are leading to higher inflation. [6]
4 Using an AD/AS diagram, analyse the effects on economic performance of the factors mentioned in the extract. [10]

Answers and quick quiz 11 online

ONLINE

Summary

You should have an understanding of:
- The distinction between short-run and long-run growth as well as the factors contributing to each type of growth.
- The advantages and disadvantages of economic growth for individuals, the economy and the environment — as well as an understanding of whether economic growth is sustainable.
- The features of each stage of the economic cycle and how to describe them — as well as explanations which may account for the nature of the economic cycle.

- The causes and consequences of unemployment within an economy.
- The causes and consequences of inflation and deflation within an economy.
- How the inflation rate is affected by expectations, changes in commodity prices and changes in other economies.
- The policy conflicts that arise in attempting to achieve multiple objectives, both in the short run and in the long run.
- How the Phillips Curve may suggest a short-run trade-off between inflation and unemployment, and how this trade-off may not exist in the long run.

12 Financial markets and monetary policy

The structure of financial markets and financial assets

The functions of money

Bartering — exchanging goods and services without money — is difficult to organise and since early civilisation societies have usually come up with a form of money. Although we think of money as being notes and coins, there are various definitions of money that are commonly used. For something to be described as money it must fulfil the **functions of money**, which include the following.

> **Function of money:** a benefit generated by the use of money.

Medium of exchange

Barter transactions rely on the 'double coincidence of wants' — the person selling must also want to buy what you have — making it difficult to complete transactions. Money accepted as a medium of exchange means no need for barter. This also means that people can specialise in work (and living standards can rise, as a result) safe in the knowledge that goods and services can be exchanged for money.

Unit of account

Giving products a monetary value enables people to compare prices and values of different products. This function works as long as inflation is low.

Store of value

Money can be stored away until needed and does not have to be spent immediately. Inflation erodes this function.

Standard of deferred payment

Money can be used now or in the future for transactions. Lending money now makes sense only if that money, once repaid, can be used at a later date.

Characteristics of money

Early civilisations used a variety of rare metals, minerals, stones, shells and other things for money. For an item to work effectively as money, it should have the following characteristics:

- acceptable — money must be accepted by (nearly) all to serve as a medium of exchange
- durable — money must physically last and must not deteriorate over time
- portable — it must be easily transportable without inconvenience, i.e. easy to carry
- divisible — money needs to be capable of being divided into smaller units of measurement (i.e. small denominations) to enable transactions of different monetary size

> **Characteristic of money:** a necessary feature of money that must be present for the item to function as 'money'.

- scarce — money needs to be limited in supply (unlike, say, leaves of common trees)
- difficult to forge — otherwise the item will not be scarce if it can be easily reproduced

Now test yourself

TESTED

1 Why is gold still seen by many as a safe alternative to money?

Answer on p. 230

The money supply

REVISED

The **money supply** refers to the quantity of money in existence in an economy. This will consist of different elements.

Notes and coins

These are issued by the Bank of England and are accepted in various denominations of coin and paper banknote. These represent only around 2% of the entire 'money supply' based on a certain definition of what constitutes money.

Bank accounts

Most people keep their money in a bank (current) account. This can be easily accessed through cash machines and used for easy payment as a debit card transaction, for contactless payment or through standing orders and direct debit payments between bank accounts.

Savings accounts may count as money but often these accounts do not offer immediate access (or do but with a loss of interest as a penalty).

Building societies are another form of financial institution with which people hold money. In effect, building societies act almost exactly like a bank (in fact, many of the current high-street banks were once building societies).

Other financial assets

Money can be held in various other forms, such as shares, bonds and bills. Some of these appear to be very similar to money in that they can be converted into cash quickly without loss in value, but other times these assets are less liquid or can be converted into cash only with a loss in value.

In reality, we have not one clear definition of money but a 'spectrum of liquidity' of assets ranging from notes and coins at one end of the spectrum to assets which have monetary value but cannot practically be converted easily and quickly into cash, such as property, at the other end. The following distinction is often made when attempting to define the money supply:

- **Narrow money:** consists of notes and coins and bank/building society current accounts. These accounts can be immediately drawn upon and fulfil a lot of the functions of cash, especially if accompanied by either a debit card or a cheque book.
- **Broad money:** consists of all of the components of narrow money but also includes other deposits, such as savings accounts that are held with banks and building societies. Central banks are often interested in this measure as it can indicate the willingness of consumers and firms to borrow and spend money.

> **Money supply:** the value of the stock of money that exists within an economy at a point in time (there are various measures of the money supply).

> **Typical mistake**
>
> Many people still think that there is an equivalent amount of gold held by the Bank of England for every pound in circulation. This is not the case.

> **Exam tip**
>
> Be clear when you mention money that you are not referring to just notes and coins — money can mean different things.

> **Narrow money:** a measure of the money supply that includes balances that can be immediately used as a medium of exchange, such as notes and coins, and accessible bank balances.

> **Broad money:** a measure of the money supply that includes notes and coins, as well as most balances held by banks and other financial institutions.

2 Arrange the following assets in descending order of liquidity:
A bonds
B bank current account
C house
D shares
E notes and coins
F savings account

Answer on p. 230

The role of financial markets

REVISED

Financial markets exist to shift money from those with a surplus of money they do not wish to spend to those who wish to spend more than they currently have. Today, financial markets operate on an international level, with money moving between people and organisations in many countries.

There are three main financial markets: the **money market**, the **capital market** and the **foreign exchange market**.

The money market

The money market provides short-term finance to individuals, firms and governments. This market mainly deals with short-term debts, ranging from loans which are due to mature (i.e. to be repaid) in hours to those due to mature in months. This will cover interbank lending and money lent to the government through the purchase of **Treasury bills**.

The capital market

The capital market deals with medium- and long-term finance to firms and governments. The capital markets typically deal with raising of finance from share or bond issues.

The capital market can be divided into the primary market and the secondary market:
- **Primary market:** this deals with the issue of new securities (**bonds** and **shares**) by firms or governments to raise finance.
- **Secondary market:** this deals with the trade in bonds and shares that have already been issued. World stock markets are largely dealing with this secondary market — with the buying and selling of existing shares. The secondary market makes it easier for bondholders and shareholders to raise money through buying and selling the shares.

The foreign exchange market

International trade and flows of investment involve the need to convert and hold different currencies. Foreign exchange transactions are divided into two types:
- spot market
- forward market

Financial markets: markets that enable transfers between those who wish to deposit funds and those looking to borrow funds.

Money market: the market which deals in short-term finance between firms, individuals and governments — focusing on debts due to be repaid in the near future.

Capital market: the market which deals with medium-term and long-term finance (such as share and bond issues) between individuals, firms and governments — focusing on debts due for repayment more than a few months ahead.

Foreign exchange market: the market that deals with transactions requiring conversion from one currency into another currency.

Treasury bill: a very short-term form of borrowing by the government, usually repaid within three months.

Bonds: a form of borrowing which gives the holder a fixed rate of interest and the money is repaid within a set period of time — bonds can be traded.

Shares: issued by firms raising finance — these give the holder the chance to receive dividends out of the firm's profits and often allow the holder to vote in company affairs. These are not repaid by the firm.

Both the **spot market** and the **forward market** are subject to large amounts of speculation — buying and selling foreign currencies in the hope of profits later when the exchange rate changes.

Now test yourself

TESTED ☐

3 Explain two reasons for buying foreign currency on the forward market.

Answer on p. 230

The role of financial markets in the wider economy

REVISED ☐

Governments often run budget deficits and issue bonds to finance the shortfall. The stock of bonds yet to be repaid represents the national debt. The significance of the national debt is explored in the next chapter.

> **Debentures**: another name for bonds — debentures are usually issued by companies (corporate bonds).

Large firms use the capital markets to raise large amounts of money, either by issuing their own bonds (referred to as **debentures**) or by issuing shares. As a result, the capital markets ensure finance is available in the economy for firms seeking to maximise their profits.

The difference between debt and equity

REVISED ☐

Equity

Equity refers to the share capital issued by firms. Firms which are seeking to raise large amounts of capital to finance business activities (such as a major expansion, takeover or start-up) can sell shares to potential investors.

> **Equity**: the value of share capital issued by firms as part of their financial capital.

Those who buy these shares are known as shareholders and they are the co-owners of the company. Shareholders usually get to vote in the running of the company, but for most this is not the motivation for buying shares. Shares are attractive to investors because their value often rises quickly (enabling capital gains) and shareholders often receive annual dividends (which are a share of the firm's distributed profits).

Historically, share prices have often risen quickly, but periodically there are sudden falls in share prices (known as crashes) where gains are wiped out rapidly.

Now test yourself

TESTED ☐

4 Explain two reasons why people who have no interest in controlling a company would buy shares.

Answer on p. 230

Bonds

Bonds are issued by firms and governments that wish to borrow money. Bonds pay a fixed rate of interest (which is known as the **coupon**) and have a fixed date when the original value of the bonds is to be repaid (its **maturity date**). Bonds typically have a ten-year term to maturity, but it is possible for bonds to have shorter or longer maturity dates (some bonds

> **Coupon**: the (fixed) interest on a bond.
>
> **Maturity date**: the date of repayment for a bond.

are issued with no maturity date). Most bondholders are institutional investors — that is, other banks and companies looking to generate returns on their investment.

In the UK, the government finances its budget deficits through the issue of new bonds. These government bonds are also called 'gilts' (gilt-edged securities).

Now test yourself

TESTED

5 Why would someone buy a bond that has no maturity date?

Answer on p. 230

The relationship between market interest rates and bond prices

Bonds are traded in the financial markets. Their price is determined by a number of factors, but a major determinant of bond prices is the current interest rate. There is an inverse relationship between current market interest rates and bond prices, meaning that if interest rates rise, we would expect bond prices to fall, and vice versa.

Calculating the yield on bonds

The yield on bonds represents the interest paid as a percentage of the bond's current price in the capital markets. This is calculated as follows:

$$\text{Yield (\%)} = \frac{\text{the coupon}}{\text{the market price}} \times 100$$

Example 1

A bond is issued with a value of £100 and has a coupon of £3 per year (i.e. it pays fixed interest of 3% to the holder). There are many years until the bond reaches the maturity date.

If the market price of the bonds falls to £75, then the yield on this bond would be:

$$\text{Yield (\%)} = \frac{\pounds3}{\pounds75} \times 100 = 4\%$$

The inverse relationship between market interest rates and bond prices is illustrated in Example 2.

Example 2

A bond is issued with a value of £100 and the coupon on this bond is £5, which offered a yield of 5% when the bond was issued, which was equivalent to market interest rates at that time.

Two years later, market interest rates have fallen to 2%. The maturity date of our bond is still many years away.

Given that our bond gives a higher rate of return than can be obtained on other financial assets (after the fall in market interest rates to 2%), we would expect the demand for our bond to rise, which would push up its price. The price of the bond would be expected to rise until its coupon of £5 gave an identical yield to the current market interest rate of 2%.

$$\text{Yield (\%)} = \frac{\text{coupon on bond}}{\text{price of bond}} \times 100$$

$$2\ (\%) = \frac{£5}{\text{price of bond}} \times 100$$

Rearranging this equation, we arrive at the following:

$$\text{Price of bond} = \frac{£5}{2} \times 100 = £250$$

The price of the bond would rise to £250.

In reality, yields on bonds are determined by a variety of factors. Expectations of future interest rate movements are a key factor in determining bond yields. If markets expect interest rates to be higher in the future than previously, we would expect the price of current bonds to fall.

The price of bonds will also be determined by how close the bond is to maturity. The closer the bond is to its maturity date, the closer will be the current price of the bond to the original nominal value of the bond.

Now test yourself

TESTED ☐

6 In each of the following cases, a bond with a face value of £100 has been issued with a coupon of £4. Calculate the yield on the bond if the market price changes to:
  (a) £80
  (b) £120
  (c) £160

Answer on p. 230

Commercial banks and investment banks

Although we often refer to the banking industry and the banking sector as if they contain only one type of bank, there are actually different types of bank in the economy.

Commercial banks

REVISED ☐

Commercial banks are referred to as 'high-street banks' as they are the banks most people use on a daily basis (even if they do not visit the 'high-street' branch of the bank). These banks accept deposits from the general public and lend money to those who wish to borrow money — often in the form of bank overdrafts and mortgages for homebuyers.

> **Commercial bank**: a bank that accepts deposits from and lends money to customers, usually for personal and business loans.

Investment banks

A key function of an **investment bank** is to help companies raise finance by assisting with the issue of new capital (in the form of a share issue or a bond issue). Investment banks do not allow the general public to open up bank accounts.

Additionally, many investment banks assist governments with shares issues for the privatisation of state-owned enterprises (for example, the Royal Mail in 2013). Income for the investment bank comes from charging a fee for the services of advising and organising the raising of finance by companies and governments.

Investment banks also engage in buying and selling securities in the secondary capital markets, as well as buying and selling financial assets in the money and foreign exchange markets. The buying and selling of securities will be carried out to generate returns for the investment bank, but also for private investors looking for someone to buy and sell on their behalf.

> **Investment bank**: a bank that doesn't accept customer deposits and normally provides financial services to other businesses, such as arranging share or debenture issues.

Dual role of banks

Many banks carry out both commercial bank and investment bank activities and some economists believe this contributed to the recent financial crisis. It has been suggested that banks should be allowed only to operate either as a commercial bank, or as an investment bank, but not both. However, legislation to enforce separation has not been passed. For banks performing dual roles, the commercial banking activities must be 'ring fenced' from their investment banking activities — i.e. the funds generated by customers' deposits cannot be used for investment banking activities, such as buying and selling investments.

> **Typical mistake**
>
> When you refer to banks, make sure you are clear what type of bank you are writing about.

Now test yourself

TESTED

7 Explain why many banks prefer to operate as both commercial and investment banks.

Answer on p. 231

The functions of a commercial bank

A key role of a commercial bank is directing funds from those with surplus money to those wishing to make use of funds that they don't have themselves. The main functions of a commercial bank are as follows:

- **Accepting deposits:** deposits from customers with a surplus of money that they wish to have securely and conveniently stored.
- **Lending to economic agents:** those (individuals and businesses) wishing to borrow money can arrange this from a commercial bank, which will offer a variety of lending instruments (e.g. loans, overdrafts, mortgages).
- **Providing an efficient means of payment:** payment for goods and services as well as settling debts with others is far more convenient if using the services of a commercial bank (e.g. through card and cheque settlements).

The structure of a commercial bank's balance sheet

The **balance sheet** of a typical commercial bank will appear as follows and is explained below.

Assets	Liabilities
Notes and coins	Share capital
Balances held at the Bank of England	Reserves (e.g. retained profits)
Money at call and short notice	Long-term borrowing
Bills (commercial and Treasury bills)	Short-term borrowing
Investments	Deposits
Advances	
Tangible non-current assets	

> **Balance sheet**: a financial statement showing the assets of an organisation alongside how those resources were financed (i.e. the liabilities of the organisation). A balance sheet must always balance.

Assets of the commercial bank

Assets represent resources available for use. They are often presented in order of **liquidity**.

- The most liquid assets are notes and coins, and balances held at the Bank of England (commercial banks generally hold a small amount of their cash at the Bank of England).
- Money at call and short notice (money borrowed from other banks on the interbank market, usually to meet short-term needs) as well as bills held by the bank are generally all very liquid assets. Either these are cash already or they can be accessed or turned into cash very quickly.
- Investments are normally bonds or shares held by the bank which were issued by other companies (including other banks) as well as the bonds issued by governments. These will be held by a bank to generate income.
- Advances are the loans made by the bank to customers. Some will be short-term loans (such as overdrafts given to the bank's customers), but some will be long term (such as mortgages given to homebuyers which may not be repaid for up to 25 years).
- Tangible non current assets are the physical assets that a bank will use to perform its activities — normally the premises in which the bank operates (e.g. headquarters and branches).

> **Liquidity**: refers to how easily an asset can be converted into cash without any loss in value.

Liabilities

Liabilities represent the amounts the bank owes to various individuals and groups.

- Share capital was issued by the bank to finance its activities. This is likely to have happened when the bank was formed, or when there was a major expansion of the bank. Many banks sold shares to the general public when converting from building societies in the 1980s. Share capital appears as a liability but it is the bank's permanent capital and will not normally be repaid.

- Reserves represent profits generated that have been placed back within the business for growth rather than being distributed to shareholders. They allow a bank to grow.
- Long-term borrowing normally consists of the bonds that a bank has issued to finance its operations (largely in the same way in which shares were issued by the bank).
- Short-term borrowing consists of money borrowed from the money markets and mainly serves to provide liquidity for any shortfall in cash needs.
- Deposits are the accounts opened and maintained by the bank's customers. These accounts are sometimes categorised as sight deposits (which can be accessed immediately) and time deposits (which require a period of time before access is allowed). However, the distinction between sight and time deposits is less clear than it used to be.

> **Typical mistake**
>
> Loans granted by a bank are an asset — they are only debt to those who have borrowed the money from the bank.

The objectives of a commercial bank

REVISED

A commercial bank is likely to be run in order to maximise its profits so as to keep its shareholders satisfied. However, its objectives can be split into three main areas:

- **Liquidity:** banks have to manage their assets carefully and need to ensure they have sufficient notes and coins to meet the needs of customers withdrawing cash. If a bank has insufficient notes and coins to meet the requirements of its customers, it will be forced to borrow money (and pay interest) from the financial markets.
- **Profitability:** holding notes and coins is not profitable as they do not generate a return. The bank will want to make a profit for its shareholders by lending out money to borrowers so that it can earn money by charging interest on any money lent.
- **Security:** banks take risks when lending money — the risk that the borrower will fail to repay. Normally, the interest on the riskiest types of loans is higher to compensate for the higher risk. Therefore there are greater profits to be made on riskier lending made by the bank.

The economy's central bank aims to ensure that commercial banks are secure and can survive by acting as a 'lender of last resort' to banks which have a short-term shortage of liquidity. This does not mean that it will continually provide money for banks that make unwise loans but it will provide short-term finance for banks to provide liquidity when required (for a fee).

Conflict between the objectives

Banks generally borrow short term and lend long term. This means that if people wish to withdraw money from their accounts, the bank risks being unable to access money from those it has lent to for long-term use (e.g. it cannot simply ask someone to repay their entire mortgage just because it doesn't have enough cash on one particular day). This discrepancy means that banks can be unstable, which is why the Bank of England steps in on occasion to maintain the stability of this industry.

A major conflict for a bank is that although it has a need for liquidity, it can make the highest profits by lending out on risky, long-term ventures, meaning money is tied up elsewhere just when the bank might need it.

Now test yourself

TESTED ☐

8 Briefly explain how there is a conflict between liquidity and profitability for a commercial bank.

Answer on p. 231

Credit creation

REVISED ☐

Banks know customers are unlikely to withdraw their full balances from accounts on a regular basis. This means banks can create credit by lending out some of their customers' deposits to others wishing to borrow, enabling the bank to profit on any loans made. If this money lent out is then redeposited in the bank as a new customer deposit, it can be lent out yet again, thus creating even more credit. This process of banks creating credit by lending out customer deposits and holding only a small amount of deposits in actual notes and coins is called **fractional banking**.

> **Fractional banking:** the ability of banks to hold a fraction of their customers' deposits at any time, thus allowing them to lend out money and earn interest.

The bank's ability to create credit is limited only by the extent to which the bank feels it must hold a portion of its customers' deposits in liquid form (i.e. as notes and coins). If the proportion held is very small, it means that any new deposits the bank receives can create large amounts of credit within the economy.

Of course, if everyone wanted to withdraw their deposits at the same time, the bank would be in trouble — it would not have the notes and coins to meet customers' demands. This is sometimes known as a 'run on the bank' — when customers fear a bank is likely to run out of money and so they demand all of their deposits back at once — and can be self-fulfilling.

Central banks and monetary policy

The functions of a central bank

REVISED ☐

Each country with its own currency has a **central bank** to manage the monetary policy for that currency. The UK's central bank is the Bank of England and it is based in London. The functions of the UK's central bank are:
- to maintain financial stability
- to help the government maintain macroeconomic stability

> **Central bank:** the bank of an economy responsible for issue of money and management of monetary policy for that currency.

Financial stability

The Bank of England achieves its role of ensuring financial stability and security by acting as the 'lender of last resort' to the banking sector — providing money for short-term needs to the sector and providing liquidity insurance, which means that the central bank will make available liquid assets for banks that need access to those funds.

Ensuring a stable financial system has taken on greater importance since the 2008 financial crisis. Up until then it was assumed that allowing financial institutions freedom to operate would be sufficient and would be self-regulating. Since the crisis, the role of achieving financial stability has been extended to include monitoring and regulating the UK's financial system.

Macroeconomic stability

The Bank of England's objective, as set by the government, is to achieve price stability in the UK. Clearly, the Bank of England provides input on monetary policy only and does not directly affect the government's fiscal policy or its supply-side policies, but it is believed that by achieving price stability it will be easier for the government to achieve other macroeconomic objectives of full employment and steady economic growth.

Monetary policy

The main focus of **monetary policy** is on the level of interest rates set in the economy. Other aspects of monetary policy include the size of the money supply, the availability of credit (i.e. money that can be borrowed by consumers and businesses) and the exchange rate of the currency.

Monetary policy is the job of the central bank of the economy, which in the UK is the Bank of England. Since 1997, the Bank of England has been largely free of government control in setting monetary policy.

This does not mean that the government has no influence: it still sets the targets for the Bank of England to achieve, and it still reserves the right to intervene in the management of monetary policy in special circumstances, such as in the financial crisis of 2008.

> **Monetary policy:** the manipulation of the price and availability of money within an economy to achieve economic policy objectives.

Objectives of monetary policy

REVISED

The key aim of UK monetary policy is to achieve the government's inflation target — using the CPI measurement of inflation — at a rate of 2% (plus or minus 1%) per year. Other objectives of government policy, such as full employment and steady economic growth, are important but should be pursued using monetary policy only if they do not conflict with the inflation target.

The inflation target of 2% is achieved through changes to the **Bank rate**. Decisions over the level at which to set the Bank rate are made monthly by the Bank of England's Monetary Policy Committee.

> **Bank rate:** the interest rate set by the Bank of England that affects interest rates set by banks and other financial institutions such as building societies across the economy.

Exam tip

Although interest rates affect the reward for savings, the main effect of interest rate changes considered in economics is the change in the cost of borrowing.

Now test yourself

TESTED

9 Explain three ways in which aggregate demand would be affected by a cut in interest rates.

Answer on p. 231

The Monetary Policy Committee

Monetary policy is mainly effected by changes in the level of interest rates. The level of interest rates is set by the **Monetary Policy Committee** (MPC) of the Bank of England.

The MPC considers how a range of economic factors will impact on the UK inflation rate. Areas of economic performance that are considered include:
- consumer spending and consumer confidence
- business investment and business confidence
- fiscal policy — government expenditure and taxation
- the exchange rate
- commodity prices
- unemployment and labour market conditions

> **Monetary Policy Committee**: this currently consists of nine members and meets monthly to consider recent developments and likely future developments of aspects of UK economic performance.

The MPC considers whether the economic conditions currently facing the UK, and those that are likely to face the UK in the short and medium term, are likely to either increase or decrease the inflation rate over the next 2 years. This is achieved by assessing how changes in the economic environment will affect both aggregate demand and aggregate supply.

If there are increased chances of inflation rising in the near future, then it is likely that members of the MPC will vote to raise interest rates. This is because a higher level of interest rates is likely to lead to lower aggregate demand which will, in turn, lead to lower pressure on demand-pull inflation.

The opposite would also be true; if there is likely to be downward pressure on prices, then members of the MPC are more likely to lower interest rates to stimulate the level of aggregate demand.

For example, a rise in the Bank rate is likely to have the following effects on the UK economy:
- lower levels of borrowing by consumers
- higher monthly repayments for those with variable rate mortgages
- increased incentives for households to save
- lower investment by businesses as the profitability of investment projects is reduced
- a rise in the exchange rate, causing UK exports to be less competitive, but imports to be cheaper, thus potentially reducing cost-push inflation as well.

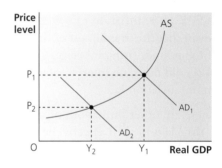

Figure 12.1 The effects of raising interest rates

All these effects will reduce the level of aggregate demand and should lead to a reduction in demand-pull inflation. In Figure 12.1, increases in interest rates will lead to a shift from AD_1 to AD_2, which is likely to bring down inflation but lower economic growth and increase unemployment.

It is worth bearing in mind that changes in interest rates usually take over a year (and perhaps up to 2 years) to work through the economy fully. This means the changes should be forward looking and the MPC should consider where inflation will be in 1–2 years' time.

Changing interest rates in response to rises in the rate of inflation is probably too late — the changes should happen well in advance. This gap in time is referred to as a **time lag**.

> **Exam tip**
>
> Changes in interest rates are not guaranteed to work immediately or exactly as planned. Remember that the predicted effects are based on consumer behaviour, which is not always predictable.

This is made harder because the data on which interest rate changes are based may take some months to become available: at any time, we may be looking at data which are at least 1 month old, if not older.

The effect of interest rates on other objectives

REVISED

There will be a policy conflict when using interest rates to reduce the rate of inflation. Higher interest rates should lead to lower inflation through the transmission mechanism of lower aggregate demand. However, the lower level of aggregate demand will have the following effects:

- higher unemployment caused by lack of spending
- lower short-term economic growth due to reduced demand
- growth of the supply side of the economy is limited due to lack of investment in productive capacity
- lower tax revenue collected due to lower economic activity
- reduced levels of exports due to a likely rise in the exchange rate, which has effects on economic growth and unemployment

Limitations of interest rates in controlling the economy

REVISED

Though the main impact of higher interest rates is on aggregate demand, there is some effect on aggregate supply, but this is less significant and less certain in terms of the size of its impact. This means that interest rates are less useful as a means of controlling rises in cost-push inflation.

In 2012, UK inflation rose well above its target level, reaching over 5%. Given that this was almost entirely due to cost-push factors (falling value of the pound, rising oil prices and rises in indirect taxes), however, the MPC did not raise interest rates as it was felt it would have little impact on the inflation rate.

There are other limitations of using interest rates to control the economy:

- time lags in their effectiveness
- uncertain effects — we cannot be sure of their impact
- when interest rates are low, further cuts may not be possible
- changes may have to be large to have any significant effect (most changes in interest rate are in steps of $+/- 0.25\%$)

Now test yourself

TESTED

10 Explain why the MPC might decrease interest rates even if the latest month's inflation rate has increased.

Answer on p. 231

Interest rates and the exchange rate

REVISED

A change in interest rates is likely to affect the exchange rate.

A rise in interest rate is likely to lead to a rise in the value of the pound on the foreign exchange markets. This occurs because a higher interest rate will attract flows of speculative short-term money (often known as 'hot money') into that currency due to the higher returns that can now be obtained. The higher demand for the currency leads to an increase in its value.

The currency's higher value will lead to downward pressure on cost-push inflation, as a higher exchange rate will lead to lower prices for imported goods and lower costs for those businesses that import materials for use in production.

The link between interest rates and the exchange rate is not as clear as the link between interest rates and aggregate demand. It will depend on what is happening to interest rates in other economies at the same time and how expected the change in interest rates was.

> **Typical mistake**
>
> The link between interest rates and exchange rates is often unclear. If an increase in interest rates is widely expected, the rise in the exchange rate may occur earlier, anticipating rather than following the change.

The effects of exchange rate changes on other macroeconomic policy objectives

REVISED

Changes in the exchange rate, whether caused by changes in interest rates or not, will affect other objectives in a number of ways:
- A rise in the exchange rate will lead to exports becoming less price competitive in foreign markets.
- A fall in the exchange rate will boost exports, leading to more jobs in the export sector.
- A fall in the exchange rate will lead to higher inflation as imported goods and services will become more expensive.
- An unstable exchange rate will make it hard for UK exporters to plan levels of production. It will also make foreign consumers less willing to buy UK goods due to uncertainty over prices, unless UK producers are willing to absorb the changes in their profit margins by accepting a fixed price, measured in foreign currency terms.

> **Typical mistake**
>
> A fall in the exchange rate will make imports more expensive but this doesn't mean UK consumers will switch away from buying imports — at least not in the short run.

The transmission mechanism of monetary policy

REVISED

The monetary policy **transmission mechanism** — specifically through changes in interest rates — is shown in Figure 12.2, taken from the Bank of England's website.

> **Transmission mechanism:** how a change in policy actually works its ways through the economy to affect macroeconomic indicators.

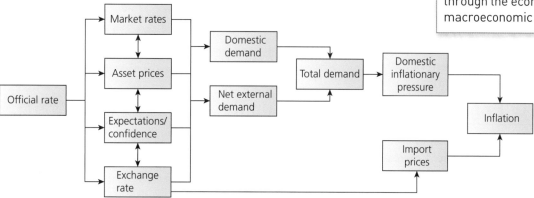

Figure 12.2 The monetary policy transmission mechanism

Source: Bank of England

A change in interest rates as decided by the Bank of England's Monetary Policy Committee will have the following effects:
- Financial institutions will react by changing the interest rates they charge to lenders. This is usually announced within the day. This may result in:
  - an effect on those wishing to borrow money

> **Exam tip**
>
> The term 'stance' is often used to describe the general effect of a policy on activity. For example, an expansionary monetary stance would be used to describe monetary policy that is promoting faster growth.

○ a change in asset prices such as shares and bonds — we would expect bond prices to fall if interest rates rise

○ possible 'wealth effects' on consumers where, if asset prices fall, there will be further falls in consumption.

● The exchange rate is likely to be affected. If the interest rate rises (especially if the change was unexpected), we would expect the exchange rate to rise (and vice versa) as investors are more willing to put their money into this currency to gain higher returns.

● In terms of domestic demand, households with variable-rate mortgages will see their monthly repayment change. Consumers who are looking to borrow money to finance consumption will be affected and the opportunity cost of saving will have been altered, all of which will change the level of consumption in the economy.

● Businesses planning for investment expenditure may change their plans, given that the cost of borrowing capital has changed. Higher interest rates reduce the profitability of business investments and thus would see investment fall.

● In terms of external demand, the change to the exchange rate will affect the demand for exports. A higher interest rate will lead to a higher exchange rate, thus decreasing the level of exports due to their being less price competitive. Import prices will be affected as well.

All of these changes affect aggregate demand, the level of GDP and unemployment levels. Depending on the current level of activity, the change in aggregate demand may lead to higher inflation — either through the demand-side factors or through the cost-push factor of import prices.

The change in interest rates takes time to 'fully work through' the economy — up to 2 years for its full effect. However, Figure 12.2 should show you how widespread the effects of interest rate change can be.

Now test yourself

TESTED

11 Draw an AD/AS diagram showing the effects of lower interest rates on the economy.

Answer on p. 231

The Bank of England and the money supply

REVISED

Growth of the money supply and of credit are both important macroeconomic indicators. Rapid increases in these often indicate inflationary pressures emerging and possible asset-price bubbles. Similarly, falling money supply and sharp reductions in credit may indicate a slowdown in economic growth or even a recession. Neither of these indicators is directly targeted by the Bank of England but will be observed with interest nevertheless.

Changes in interest rates affect people's willingness to borrow, which affects the rate of monetary growth and the amount of credit within the economy. In addition to the interest rate, the Bank of England has other policies it can use to affect the rate of growth of both the money supply and the amount of credit.

Now test yourself

TESTED ☐

12 Explain why the UK government relinquished power in setting interest rates to the Bank of England.

Answer on p. 231

Quantitative easing

Quantitative easing (QE) is a useful way of increasing borrowing and spending in the economy when interest rates cannot easily be reduced.

The Bank of England creates new money which is used to buy bonds from private investors. It is hoped then, due to the low rate of return available on the money now held, private investors will use it to buy corporate bonds and shares, which in turn helps businesses issuing the bonds and shares, which should stimulate spending in the economy. In other words, it attempts to help businesses raise finance for bonds and share issues without the need for approaching banks directly.

QE was introduced in the UK in 2009 because it was felt that banks were reluctant to lend to businesses when they were still facing a liquidity shortage. Also, interest rates reached historic lows after the financial crash and it was felt that they could not be lowered any more. Although it may appear to be the case, QE does not involve the Bank of England 'printing money'.

> **Quantitative easing:** increasing the money supply by government buying bonds so as to increase liquidity within the economy and thus encourage more borrowing.

Funding for Lending Scheme

In 2012 the Treasury and the Bank of England introduced the Funding for Lending Scheme (FLS). It is designed to boost bank lending to generate more loans and more economic activity as a result. Banks and other lenders can approach the Bank of England to swap assets they already have — say loans — with the Bank of England for Treasury bills. The Treasury bills are very liquid assets and can therefore be used to borrow money from other money markets at low interest rates.

Being able to access money market funds at low interest rates should, in theory, encourage the commercial banks to lend money more readily (it will be more profitable lending from the banks' point of view as they have been able to access the funds to finance the lending at low interest rates).

FLS, originally planned to end in 2015, was extended until 2018 in the UK but can no longer be used to support mortgage lending.

Forward guidance

Forward guidance is used by the MPC to make it easier for households and businesses to plan their spending and investment decisions. Forward guidance involves Bank of England announcements of expected future changes in monetary policy.

When first used in the UK, forward guidance took the form of the announcement that the country's interest rates were unlikely to rise until unemployment had fallen below a certain level (7%). Unemployment then dropped more quickly than expected and fell below the 7% rate. This surprise fall led to the Bank of England announcing an adapted forward guidance policy where it specified that interest rates would be increased based only on changes in a number of economic indicators, such as the output gap.

> **Forward guidance:** announcements made by the central bank as to the likely future direction of monetary policy in advance of actual changes.

Forward guidance is meant to provide confidence to households and businesses as to how long interest rates are expected to remain at a certain level. This allows the private sector to make borrowing and spending decisions with greater confidence.

The regulation of the financial system

The financial markets were subject to minimal regulation through most of the 1990s and early 2000s. It is believed that this 'light touch' approach helped magnify the size of the financial crisis. In the UK this approach has been reversed since the crisis, with, for example, the passing of the Financial Services Act of 2012. This established a number of institutions designed to improve financial stability:

- Prudential Regulation Authority (PRA)
- Financial Policy Committee (FPC)
- Financial Conduct Authority (FCA) — which unlike the PRA and the FPC is independent of the Bank of England

The FPC is responsible for **macroprudential** regulation whereas the PRA and the FCA are mainly concerned with **microprudential** regulation.

> **Macroprudential regulation**: identifying, monitoring and acting on risks which threaten the whole financial system of an economy.
>
> **Microprudential regulation**: identifying, monitoring and acting on risks to individual banks and firms.

Prudential Regulation Authority

REVISED

The PRA is responsible for the supervision of the banks, building societies, credit unions, insurers and major investment firms. It supervises individual financial institutions and sets standards for these financial organisations to follow.

The PRA aims to improve financial stability by taking action to ensure financial institutions are managed properly, and it can specify that individual institutions maintain certain capital and liquidity ratios. The PRA will allow banks and other financial institutions to fail as businesses, but only if their failure does not disrupt the overall financial system.

Financial Policy Committee

REVISED

The main purpose of the FPC is to identify, monitor and take action to remove **systematic risks** to the whole financial system and to take action to make the system more robust. An example would be where a collapse in one bank could lead to a 'run' on other banks, triggering a collapse of the financial system. The FPC can make recommendations to banks and other institutions if it feels that they are at risk of failure. Risks are judged by **stress tests**.

> **Systematic risks**: risks that could lead to a collapse in the whole or a significant part of the financial system.
>
> **Stress tests**: hypothetical exercises that see how banks and other institutions would be affected by various economic shocks.

Financial Conduct Authority

REVISED

The FCA is separate from the government and is funded by charging financial institutions a fee. The FCA's aim is to protect consumers and to ensure healthy competition between financial institutions. If it is felt that financial institutions are not acting appropriately, it has the power to regulate and to set standards and rules for behaviour. It can also order investigations into the industry if it is felt that behaviour is not acceptable.

Why banks fail and moral hazard

If banks do not have sufficient capital, they are at risk from a fall in the value of their assets. This may occur if a number of loans made by a bank fail to be repaid (due to a housing market collapse, for example).

Insufficient liquid assets (especially notes and coins) make a bank vulnerable to a run on the bank, in which customers fight to withdraw their deposits before the bank runs out of cash — thus creating a panic as each customer fights to ensure that they get their money back before the bank runs out of cash.

The Bank of England acts as the lender of last resort and provides liquidity insurance, which should minimise the likelihood of a collapse in a bank. However, the fact that the banking sector is backed by the Bank of England (and also by the government) creates a culture in which banks will take more risks than they should as they feel they will always be supported if they run short of cash.

Moral hazard was present in the run-up to the banking crisis and resulted in some banks taking too many high risks. The high-risk investments and the high-risk lending undertaken had the potential to generate significant profits for the banks, but if the risks failed, the cost of the failure would be covered by the government, which would not allow significant parts of the banking industry to fail. Part of this moral hazard came from banks engaging in both commercial and investment bank activities. As a result, some have suggested that the activities of commercial banks and investment banks must be separated out.

> **Moral hazard:** occurs when one institution takes on too much risk, knowing that if the risk fails, someone else will cover the costs of the failed risk.

Now test yourself

TESTED

13 The government will back individuals' savings up to £75 000 per bank if the bank should fail. Explain why the government feels this is necessary.

Answer on p. 231

Liquidity and capital ratios

REVISED

Another way the authorities can regulate the financial industry is through the use of **liquidity ratios** and **capital ratios**.

- **Liquidity ratios:** also known as cash ratios or reserve ratios, these are a requirement on banks and other institutions to hold a particular amount of their deposits in the form of cash (either at the Bank of England or at their own premises). The higher the liquidity ratio, the less a bank can lend out — and the less able it is to 'create credit'. Liquidity ratios are meant to provide assurance that commercial banks have sufficient liquid assets in case of a shortage. In the UK, liquidity ratios were abolished in 1981.
- **Capital ratios:** these are a ratio of the bank's equity (money raised through shares issued plus reserves earned) to the amount of lending made by the bank. It is believed that specifying a capital ratio will stop a bank building up a large number of amounts lent compared with its permanent capital. A higher capital ratio will mean a bank can lend out a smaller proportion compared with its capital base.

> **Capital/liquidity ratio:** where banks hold set amounts of liquid assets as a proportion of their overall lending or capital.

In 2019, a new capital ratio known as the 'liquidity coverage ratio' will be introduced for UK banks (as part of the Basel III agreement, a set of rules applied on a global level designed to improve the supervision and regulation of the banking sector), which will mean banks need to hold 7% of their lending in the form of capital. For example, if a bank has lent out £100 billion of loans but has only £5 billion of capital, it will need to increase its capital to £7 billion (7%) by issuing new shares, or it could halt dividend payments to build up its retained profits, or it could reduce its lending until it reaches just over £71 billion (when the ratio of capital to lending would be 7% again).

Now test yourself

TESTED

14 A bank has lent out £80 billion in loans and has capital of £6 billion. If capital ratios are increased to 12%, then assuming it is to reduce its level of lending, what is the maximum amount of loans it can now make?

Answer on p. 231

Systemic risk

REVISED

Financial crises that affect the whole of the financial sector often occur after a period of prolonged economic activity. Speculative bubbles do occur and, in the case of house prices, are not easy to control. Financial institutions will be involved in speculative bubbles as they provide loans to fund speculative activity.

> **Systemic risk**: a risk that applies to the whole sector (the banking sector is the most common usage of the term).

After a financial crisis, banks are likely to be less willing to lend money as they are likely to be suffering liquidity problems. This reduced bank lending will affect the real economy because of low aggregate demand and rising cyclical unemployment. Any financial crisis is likely to damage confidence in the economy, which leads to further falls in spending as people are reluctant to borrow to spend. Therefore financial instability and economic instability are interconnected: one causes the other and it is hard to separate these out.

Tighter regulation reduces the chances of a financial crisis occurring, but regulation is not without its own problems.

Issues with regulation

- Regulation restricts economic activity — if lending is more difficult to obtain, then economic activity will not be as high as it would be with easier lending conditions.
- Regulation may divert financial services industry output to other countries (with jobs being lost).
- Regulation requires time and money to plan, implement and monitor.
- Any penalties will need to be used so as to maintain the regulation's credibility.
- Unintended consequences are likely — e.g. development of a shadow banking sector.

Exam practice

In 2015, the Bank of England — through the FPC — conducted its second stress test on the banking system. This was designed to see whether banks would cope with a number of economic shocks and tested their ability to survive these shocks. In 2015, the banks were tested on their ability to survive a sustained oil price fall and a slump in the global economy.

The results of the test were that a small number of banks were found to have insufficient capital to cope with the shock. This led to these banks increasing their capital relative to the amounts that they had lent out. The stress test was a good predictor of what was to come as oil prices did fall to low levels during 2015 and had barely recovered in the first half of 2016. This is worrying for countries that rely on earnings from sales of oil stocks.

One way that the Bank of England can force banks to increase their capital is through the use of capital ratios. For example, a capital ratio of 12% would mean that for every £100 of loans granted by a bank, it must have at least £12 of capital.

1 If capital ratios of 12% are imposed, calculate the change in a bank's advances if it has currently granted £250 billion of loans with capital valued at £15 billion (and cannot increase its capital). [4]
2 Explain the term 'stress test'. [3]
3 Using an AD/AS diagram, show how a slump in the global economy would affect the UK economy. [4]
4 Analyse the ways in which the government has increased regulations on the UK financial system. [10]
5 To what extent is increased regulation on the financial system a good thing for the UK economy? [25]

Answers and quick quiz 12 online

ONLINE

Summary

You should have an understanding of:
- What is meant by money and the functions and characteristics money must fulfil.
- The role of financial and money markets in the economy.
- The different types of bank that operate in the UK, the roles these banks fulfil and how they are structured.
- The difference between debt and equity and how bond prices are calculated.
- How banks create credit.

- What a central bank is and how the central bank operates monetary policy.
- The effects of changes in monetary policy, especially when interest rates change.
- The transmission mechanism of monetary policy.
- How the banking system is regulated in the UK, including the workings of the PRA, the FPC and the FCA.
- How moral hazard has affected the banking system.

13 Fiscal and supply-side policies

Fiscal policy

Fiscal policy involves making deliberate changes in either government spending or taxation. Government spending is generally financed by the collection of taxation revenue. The difference between the level of government spending and the tax collected is referred to as the budget balance.

Given that the government spends huge sums of money (over £750 billion in 2015/16), it would be highly unusual if it managed to spend the exact amount collected in tax revenue. Each year there will be either a deficit or a surplus. In the last 40 years, there has been a surplus in around 5 years only, with the deficit becoming increasingly large in the last 10 years.

Budget deficits are financed by borrowing. The government issues bonds (a form of IOU) that people purchase from the government, which enable the excess spending to be financed. The bond will pay the holder a fixed rate of interest until it has to be repaid. Typically bonds have a 10-year life before they are repaid.

> **Fiscal policy:** fiscal policy involves deliberate changes in either government spending or taxation.

> **Typical mistake**
>
> Cutting taxes should boost economic activity, but do not assume the tax cut to be self-financing; the boost in economic activity will not lead to tax revenues rising *in excess* of the tax cut.

Taxation

REVISED

Taxation revenue collected by the government finances government expenditure. In general, the following types of tax exist.

Direct taxation

Direct taxes are normally placed on incomes and are often taken away by the employer before the employee ever receives them.

Indirect taxation

Indirect taxes are placed on expenditure. When we buy goods and services, they are often subject to indirect tax, which means part of the selling price is not kept by the seller but is collected by the government.

> **Direct tax:** a tax that cannot be passed on to another person and is usually levied on incomes.
>
> **Indirect tax:** a tax on spending. It is termed indirect because the seller can pass on the tax to the buyer, i.e. the seller can avoid the tax by increasing the selling price, though the tax cannot always be passed on in full.

Progressive, regressive and proportional taxation

REVISED

One objective of the government is to create a favourable distribution of income. This involves ensuring that the gap between the richest and the poorest households is less than it might be if left to the market. Inequality may be seen as undesirable if it becomes too great. As a result, governments regularly use the taxation system to create a more equitable distribution of income.

Exam practice answers and quick quizzes at **www.hoddereducation.co.uk/myrevisionnotes**

Progressive taxes

Progressive taxation is achieved by having different tax bands. In the UK, the current tax bands are as follows:

Tax rates for 2016/17	Income range (£)
Tax-free allowance	0–11 000
Basic rate of 20%	11 001–43 000
Higher rate of 40%	43 001–150 000
Additional rate of 45%	150 000+

Progressive taxes: where those on higher incomes pay a higher proportion of their income in tax compared with those on lower incomes.

Those earning above £100 000 would see their personal allowance gradually reduced until it is withdrawn fully, depending on their earnings.

What makes this system of tax progressive is that it is paid only on any additional income earned. For example, a person earning over £43 000 would pay 40% only on their earnings above that level. On the income earned below that, they would pay 20%, apart from £11 000 on which they would pay no tax at all.

This means that low earners pay a relatively low rate of tax: someone earning around £14 000 would pay only £600 in income tax, a rate of less than 5%.

At the other end, the rates paid by above-average earners rise from 20% to 40% and higher if they earn very large amounts. Hence, the income of above-average earners reduces more quickly than that of below-average earners.

Now test yourself

TESTED

1 (a) Based on the table of different tax bands for the UK shown above, calculate how much income tax someone would pay if they earned:
   (i) £15 000
   (ii) £30 000
   (iii) £45 000
   (b) Express the amounts paid in tax by each of the people described in (a) above as a percentage of their income — this gives you the average rate of tax paid by that person.
   (c) What do the answers in (b) tell you about the UK system of income tax?

Answer on p. 231

Regressive taxes

An example of a **regressive tax** in the UK was the 'community charge', which existed before the council tax was introduced. Every person had to pay the same amount, regardless of income. The tax was seen as very controversial as it hit the poorest earners hardest.

Regressive taxes: taxes that increase in relative size on lower income earners.

Some think VAT is also a regressive tax but this would be true only if it were charged on items that poorer earners have to buy in the same quantities as others in the population. This is one reason why food is exempt from VAT: if food were subject to VAT, it would account for a higher proportion of a poorer earner's income.

Proportional taxes

Economists sometimes refer to **proportional taxes** as 'flat taxes'. A tax with one uniform percentage rate and no tax-free thresholds would

Proportional taxes: taxes that are paid in equal proportions by everyone.

fall into this category. VAT can be seen as proportional if it is on non-essential items (items that poorer households do not have to buy in the same quantities as others).

Now test yourself

TESTED

2 Why do some people think VAT is a regressive tax?

Answer on p. 231

The main taxes used in the UK

REVISED

The main taxes used in the UK are as follows.

Income tax

This is the main direct tax used in the UK, paid on earnings from employment. The rate levied on incomes varies due to the progressive nature of UK income tax and there is a tax-free allowance before any is paid.

National insurance

National insurance contributions (NICs) appear very similar to an additional income tax. They were originally levied by the UK government to raise finance for health and welfare expenditure. The rate of NICs charged on incomes varies according to whether the worker pays into a private or occupational pension scheme.

Corporation tax

This is a tax on the profits earned by companies in the UK. In 2016, company profits were taxed at the rate of 20%, but this was set to be reduced over the next two years.

Inheritance tax

This is a tax based on the value of a person's wealth (known as the 'estate') when they die and is calculated as 40% of the net value. However, most people's estates would not be subject to this tax as the estate on a single individual has to be worth more than £325,000 before it becomes liable for inheritance tax.

Capital gains tax

This tax is based on the profit earned from the sale of assets (physical assets such as houses, and financial assets such as shares and bonds). The profit on the sale is subject to tax at a rate of either 10% or 18% (or higher if the person is a higher-rate taxpayer) but is only paid if the profit exceeds a threshold of £11,100 (in 2016). Additionally, profits made on the sale of property are exempt if the property was the person's main place of residence.

Value added tax (VAT)

This is the main UK indirect tax. It is a tax of 20% on spending on most goods and services (though some items are zero rated and some are taxed at 5%). VAT is one of the main sources of tax revenue for the UK government. VAT is an **ad valorem tax**.

Ad valorem tax: a tax based on a percentage of added value on top of the original price.

Excise duties

These are additional indirect taxes placed on alcohol, tobacco and fuel (at different rates on each). Excise duties are all **unit taxes**. Excise duties are normally raised broadly in line with inflation in each year's budget so as to maintain their real value.

> **Unit tax:** a tax where a fixed amount is placed on the item sold.

Council tax

Administered by the local government, council tax is based on the value of property. The higher the estimated value of a property, the higher the annual council tax charge. Given that the cost of valuing all properties in a town or city is high, the values used to assess properties can be very out of date.

Stamp duty

This is based on a percentage of the purchase price of property and is paid by the purchaser when buying a house. The percentage rises in bands with the value of the property so as to make this tax progressive.

The merits of different taxes used in the UK

REVISED

Each type of tax has both advantages and disadvantages for the government that levies the tax. Some of main merits (and drawbacks) of taxes commonly used in the UK are shown in the table.

Type of tax	Advantages	Disadvantages
Income tax	Seen as fair — is based on earnings and can be progressive Progressive nature can be used to alleviate relative poverty Calculated and administered by employer for most workers	Acts as a disincentive to work Progressive system makes it more complex
VAT	Does not affect work incentives Hard to avoid	Regressive in many cases Changes in VAT rate can be inflationary
Excise duties	Can change patterns of expenditure (e.g. different rates used for petrol and diesel) Can be used to discourage consumption of demerit goods	May lead to unemployment in those industries Regressive in some cases Can lead to 'black markets' where consumers get the product through alternative means to avoid the tax
Council tax	Seen as fair as based on wealth of household Raises money for local services	Poverty values used to set 'bands' are very out of date May be difficult to pay for those who are 'asset rich and cash poor'
Corporation tax	Based on success of companies — i.e. does not hit less successful companies as hard	May deter foreign direct investment Encourages tax avoidance May discourage business investment

Now test yourself

TESTED

3 Explain two ways in which higher direct taxes reduce incentives.

Answer on p. 231

Why governments levy taxes

Governments **levy** a variety of taxes on economic activity and transactions. The reasons for taxes include:

- **to raise revenue to finance government expenditure:** the UK government spends around £800 billion per year, which is financed out of revenue collected through taxation — though usually the government still has to borrow money to maintain its desired level of expenditure
- **to change patterns of economic activity:** taxes can be changed on different products to encourage a shift away from one product and towards another. For example, taxes can be lowered on renewable energy sources in order to encourage people to switch away from non-renewable sources
- **to discourage consumption and production of certain products:** governments often tax demerit goods to discourage their consumption. In the UK, tobacco and alcohol are subject to excise duties, which should lead to a lower quantity demanded. If demand is price inelastic then demand may not fall by a significant amount, but at least in this case it would generate significant tax revenue
- **to redistribute income:** progressive income taxes mean the gap between rich and poor households will be narrowed as proportionally more tax will be taken from higher earners. This will reduce relative poverty

> **Levy:** to impose or to place (often used to refer to taxes being imposed).

Hypothecated taxes

Economists have suggested governments should make more use of **hypothecated taxes**. For example, the Labour government of 1997–2001 imposed a windfall tax on certain privatised business to raise money which funded its employment programmes. Hypothecated taxes on demerit goods and those activities generating negative externalities could raise money to deal with the problems that their consumption and production impose on society.

Some economists have claimed that hypothecation restricts the government's ability to use revenue as it chooses and limits its flexibility when deciding how to finance spending.

> **Hypothecated tax:** a tax levied to raise money for a specific purpose.

> **Typical mistake**
>
> Be clear when talking about cuts in taxation — do you mean cuts overall in the tax burden or just cuts in one type of tax?

Principles of taxation

Governments have to raise taxes to finance spending, but raising taxes is unpopular. Therefore it is important to consider what a 'good' tax would look like. The economist Adam Smith put forward suggestions to answer this question and these suggestions became known as the canons of taxation.

Originally, there were four canons of taxation but these have been added to with two further principles of taxation. Combining the original canons of taxation with the modern additions, the principles of taxation would be as follows:

- **economical:** relative to the revenue the tax generates, the tax should be inexpensive to collect
- **equitable:** the tax should be fair and should be based on people's ability to pay, which appears to justify a progressive taxation system.

Equity can be measured in terms of both **horizontal equity** and **vertical equity**

- **efficient:** the tax should have few side effects or unexpected consequences
- **convenient:** the tax should be easy and convenient to pay
- **certain:** a taxpayer should be able to work out broadly the amount of tax that they will pay
- **flexible:** the tax should be able to be changed and modified if circumstances change

> **Horizontal equity:** where people with similar income levels pay similar amounts of tax.
>
> **Vertical equity:** where the tax paid is based on the ability to pay.

Public expenditure

REVISED

Currently the UK government spends around £800 billion per year — equivalent to almost £30,000 per household or around 40% of GDP. The amount spent is referred to as total managed expenditure (TME).

UK public expenditure is officially divided into a number of components:

- **Departmental expenditure limits (DEL):** the amounts spent by the individual government departments. These include both the current day-to-day running costs of these departments — such as health, education, defence, etc. — and the capital investment undertaken by these departments (e.g. infrastructure projects, such as building new hospitals, schools, roads, etc.).
- **Annually managed expenditure (AME):** consists of items affected by macroeconomic change (and which, as a result, are less easy to control). These include welfare expenditure, pensions and interest on the national debt.

Another way of classifying public expenditure is to divide it between **current expenditure** and **capital expenditure**. This may make it easier to spot if the government is spending more than is beneficial for an economy.

> **Current expenditure:** government spending on the day-to-day running of its services (e.g. paying salaries for those in public services).
>
> **Capital expenditure:** government spending on investment projects, such as new infrastructure.

In terms of the major areas, public expenditure includes:

- public good provision — those services that cannot easily be provided by the marketplace, such as roads, defence, police, etc.
- merit good provision — to ensure that the service is consumed at a sufficient level, such as health, education, pensions, etc.
- welfare expenditure — so as to prevent poverty, to help those less fortunate and to provide income for those who cannot earn for themselves (either temporarily or on a more long-term basis)
- debt interest — the government regularly borrows money to finance expenditure and this borrowing generates interest payments

Fiscal policy and aggregate demand

REVISED

Changes in the government's fiscal stance, i.e. changes in either tax or government spending, will affect aggregate demand. Changes to AD resulting from fiscal policy are sometimes referred to as 'demand management'.

Expansionary fiscal policy would refer to either increases in government spending or reductions in taxation, or to both. This will shift the AD curve to the right.

Contractionary fiscal policy will shift the AD curve to the left.

> **Exam tip**
>
> The terms 'tight' and 'loose' are sometimes used to describe 'contractionary' and 'expansionary' policies, both monetary and fiscal.

As a component of AD, changes in government spending will directly affect the overall total of AD.

As we know, changes in AD, whether caused by changes in government spending or not, will change the following macroeconomic indicators:

- the level of real GDP
- the level of unemployment
- the price level

There will be multiplier effects caused by the change in government spending, which are also likely to affect the macroeconomic indicators mentioned above.

Effects of changes in tax

Changes in taxes on incomes will affect the disposable income of households (income after tax deductions), which will affect the level of consumption — higher taxes act to reduce consumption.

Changes in taxes on business profits will affect the level of investment as they increase or reduce the funds available for investment in the business.

Again, there will be multiplier effects. These will be less certain. For example, a tax cut which increases disposable incomes may not always lead to higher consumption; households may decide to save some of this extra income, or spend it on imports.

As with government spending, whether or not the fiscal policy is designed to increase AD (through lower taxes) or reduce AD (through higher taxes), there will be potential effects on real GDP, unemployment and the price level.

Exam tip

Changes in tax can influence behaviour but will not always have a precisely predictable effect — a cut in income tax may simply encourage households to save more. Be careful of making snap judgements.

Fiscal policy and aggregate supply

REVISED

Change in fiscal policy can also have effects on the aggregate supply curve (both the SRAS and the LRAS curves).

Effects of changes in indirect taxes

Increases in any indirect tax, such as VAT or excise duties, which affect businesses will shift the SRAS curve to the left, and reductions will shift it to the right.

This is because higher indirect taxes cannot always be fully passed on to the consumer in the form of higher prices. Thus, the firm's profit margins drop per unit sold.

This reduces the incentive for firms to supply output at any given price level.

Supply-side fiscal policies

Fiscal policy deliberately designed to affect aggregate supply is often referred to as **supply-side fiscal policy**. Common examples of supply-side fiscal policies include:

- Targeted government spending on improvements to the economy's production capacity, shifting the LRAS curve to the right. This would involve spending on infrastructure, such as transport networks, or subsidising investment in new technology.

Supply-side fiscal policies: policies that involve changes in fiscal policy that are designed to improve the LRAS of the economy.

- Tax incentives can be given to firms to encourage them either to take on more workers, or to spend more on investment. For example, corporation tax in the UK has been steadily reduced by the government to attract more firms to set up in the UK.
- Reducing direct taxation (especially income tax) to make work more attractive.

Now test yourself

4 Show on an AD/AS diagram how a cut in income tax can have two effects on the economy.

Answer on p. 231

Fiscal policy and microeconomics

Fiscal policy can also be seen as having microeconomic effects where it involves intervention in individual markets.

Government spending on subsidies can encourage consumption or production of certain desirable products (e.g. merit goods like education and health).

Indirect taxes can be used to discourage consumption and production of certain products (e.g. demerit goods like cigarettes).

Often these microeconomic interventions are intended to change the pattern of economic activity. For example, if an industry is in decline and a new one is set to replace it, the government may speed up the growth of the new industry through subsidies, such as the UK government subsidising solar panels to encourage households to install them.

High indirect taxes on an industry will also affect the success of those businesses. For example, some blame the high excise duty on beer for the closure of many pubs (whereas others blame this on the smoking ban introduced in pubs and other venues in 2007).

Fiscal stance

- Expansionary fiscal policy is that which adds to the level of aggregate demand. This is also referred to as an 'easing' of policy, or a 'loose' policy.
- Contractionary fiscal policy (also called a 'tight' fiscal policy) would be where changes in fiscal policy reduce the level of aggregate demand.

Using fiscal policy to affect the level of aggregate demand is referred to as demand management.

Clearly, the **fiscal stance** will affect the budgetary balance — with an expansionary fiscal policy moving the budgetary balance closer to, or further into, a budget deficit, and a contractionary fiscal policy moving it towards a budget surplus.

> **Fiscal stance:** the extent to which fiscal policy is likely to add to or subtract from aggregate demand.

The rate of economic growth will affect the budgetary balance. A downturn or recession reduces tax revenue collected by a government. It is also likely that higher unemployment will require higher levels of government welfare expenditure. Therefore, a downturn or recession is likely to increase a budget deficit. The opposite would also be true: as the economy moves towards a boom, the budgetary balance is likely to move closer to (or further into) a budget surplus.

Cyclical and structural budget deficits

Given that a budget deficit could be the result of either a contractionary fiscal stance or a fall in the rate of economic growth (or both), economists can analyse a budget deficit into two components: the **cyclical budget deficit** and the **structural budget deficit**.

The cyclical budget deficit is the portion of any budget deficit that changes when the rate of economic growth changes. Over time, the cyclical deficit will be eliminated as the economic growth rate recovers towards its long-run average rate (and would move into a cyclical budget surplus if the economy were growing at an above-average rate).

The structural budget deficit is the portion of a budget deficit that remains even if the economic growth is at its normal long-run rate. This means any structural deficit will not necessarily be eliminated after a prolonged period of growth.

Recently, the UK government has attempted to reduce a very large budget deficit caused partly by the deep recession of 2008–09, which significantly boosted the cyclical deficit, but also partly by a structural deficit where government expenditure would have exceeded tax revenue regardless of the rate of economic growth.

A cyclical budget deficit will eventually be eliminated by economic growth returning to its average rate. A structural budget deficit will be eliminated only if contractionary fiscal policy is implemented.

> **Structural deficit (surplus):** where the government finances remain in deficit (surplus) even if the effects of economic growth are removed.
>
> **Cyclical deficit (surplus):** where the balance on the government's finances moves into deficit (surplus) largely because of effects of the economic cycle on tax and spending plans.

> **Exam tip**
>
> Be careful when analysing the causes of budget deficits or surplus — is it because of economic growth or actual policy changes?

Consequences of budget deficits and budget surpluses

The budgetary balance will have a number of effects on macroeconomic performance. We must be careful in our analysis here as we must distinguish between whether economic performance is causing a change in the budgetary balance or whether a change in the budgetary balance is causing a change in economic performance.

Economic growth

A budget deficit implies that fiscal policy is adding to aggregate demand and a surplus would mean that fiscal policy is subtracting from aggregate demand. Clearly, these changes to aggregate demand will affect short-run economic growth. However, the rate of economic growth will, in turn, affect the budgetary position in that slower growth will require higher welfare expenditure and will mean lower tax revenue collected.

> **Typical mistake**
>
> A budget deficit may be caused by low economic growth, but a budget deficit can also increase economic growth. Check what's happening with economic indicators before drawing conclusions.

Unemployment

A government can reduce unemployment levels through expansionary fiscal policy. Higher government spending and a larger budget deficit may mean there is a greater demand for workers as a result. However, in the long run, some economists would argue that unemployment will return to its natural rate and will be independent of the budgetary policy.

Inflation

Demand-pull inflation is the result of excessive aggregate demand, which may be the result of expansionary fiscal policy. A rise in the budget surplus (through a combination of tax rises and cuts in government spending) will help to reduce demand-pull inflation.

Fiscal policy and the national debt

REVISED

Any time the government runs a budget deficit as part of its fiscal policy, it will have to borrow the shortfall. As stated earlier, this is done through the issue of debt in the form of interest-bearing government bonds. These bonds will eventually be repaid, but until that date, they form part of the **national debt**.

> **National debt**: the stock of all outstanding government debt that has yet to be repaid.

At any one time, the government is likely to be paying back past debt as bonds reach their maturity date (repayment date), but as stated earlier, budget deficits occur much more frequently than budget surpluses. As a result, even as debt is repaid, more debt is taken on, meaning that the national debt does not necessarily shrink.

It is this outstanding debt on which interest has to be paid each year. In 2015/16, around £50 billion will be spent by the government on these interest payments.

The size of the national debt is high when compared with the national income (it is normal to express national debt as a percentage of national income), but this is not necessarily worrying: most households, for example, regularly fund house purchases with mortgages that are in excess of the households' annual income. The UK national debt is currently around £1.6 trillion (or £1600 billion). This is equivalent to almost 90% of the UK's GDP.

> **Typical mistake**
>
> Do not confuse the national debt with the budget deficit; the budget deficit adds to the national debt, but the debt will still be there even if there is a budget surplus.

Why do we appear always to run deficits? This is largely due to the popularity of government spending among voters. People like well-funded schools and hospitals, and good roads. Few politicians would get elected if they promised tax rises. If the debt is to be paid off some years in the future, politicians seeking election today are unlikely to worry.

> **Exam tip**
>
> Think about why budget deficits are so commonplace.

Now test yourself

TESTED

5 Why will national debt as a percentage of national income fall even if the government runs continual budget deficits?

Answer on p. 231

The significance of the national debt

REVISED

The size of the national debt is enormous. Even at its lowest level (as a percentage of GDP), reached in 2002, it still totalled hundreds of billions of pounds. In 2009, the size of the national debt was close to 90% of GDP (i.e. more than £1500 billion). The reasons why this may be significant include the following:

- If the government runs budget deficits in the future, these will add to the national debt (and budget surpluses would reduce the size of national debt).

- Clearly a larger national debt requires a greater amount of interest to be paid on the debt, which will require the government to make choices as to how it will finance those interest payments.
- Those who buy government debt (bonds) will demand higher interest on the debt if they feel there is a danger that the size of the national debt will get out of control (and the risk of default increases). This is to do with the UK's credit rating. The Chancellor at the time of writing was keen to keep the UK's high credit rating as it means future borrowing will be at lower rates of interest.
- The national debt (as a percentage of GDP) will fall if the rate it grows is lower than the rate at which GDP grows (i.e. the national debt may grow but it will represent a smaller proportion of GDP).
- Although large in absolute terms, the UK's national debt is not large when compared with that of plenty of our trading partners and is also lower than at previous points in history — though at the time of writing it was at its highest for around 40 years.

Now test yourself

TESTED

6 Explain two reasons why a budget deficit may have undesirable effects on the macroeconomy.

Answer on p. 231

Office for Budget Responsibility (OBR)

REVISED

The Office for Budget Responsibility was set up by the government in 2010 to provide independent analysis of fiscal policy. It was hoped that this would make it harder for the government to implement changes in fiscal policy which might be politically rather than economically motivated.

The main functions of the OBR are as follows:
1 Economic forecasting — especially focusing on forecasts of the government's finances.
2 Evaluating fiscal policy (against the government's own previously set targets).
3 Analysis of the sustainability of public finances.
4 Evaluation of fiscal risks.
5 Analysis of tax and welfare costing.

Supply-side policies

The supply side of the economy refers to the level of aggregate supply, both short term and long term. This is connected with the productive capacity of the economy (i.e. how much can be produced over time). Factors of production, such as labour, as well as the quantity of capital stock (buildings, machinery, infrastructure) will determine how much can be produced.

Successful **supply-side policies** will shift the LRAS to the right, allowing for expansion of AD without upward pressure on prices emerging. In Figure 13.1, we can see output increase from Y_1 to Y_2 but there is no change in the price level.

If successful, supply-side policies increase the amount that an economy can produce without inflationary pressures emerging. By increasing the

> **Supply-side policies**: deliberate actions taken by the government designed to increase the LRAS of the economy (i.e. shift the LRAS curve to the right).

potential output level, more can be produced before there is upward pressure on prices.

Many (but not all) supply-side policies are microeconomic in origin. This means the policy may concentrate on one particular market or one particular industry, rather than the economy as a whole.

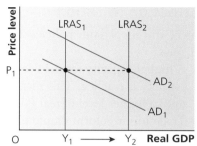

Figure 13.1 Impact of successful supply-side policies

Supply-side improvements

We should distinguish between supply-side policies and **supply-side improvements**. Whereas supply-side policies are direct actions taken by the government to improve the productive capacity of the economy, supply-side improvements are slightly different.

Firms themselves have a desire to increase output (if possible) and this can be seen as a natural consequence of allowing markets to work reasonably freely.

Having said that, direct supply-side policies adopted by the government will also lead to supply-side improvements in the economy.

> **Supply-side improvements**: these arise out of general increases in productive capacity resulting from businesses acting out of their own interest in improving efficiency and the quantity of their output.

> **Typical mistake**
>
> Improvements in the supply side of the economy can occur without action being taken by the government.

The economic effects of supply-side policies

We have stated that successful supply-side policies will shift the LRAS curve further to the right by increasing the capacity of the UK economy. There are other effects on macroeconomic indicators.

Effect on GDP

Increasing the capacity of the economy should lead to higher GDP. It should certainly increase the trend rate of growth in the economy. Of course, GDP requires both AS and AD, and so far we have only referred to AS. Therefore, for supply-side policies to boost GDP, they need to be used in conjunction with policies to manage aggregate demand.

Effect on unemployment

Successful supply-side policies should lead to lower unemployment in a number of ways:

- Lower income taxes will encourage people to take jobs as work becomes financially more worthwhile.
- Reduced welfare benefits will discourage people from remaining out of work.
- Deregulation of markets should increase competition and this should mean higher output and more jobs (though the increases in output may come from efficiency gains rather than employment gains).
- Improvements in education and training should lead to reduced occupational and possibly geographical immobility.
- Investment in infrastructure should attract more businesses and jobs to the UK, and should also reduce geographical immobility as people find it easier to work further from their home.

Effect on inflation

Successful supply-side policies should lead to lower inflation in a number of ways:

- A higher capacity for the economy means AD can be increased before capacity is reached. This means demand-pull pressures will not emerge until a higher level of real GDP is achieved.
- Trade union reform should ease cost-push pressure as there will be less upward pressure on wages by trade unions.
- More competition in certain industries will mean it is harder for firms to increase their prices due to declining monopolistic powers.

Effect on the balance of payments on current account

Supply-side measures should improve the balance on the current account:

- The downward pressure on prices outlined above should make UK exports more price competitive.
- A more productive workforce should also lead to lower-priced UK output.
- Quality of output should improve if investment takes place in education and training, and this should also lead to greater demand for UK exports.

Free market supply-side policies

Free market supply-side policies involve removing barriers that prevent the market reaching the most efficient equilibrium and allowing the market to work as 'freely' as possible. These policies focus on tax cuts, the labour market, and **privatisation** and **deregulation**.

Income tax cuts and personal incentives

Cuts in income tax rates normally increase aggregate demand but also function as a supply-side policy. This is because high income tax rates act as a disincentive to work. Higher income tax rates mean each extra hour of work earns reduced disposable income and makes work seem less worthwhile. Cutting income tax rates will therefore incentivise workers to increase the amount of labour they supply.

This supply-side policy can be described using the **Laffer Curve** (see Figure 13.2). This shows how reductions in rates of income tax towards T* will actually increase tax revenues collected by the government because lower tax rates increase personal incentives to work.

If lower income tax rates improve personal incentives, it is likely that lower income tax rates could increase long-run aggregate supply, as they may lower the rate of frictional unemployment that high income tax rates contribute to, and will reduce voluntary unemployment as well.

The UK government has gradually shifted taxes away from direct to indirect partly based on this idea. Income tax rates have been reduced over the past 30 years and indirect tax rates have risen. There has also been a rapid increase in the

> **Free market supply-side policies:** those policies designed to make markets work more efficiently and thus increase aggregate supply for the economy.
>
> **Privatisation:** the sale of state-owned enterprises to the private sector.
>
> **Deregulation:** the removal of barriers to competition in an industry.
>
> **Laffer Curve:** shows how high income tax rates can actually reduce tax revenue due to the reduced incentive to work.

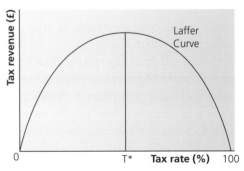

Figure 13.2 The Laffer Curve — showing how lower rates of tax can actually increase tax revenue

tax-free allowance given to all workers, meaning low-paid workers pay very little income tax.

Evidence supporting the effect of tax cuts on the labour supply has been limited. Most workers are on full-time contracts and are salaried rather than paid an hourly rate, which means they cannot easily adjust their quantity of hours supplied. Also, very high tax rates may act as a disincentive, but cutting tax rates once they are reasonably low (say, from 21% to 20%) may have little effect on workers' incentives.

Now test yourself

TESTED

7 Explain how a tax cut can have both microeconomic and macroeconomic effects.

Answer on p. 231

Reduction in trade union power

Trade unions can use their collective strength and the threat of potential industrial action to force wages higher than the free market rate. Also, trade unions will press for better conditions for workers and this will impose higher production costs on firms. This will reduce firms' demand for labour and will lead to a lower level of unemployment as a result.

> **Trade union:** an organisation designed to protect the workforce by pushing for improvements to pay and conditions.

Reduction or elimination of minimum wage legislation

The minimum wage is a guaranteed minimum rate paid to workers, which should be higher than the free market wage rate. This may increase real-wage unemployment (see Figure 11.7 on page 150). The decision to increase the UK's minimum wage (for those aged 25 and above) in 2016 to £7.20 per hour was criticised by some businesses which claimed that as a result they might reduce the number of workers they employ.

Reduction in unemployment benefits

If unemployment benefits are too generous, this may act as a disincentive for any unemployed person to find work. This may lead to higher levels of frictional and voluntary unemployment.

Cutting unemployment benefits should create greater incentives for the unemployed to find jobs as they will have to survive on lower benefits otherwise. This can add to greater levels of poverty and also lead to a more unequal distribution of income.

Now test yourself

TESTED

8 Explain why a government would want to raise the minimum wage.

Answer on p. 232

Reduction in labour protection

Workers benefit from a number of regulations designed to protect them in the workplace. Examples include holiday pay, sick pay, maximum working hours per week, and entitlements to maternity and paternity leave. However, all these regulations and payments increase business costs.

> **Labour protection:** laws and regulations designed to protect the pay and conditions of those in the workplace.

If the non-wage cost of the workforce increases, it is likely to lead to lower demand for labour and a higher level of unemployment. This is because firms will realise that employing extra workers generates extra costs. Therefore a supply-side policy would involve reducing these benefits that workers currently receive.

Zero-hour contracts

This is where a worker has no guaranteed hours of work in their job. Although it might seem insecure for workers, the effect of increased numbers of zero-hours contracts (around 700,000 in the UK) is to make it easier for firms to hire workers only as required.

Privatisation

Theory suggests that moving businesses into the private sector increases efficiency as private businesses will pursue profit maximisation. This means that businesses should be looking to cut costs so as to increase profits and may also seek to increase output.

Privatisation is often accompanied by a policy of deregulation. It is hoped that a deregulated market will encourage greater competition within the market and this will lead to lower prices and higher output overall — with a rightward shift in aggregate supply. In some cases, industries have had to be broken up into smaller businesses to make competition a realistic prospect. For example, for UK railway privatisation, the tracks and stations are owned by a state-backed provider (Network Rail) and competition occurs only among the train operation companies.

Although controversial, most people now accept the principle of private sector involvement in the provision of services previously provided by the government. Where this policy is problematic is where deregulated markets have not led to significant changes in the market's competitive structure. These issues were explored in more detail earlier in this book (see Chapter 5).

Now test yourself

TESTED

9 Analyse reasons why privatisation may not work as a supply-side policy.

Answer on p. 232

Interventionist supply-side policies

REVISED

Interventionist supply-side policies will often affect aggregate demand as well as aggregate supply (though the effects on aggregate supply are likely to take longer to emerge than the short-run effects on demand).

> **Interventionist supply-side policies**: designed to increase aggregate supply by intervening more in markets — often accompanied by higher targeted government expenditure.

Education

Educational reform and greater investment in education should help to increase aggregate supply in the economy. This will occur for two reasons:
- Giving the workforce (current and future) a greater set of skills should reduce occupational immobility as workers find it easier to move between different occupations. This would lead to lower structural unemployment.
- Increasing the quantity of training and improving the quality of education (as well as increasing participation rates) should increase the productivity of the workforce, which will increase the productive capacity of the economy.

Training

Increasing both the quality and quantity of training undertaken in the economy will have similar effects to the reform and investment in education. Training schemes can be provided as follows:

- by the government directly (sometimes welfare recipients receive benefits on condition of completing training)
- subsidies by the government, or as part of a tax break given to firms

Now test yourself

TESTED

10 Explain why a government would want training to be provided in larger quantities.

Answer on p. 232

Industrial policy

Governments can increase business investment and improve the functioning of the business sector through a set of policies known as industrial policies. These may be centred on changes in legislation affecting the labour market (such as trade union reform and labour market regulations). There is also the possibility of changes in laws on how businesses operate — in terms of grants given to businesses, tax breaks that encourage investment and how businesses are subject to tax and regulations.

Research and development subsidies

By increasing spending on research and development (R&D), firms can make breakthroughs that lead to improved production techniques or advances in technology, both of which increase the productive capacity of the economy.

In order to increase spending on R&D, the government could give grants to research institutes (such as universities) or it could offer tax incentives to private sector businesses that encourage them to spend more on research.

> **Exam tip**
>
> Supply-side policies often require you to explain concepts which would ordinarily be found on Paper 1 of the exams — this is a good synoptic link to make in your analysis.

Other supply-side policies

REVISED

Infrastructure

Infrastructure refers to the physical capital that facilitates business activity and includes railways, roads, communication systems, etc. Governments can invest in these to make it easier for business to operate. For example, the proposed high-speed railways between London and Scotland will make it easier for business to be conducted throughout the UK. Similarly, expansion of London airports should make London and the UK more attractive to overseas businesses.

Entrepreneurship

Governments can make it easier for people to set up their own businesses. Either directly or (more recently) indirectly, the government can offer assistance to entrepreneurs. Reduced 'red tape' in the sense of fewer administrative and legal burdens on small business will encourage people to set up their own enterprises.

Supply-side policies and the natural rate of unemployment

Successful implementation of supply-side policies should lead to a fall in the natural rate of unemployment. This is the rate of unemployment that exists because of structural and frictional causes. Factors leading to this fall include the following:

- Improvements to education should reduce occupation immobility as workers should be able to perform a greater variety of jobs.
- Incentives to increase training should also reduce occupational immobility.
- Higher investment (especially in transport infrastructure) should reduce geographical immobility as workers find it easier to move to vacancies elsewhere.
- Lower taxes on incomes should create incentives for people to work — reducing frictional and voluntary unemployment.
- Less generous unemployment benefits encourage workers to accept jobs earlier — again reducing frictional and voluntary unemployment.
- Subsidising research and development may encourage the development of new industries, which may create jobs for the occupationally immobile (assuming they can be trained for these positions).

A lower natural rate of unemployment means national income can be increased and it should mean that aggregate demand can be increased to higher levels with less risk of inflationary pressures emerging.

In the UK, the natural rate of unemployment is estimated at around 5%. In other European economies, the estimate for the natural rate of unemployment is higher.

> **Exam tip**
>
> Supply-side policies may not automatically reduce unemployment but may only create the conditions which allow other policies to reduce unemployment.

Now test yourself

11 Explain why the natural rate of unemployment is lower in the UK than in other major European economies, such as France.

Answer on p. 232

Limitations of supply-side policies

Supply-side policies have not always been popular with the country as a whole. This is probably because:

- Tax cuts often favour those with high incomes (e.g. cutting the 'top' rate in the UK from 50% to 45%).
- Cutting benefits is more likely to increase poverty.
- Reducing the rights of workers may prove unpopular with workers, who make up three-quarters of those of working age.
- These policies often take many years to show significant effects.

> **Typical mistake**
>
> Although supply-side policies resolve many of the policy conflicts, do not forget to include limitations of these policies when evaluating what policy is best.

Exam practice

HS2 — the proposed high-speed rail link

One factor that determines the long-run growth of an economy is its infrastructure. More investment in infrastructure should improve the economy's potential growth rate. Therefore it would appear that the building of HS2, a high-speed rail link between London and Scotland (via Birmingham, Manchester, Sheffield and Leeds) is a good idea. However, opinion is divided.

The government believes that it will create jobs outside London, which are needed given the fear that too much investment in the UK goes to London. It will also cut journey times significantly, in some cases slashing the journey time to London in half. Quicker journey times can also improve long-term growth and can encourage more businesses to locate in the UK due to improved travel time for workers. However, some argue it will result in more people working in London, so taking money away from other cities.

Critics say that HS2 is too costly, with the first estimate of its total costs of £33 billion now having to be revised to over £40 billion. The flipside of this is that it will provide an enormous boost to the economy, creating 22000 jobs in building the line and 10000 jobs in running the line once finished. Others claim this boost could have been injected elsewhere in the economy, for instance by upgrading existing railway lines or extending airport capacity.

1 Define the term 'long-run growth'. [3]
2 Explain two ways in which the building of HS2 might affect the current account of the balance of payments. [6]
3 Explain two ways in which the building of HS2 will generate higher economic growth in the UK. [8]
4 Analyse the negative consequences for UK economic performance of spending £40 billion on HS2. [10]

Answers and quick quiz 13 online

ONLINE

Summary

You should have an understanding of:
- What is meant by fiscal policy and how it has both microeconomic and macroeconomic functions.
- How fiscal policy can affect both aggregate demand and aggregate supply.
- The types of tax used and the reasons for taxation (including the principles of what makes a 'good tax').
- The merits of different types of tax.
- The types of and reasons for government expenditure.
- The measurement and the effects of a budget deficit or budget surplus on the UK economy.
- The relationship between the budgetary balance and the national debt.
- The size and significance of the national debt.
- The role of the Office for Budget Responsibility.
- The difference between supply-side policies and supply-side improvements.
- The main types of free market and interventionist supply-side policies.
- The microeconomic and macroeconomic effects of supply-side policies.
- How supply-side policies affect the main macroeconomic indicators, such as growth and unemployment.
- How supply-side policies affect the natural rate of unemployment.
- The limitations of supply-side policies.

14 The international economy

Globalisation

The causes of globalisation

Globalisation has increased rapidly over the last 100 years. The causes of this globalisation and its increasing speed include:

- improvements in communication, in terms of speed, availability and the falling cost of international communications (e.g. online and mobile technology)
- improvements in transport, in terms of both speed and cost reduction
- **containerisation** — which has generated massive increases in efficiency for firms transporting goods globally
- increased free trade — the reduction of trade barriers has made foreign trade more worthwhile
- closer political ties between countries — especially since the end of the cold war
- abolition of capital controls by many governments

> **Globalisation:** increasing integration and interconnectedness between the countries of the world.
>
> **Containerisation:** the use of uniform-sized containers for transportation of goods, which significantly reduces the cost of transportation.

The main characteristics of globalisation

Increasing globalisation can be observed through a number of characteristics. These include:

- greater trade in goods and services between countries
- higher levels of labour migration between countries
- increasing transfers of capital (money) between countries through FDI and portfolio investment
- increased regional specialisation — i.e. greater division of labour
- greater use of **outsourcing**/offshoring
- more global brands being developed

These characteristics are ongoing in that they are part of a process of increasing globalisation.

> **Outsourcing:** part of a firm's production is performed by another firm (or in the case of offshoring, the work is done by a firm in another country).

> **Typical mistake**
>
> Globalisation has been taking place for hundreds if not thousands of years — it did not start with the invention of the aeroplane or the internet.

The consequences of globalisation

There are consequences for both more developed and **less developed countries**.

> **Less developed economies:** economies with low income per capita and less development in terms of human capital and infrastructure.

Consequences for more developed countries

- Increasing ability to outsource production to low-cost countries.
- Potential for higher sales and output by targeting products at fast-growing less developed economies.
- Economies of scale may be exploited by producing on a global scale (though products might need some adaptation to meet local needs).
- Increased competition for firms in developed economies from low-cost producers.
- Need to diversify away from manufacturing as less developed economies build up their absolute and comparative advantage in this sector.

- Ability of firms to recruit on a larger scale — though this may push down wages in the local economy.
- Possible 'brain drain' as skilled workers seek opportunities overseas.

Consequences for less developed countries

- Increasing dominance by global brands from developed economies (although many global brands have succeeded by adapting their global products to local needs and tastes, a process referred to as 'glocalisation').
- Issues of treatment of local workforces — subject to potential exploitation by global corporations.
- Having to adopt free market macroeconomic policies in order to attract FDI.
- Having to open up markets to foreign competition, even if the result is the failure of local businesses.

Role of multinational corporations

REVISED

Multinational corporations (MNCs) are significant players in the global economy. Their size means that they cannot easily be overlooked. As a result, governments cannot easily ignore them given their potential economic impact.

Benefits of MNCs to economies include:
- employment — MNCs will often generate many new jobs with an obvious boost to GDP (with potential multiplier effects)
- wages — MNCs may have to offer higher wages to attract workers
- tax revenue — coming from profits generated, incomes earned and any extra spending

Drawbacks of MNCs to economies include:
- they will pay the lowest wage possible to recruit sufficient numbers — if there is a significant labour surplus, pay will be offered at very low rates
- the effect on employment levels may not be as significant as hoped for — many MNCs will bring in skilled labour from developed economies and will recruit workers only for less skilled jobs
- property rights and other regulations are usually less clear in less developed economies and MNCs can exploit this by depleting natural resources and not producing output in a clean way — damage for the environment that may be irreversible
- tax revenue may not rise significantly as profits can be transferred around the global business to ensure that taxes are paid only in economies with low rates of tax (tax avoidance)
- workers may be treated in an unethical manner — many less developed economies do not provide workers with clear protection. MNCs can exploit this for their advantage

> **Multinational corporations (MNCs):** businesses that operate in at least two countries (also known as TNCs — transnational corporations).

> **Typical mistake**
>
> When an MNC is accused of paying low wages to workers in less developed economies, these may be low only in comparison with the wages of developed economies.

> **Typical mistake**
>
> Although tax avoidance may be unethical (or not), it is not illegal — it is tax evasion that is illegal.

> **Exam tip**
>
> When assessing the impact of MNCs, try to base your judgement on economic criteria rather than personal feelings.

Trade

We would expect all countries to engage in foreign trade. The benefits of foreign trade are as follows:
- access to cheaper goods and services
- greater range of goods and services
- ability to lower average costs through specialisation

The gains from specialisation and international trade can be examined by looking at the theory of comparative advantage.

Absolute advantage

Example 1

Here, the world consists of only two countries producing two goods (food and clothing). If each country divides equally its resources (workers, machinery, etc.) for production of food and clothing then the following shows how much each country produces when it is self-sufficient (i.e. no trade takes place).

	Food (units)	Clothing (units)
Country A	200	100
Country B	100	200
World total	300	300

As we can see, Country A can produce more food than Country B and Country B can produce more clothing than Country A. This tells us:
- Country A has an **absolute advantage** in food production
- Country B has an absolute advantage in clothing production

If both countries completely specialise in the industry in which they have absolute advantage, the output of both countries will become:

	Food (units)	Clothing (units)
Country A	400	0
Country B	0	400
World total	400	400

> **Absolute advantage**: a country has an absolute advantage in the production of a product if it can be produced for a lower cost than in another country.

Specialisation has increased world output. If we allow trade, then each country can be made better off and the country can consume beyond its internal PPC.

Comparative advantage

It is likely, however, that one country may be better at producing both products. Even so, specialisation and trade can still be beneficial.

Example 2

Again, if a country puts half of its resources into the production of each good, then with self-sufficiency the following output would be produced:

	Food (units)	Clothing (units)
Country A	200	400
Country B	100	25
World total	300	425

> **Comparative advantage**: a country has a comparative advantage in the production of a product if it can be produced at a lower opportunity cost than in another country.

It may appear that it is not worth specialising as Country A has the absolute advantage in both food and clothing production. However, specialisation may still be beneficial if each country specialises in the industry in which it has **comparative advantage**.

Comparative advantage occurs when the opportunity cost of producing one product (i.e. how much of the other product has to be given up when producing an additional unit) is lower than in another country.

- In Country A, 200 units of food 'cost' 400 units of clothing — i.e. 1 unit of food 'costs' 2 units of clothing.
- In Country B, 100 units of food 'cost' 25 units of clothing — i.e. 1 unit of food 'costs' ¼ unit of clothing.

The opportunity cost of food production is lower in Country B, so we would say it has a comparative advantage in food production.

The opportunity cost of 1 unit of clothing in Country A is ½ unit of food and in Country B is 4 units of food — therefore Country A has a comparative advantage in clothing.

If both countries specialise(★) according to their comparative advantage, we will arrive at the following:

	Food (units)	Clothing (units)
Country A	100	600
Country B	200	0
World total	300	600

(★ Country B completely specialises, whereas Country A partly specialises, with ¾ of its resources devoted to clothing production)

As we can see, specialisation where each country has comparative advantage has improved global output — the world has gained 175 extra units of clothing for no reduction in food production.

Trade will be beneficial to both countries as long as it takes place at a mutually beneficial exchange rate (which would have to be lower than the opportunity cost of production in each country).

Assumptions of the model of comparative advantage

The model of comparative advantage makes the following assumptions, which may not be completely realistic:

- Each country's factor endowment is fixed and cannot be improved upon.
- Factors of production are immobile between countries (e.g. workers cannot work in another country, etc.).
- There are constant returns to scale — the opportunity cost is constant. However, if there are economies of scale, that would actually increase the case for specialisation.
- Transport costs are small enough not to cancel out the benefits of specialisation and trade.
- There are no barriers to trade — i.e. tariffs or quotas, etc.

Governments can acquire an advantage that the country did not have with strategic investment in particular industries.

The model of comparative advantage makes a strong case for governments to allow free trade: efficiency on a global scale will be increased if countries specialise where they have comparative advantage and trade

Exam tip

Ensure you don't confuse absolute with comparative advantage — they are different!

freely with other countries. However, in reality, countries will not specialise completely due to transport costs, lack of perfect knowledge, and for strategic reasons.

1 Using a numerical example, show how comparative advantage does not exist when opportunity cost ratios are identical.

Answer on p. 232

> **Typical mistake**
>
> Comparative advantage does not always exist — it requires there to be a difference in the opportunity cost ratios.

Changing pattern of UK trade with the rest of the world

REVISED ☐

The UK is a fairly open economy — where foreign trade counts for around 30% of the country's GDP. There has been a gradual change in the pattern of UK trade, including:

- a shift away from trading with Commonwealth countries and towards the EU and North America
- the EU now accounting for the majority of both UK imports and exports
- a gradual decline in the export of manufactured goods from the UK — though this is still the largest category of exports
- growth in services exports (especially those in the financial services industry)
- faster growth in imports compared with exports — meaning the current account is in a persistent and fairly large deficit
- China and India becoming more significant for UK exports (though still accounting for a small share)

Protectionist policies

REVISED ☐

If a government wants to attempt to reduce the quantity of imports into its economy, there are a number of **protectionist** policies it can adopt.

- **Tariffs:** these work by increasing the price of imported products relative to domestic output. This should lead to a contraction of demand and also encourage a switch to domestic substitutes (if they exist). The tariff can be shown on a diagram, as in Figure 14.1.

In the figure, the domestic equilibrium would be at P_D and Q. Once we allow foreign trade, domestic consumers can import at the lower price of P_W, meaning they will buy a total of Q_2, of which Q_1 will be domestically produced and $Q_2 - Q_1$ will be imported.

A tariff shifts the world supply curve upwards and increases price to P_T. Now, consumers reduce consumption of the product to Q_3, of which domestic producers will supply Q_4 and imports will fall to $Q_4 - Q_3$. Hence the tariff has encouraged a shift from imports to domestically produced goods.

- **Quotas:** these are a limit on the physical number of imports allowed into a country.
- **Export subsidies:** a government provides subsidies for firms which produce exports.

> **Protectionism:** implementing policies that will protect an economy through restrictions on imports.
>
> **Tariff:** a tax on imported goods and services.
>
> **Quota:** a restriction on the number of a particular kind of import into an economy.

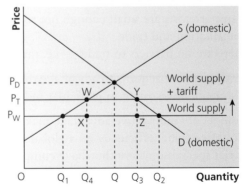

Figure 14.1 The effects of a tariff on imports

2 Draw a diagram showing a tariff being imposed, indicating clearly the tax revenue raised and any welfare loss that results.

Answer on p. 232

Arguments for protectionist policies

REVISED

Protection of jobs

Often jobs will be lost to lower-cost producers overseas. Protection can be justified on the basis that it will protect those jobs that would otherwise be lost (though consumers will lose out by now having to pay a higher price for their goods and comparative advantage theory would suggest that jobs can be gained elsewhere if any country specialises).

Infant industry argument

Small, newly established businesses do not benefit from economies of scale in the way that large, long-established businesses can. This may justify protection of these 'infant industries' until such a time that they have grown and can compete (though protection may mean the incentive to become efficient is removed and the 'infant' never 'grows up').

Anti-dumping

Protectionist measure may be imposed to prevent the harm to domestic businesses when faced with **dumping** by overseas low-cost producers. Dumping is seen as 'unfair' competition but is difficult to prove.

Sunset industries

Industries in long-term decline may benefit from protection so as to allow them to decline in a more gradual rather than sudden manner, minimising demand shocks to the domestic economy.

Strategic reasons

Government may wish to keep industries running despite cheaper imports being available due to the industry being seen as strategically important and one that should not be allowed to fail, such as agriculture.

Customs unions

REVISED

Customs unions are a form of economic integration and cooperation between two or more countries which are more closely integrated than a **free trade area** but are not as closely integrated as a single or common market. The main economic benefit of a customs union would be the gains that can be made from free trade, allowing consumers access to a wider choice of goods and services at the lowest possible price.

Infant industry: a small, developing industry which cannot yet benefit from economies of scale (and this may justify protection).

Dumping: where a low-cost producer 'dumps' large quantities of a product onto another country's market below cost price — often leading to the closure of local firms which cannot compete with the low-cost producer.

Exam tip

Just remember: in reality, any attempt to use protectionist policies is likely to lead to rapid retaliation by any country affected by your policies.

Customs union: a free trade area between two or more countries with a common external tariff applied to all outside countries.

Free trade area: trade without barriers, such as tariffs, between two or more countries.

The European Union is a **common market** but has elements of both economic and political union, with EU members using the euro sharing monetary policy as well as some small attempts at fiscal harmonisation.

> **Common market**: a customs union that has other forms of economic integration, such as free movement of factors of production between members, or harmonisation of laws and product standards.

The Single European Market

REVISED

The Single European Market (SEM) of the EU came into existence in 1993. The main features of the SEM are:
- free movement of goods and services, i.e. free trade (in nearly all areas)
- free movement of workers and capital
- common product standards and regulations
- some fiscal coordination (e.g. members must have a sales tax — such as VAT — of at least 15%)
- a common external tariff on imports into the EU

The SEM is not fully complete as there is not yet a free market across the EU in certain industries such as energy and financial services.

Now test yourself

TESTED

3 Explain why tariffs imposed on products coming into the EU are the same in each country.

Answer on p. 232

> **Typical mistake**
>
> A common external tariff does not mean that the same level of tariff is imposed on different types of goods and service.

EU membership for the UK

REVISED

The UK joined what became the EU in 1973. Membership has not always been popular and this was shown with the slight majority for leaving the EU in the 2016 referendum.

Clearly, the EU did change during the period of UK membership. Attempts at closer political integration were made, but turnout at elections for the European Parliament was generally low and people's view of the EU administration and bureaucracy was generally not positive. However, many would argue that, as a fairly open economy, the UK did benefit from the ability to trade freely with other EU members.

There are arguments that can be made both for remaining and for leaving the EU.

Arguments for leaving the EU

- Greater threat to the competitiveness of domestic business, especially those with lower wage costs in poorer EU countries.
- Trade diversion — this occurs because, for example, the UK cannot buy goods tariff free from non-EU members and as a result may be forced to buy from higher-cost suppliers from within the EU.
- The financial contribution made to the EU budget (estimated at a net total of around £9 billion per year).

- Wages may be forced downwards due to competition for jobs from poorer countries.
- Need to comply with rules and regulations, which may impose extra costs on businesses.
- Decisions taken by the EU as a whole may go against national interests of the UK.

Arguments for remaining an EU member

- Wider choice for consumers, who are presented with a greater variety of goods and should benefit from more price competition.
- Wider markets for businesses to aim their products at (the EU population is approximately 500 million).
- Potential economies of scale gained by selling to many more people.
- Trade creation — the benefits of being able to buy products tariff free, which would not be possible if not a member of the EU.
- Access for businesses to a larger supply of labour (possibly cheap labour as well).

> **Typical mistake**
>
> Just be careful: EU membership doesn't always mean adopting the euro as a currency.

The World Trade Organization (WTO)

The WTO attempts to promote **trade liberalisation** and the reduction of trade barriers that exist between its members. More than 100 countries are members of the WTO and they are invited to 'rounds' of talks among themselves, which are meant to serve as a process of trade barrier reduction. Rounds often taken many years to complete, but there have been achievements evidenced by the reduction in many import barriers on manufactured goods among WTO members.

> **Trade liberalisation:** trade without barriers (or with reductions in trade barriers).

One recent trend is the growth of regional trade blocs, where groups of geographically close countries form a regional free trade area between themselves. These regional trade blocs include the North American Free Trade Agreement (NAFTA), the EU and the Association of Southeast Asian Nations (ASEAN).

> **Balance of payments:** a record of all the financial transactions taking place between the UK and any other country.

The balance of payments

The **balance of payments** looks at all the inflows and outflows of money that take place in the UK as a result of transactions with other countries.

Transactions between the UK and the rest of the world do matter. Trade in goods and services is important and jobs depend on the UK's ability to export goods and services. Even though imports do not directly create jobs in the UK, the goods and services that we buy from abroad will often be used by UK firms as part of their production process.

> **Exam tip**
>
> The capital account is of minor significance — you should focus on the financial account and the current account.

The balance of payments is divided into three sections:
1 Capital account.
2 Financial account.
3 Current account.

> **Typical mistake**
>
> Many commentators talk about a UK balance of payments deficit when they really mean a current account deficit — try to avoid making the same mistake.

The capital account

REVISED

The capital account is a minor component of the balance of payments and includes capital transfers as well as purchases and sales of some non-financial assets.

The financial account

The financial account measures the flows of financial capital into and out of the country. It consists of three main components:

- Net **foreign direct investment (FDI)**: opening up a new business or buying an existing business located outside the UK would count as an outflow of FDI. Net FDI compares the flow of FDI into the UK with the flow of FDI out of the UK.
- Net **portfolio investment**: for example, a foreign investor buying shares in a UK business would appear as an inflow of portfolio investment. Net portfolio investment refers to the flows of money into the UK less the flows of money leaving the UK in respect of buying financial assets.
- Short-term movements of capital: money can easily move into and out of countries looking for the best rate of return available. These movements of **short-term speculative capital** — often referred to as 'hot money' — contribute to the financial account.

> **Foreign direct investment (FDI)**: the buying of productive assets located outside the country of ownership.
>
> **Portfolio investment**: refers to the buying of financial assets located outside the country of ownership.
>
> **Short-term speculative capital**: money which can be moved immediately between currencies to maximise its return (also known as 'hot money').

Current account of the balance of payments

The current account is concerned with the flows of income from trade, the use of factors of production and other transfers between countries. It looks at earnings made by the use of assets rather than the assets themselves.

The current account consists of these sections:

- **trade in goods** — exports and imports of goods
- **trade in services** — exports and imports of services
- **primary income** — net investment incomes
- **secondary income** — transfers of money between countries

Trade in goods

- The balance of trade in goods calculates the value of goods exported by the UK less the value of goods imported by the UK.
- The UK typically runs a fairly large deficit on the trade in goods balance.
- The balance on the trade in goods is sometimes known as the 'visible' balance.

Trade in services

- The balance of trade in services calculates the value of services exported by the UK less the value of services imported by the UK.
- The UK typically runs a surplus on trade in services, though this is not as large as the deficit on the trade in goods balance.
- Major services exported by the UK relate to the UK's financial services industry (e.g. banking and insurance).
- This balance is refered to as the 'invisible' balance.

Primary income

- **Primary income** refers to the net investment income flows earned by the UK.
- This is calculated as investment income received from abroad less any investment income paid abroad.

> **Primary income**: flows of income from investments abroad less flows of income from foreign investments located in the UK.

- Investment income relates to the earnings from assets located outside the UK. This includes earnings on financial assets, such as dividends and interest earned from overseas, as well as the profits and wages paid by UK-owned direct investments in businesses located overseas.
- The inward flow of investment income will be accompanied by an outward flow of investment income, which relates to foreigners who own assets located in the UK. The inward flow of income less the outward flow of income gives the net investment income position.
- The balance on net investment income in the UK used to be a large surplus but this has moved into deficit recently.
- The deficit on net investment income is explained by rapid growth in investment in the UK by investors in countries like China and India (thus creating flows of investment income back to those countries).

Secondary income

Secondary income refers to the transfers of money between countries. This usually arises from:

- private transfers, e.g. wages of overseas workers sent back to their family at home
- foreign aid
- grants
- gifts

> **Secondary income**: transfers of money received in the UK from abroad less transfers of money paid by the UK overseas.

The biggest two components of the current account are the trade in goods and the trade in services. The deficit on goods outweighs the surplus on services, which means that overall the current account balance is normally in deficit.

Now test yourself

TESTED ☐

4 Decide whether each of the following transactions would improve or worsen a current account deficit:
(a) sale of goods abroad
(b) wages paid by workers overseas sent back to families in the UK
(c) purchase of services provided by a French investment bank
(d) UK tourists on holiday in Greece
(e) aid given to developing countries
(f) dividends received by UK residents on shares held in a German company

Answer on p. 232

Balance on the current account

REVISED ☐

Factors determining exports

Foreign GDP

As foreign GDP rises, spending in those countries will also rise and this will lead to a greater demand for UK goods and services (i.e. they will import more as their spending increases).

Productivity

If UK productivity rises relative to foreign productivity, this means UK firms can produce more output for a proportionately smaller amount of inputs. This increased efficiency means that costs per unit of output fall, which allows firms to price their goods more competitively compared with foreign substitutes. This should boost the demand for UK goods — thus leading to increases in exports.

Inflation

If UK inflation is higher than foreign inflation, it means that the prices of UK goods are rising faster than those of goods produced overseas. This means UK goods will become less price competitive and foreign buyers will switch away from buying UK goods — thus leading to lower exports.

The main issue here is not the rate of inflation, but the level of relative inflation (i.e. UK inflation compared with foreign inflation).

The overall balance of payments

REVISED

The individual components of the balance of payments can be in either deficit or surplus. However, the balance of payments overall must balance. For example, a current account deficit can be, in effect, 'financed' by a surplus on the financial account.

A deficit on combined totals of the current, capital and financial accounts would be 'financed' by a reduction in the foreign currency reserves held by the UK. If there were insufficient reserves held, the government would have to borrow money to finance the shortfall.

> **Exam tip**
>
> Focus on the calculation of the current account balance — this is the balance you are more likely to face calculating in an exam.

Now test yourself

TESTED

5 From the following information, calculate the current account balance:

	£ million
Exports of goods	534,531
Imports of goods	524,131
Exports of services	133,011
Imports of services	98,080
Primary income balance	−4,580
Secondary income balance	−2,199

Answer on p. 232

Policies to correct a deficit on the current account

REVISED

There are a number of policies that a government can implement which should correct (eliminate or at least reduce) the current account deficit:
- **expenditure reducing policies** — deflationary policies
- **expenditure switching policies** — protectionist policies and devaluation

Expenditure reducing policies

Imports are determined by UK consumers' purchasing power — the faster incomes rise, the more is spent on imports. Therefore, if we wanted to reduce UK spending on imports, one policy would be to reduce the ability of UK consumers to spend money.

> **Expenditure reducing policies**: policies to improve the current account balance by reducing spending in the economy.
>
> **Expenditure switching policies**: policies to encourage a switch away from imports and to encourage a growth in exports.

An expenditure reducing policy includes any policy designed to reduce the level of consumption and, in turn, reduce the quantity of import spending. These policies include any combination of the following:

1 Higher taxation
2 Lower government expenditure
3 Higher interest rates

Issues with this policy

The problems associated with deflationary policies include:

- deflationary policies reduce the rate of economic growth and this will lead to higher (cyclical) unemployment
- they are not popular with those who vote as they reduce living standards
- higher interest rates may increase the exchange rate, leading to lower volumes of exports — cancelling out to some extent the current account improvements that deflationary policies set out to achieve

Exam tip

It would be a good idea to explain the impact of expenditure reducing policy on other economic objectives — i.e. the trade-offs that exist.

Expenditure switching policies

Expenditure switching policies attempt to correct a deficit by encouraging a reduction in the quantity of imports accompanied (where possible) by a rise in the quantity of exports. The specific policies that achieve this are as follows.

Devaluation

A **devaluation** of the currency means that each unit of currency can buy less foreign currency than before the devaluation. The effects on the current account are:

- exports appear cheaper to foreign customers (a lower exchange rate means each unit of foreign currency buys more of our currency), meaning we would expect the level and value of exports to rise
- imports will be more expensive as the lower exchange rate means more currency is needed to buy the same amount of foreign currency as before. This should lead to a lower quantity of imports

Devaluation: a sudden and significant fall in the value of the exchange rate.

Issues with this policy

Devaluing a currency may improve the current account balance but this will depend on the elasticity of demand for both exports and imports.

Marshall–Lerner condition

The effect of the devaluation is to make imports more expensive for domestic consumers and to make exports appear cheaper for foreigners. However, we need to know how consumers respond to this change in relative prices. This depends on the price elasticity of demand for both imports and exports, which needs to be sufficiently price elastic to ensure that the demand for exports rises and the demand for imports falls when the devaluation changes their relative prices.

If the demand for both imports and exports is highly price inelastic, the devaluation will not lead to significant enough changes in exports and imports to improve the current account balance.

The **Marshall–Lerner condition** states that devaluation will improve the current account balance only if the price elasticity of demand for exports

Marshall–Lerner condition: the requirement that devaluation will improve the current account balance only if the total of the price elasticities for imports and exports is greater than 1.

and imports together is greater than unity (1). If not, then the devaluation will not improve the current account balance.

PED (exports) + PED (imports) > 1

The J Curve

Demand usually becomes more price elastic over time as more substitutes are found. This also applies to the demand for foreign goods. This has two effects on the current account balance following devaluation:

- For foreign customers, export prices fall but this does not immediately lead to significantly higher exports. The increase in exports will occur only once demand becomes more price elastic — over time.
- Imports become more expensive after the devaluation but the demand for these will not fall much in the short term as demand is initially price inelastic. Therefore, the value of imports will rise initially and fall only once consumers switch away from the now more expensive imports (i.e. as demand becomes more price elastic).

Therefore, the current account balance may worsen in the short term. This is known as the 'J Curve effect' because of its appearance, which shows how the balance moves further into deficit before it improves in the longer term (see Figure 14.2).

Protectionist policies

Another form of expenditure switch policy is that where protectionist policies are adopted by an economy. The purpose of trade barriers is to restrict the flow of imports into a country so as to switch expenditure to domestically produced goods instead. As a result, the balance on the current account should improve.

Issues with this policy are:

- countries that have restrictions placed on their exports are likely to retaliate with similar measures, which may mean we sell fewer exports and the current account balance does not improve
- if a tariff is used to restrict the flow of imports, an assumption is being made that demand for the import is relatively price elastic (and the import subject to the tariff has domestic substitutes available)

Supply-side policies

A longer-term policy would be to improve the supply side of the economy. This should improve the current account balance through improvements in productivity and keeping inflation low, thus helping to boost the competitiveness of UK exports.

The significance of current account deficits and surpluses

REVISED

Achieving balance on the current account is one of the government's macroeconomic objectives. However, the government sees the pursuit of full employment, price stability and steady economic growth as more important.

> **J Curve:** the observation that after a devaluation the current account balance worsens initially before improving.

> **Exam tip**
>
> Remember: a devaluation will improve the current account balance only if the Marshall–Lerner conditions are satisfied — if they are not, there will be no improvement.

> **Typical mistake**
>
> Devaluation is not pain-free — import price rises may lead to significant cost-push inflation pressure.

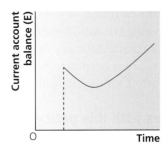

Figure 14.2 The J Curve

Nevertheless, even if only a minor objective, current account balance must still be seen as a desirable goal. The reason why current account deficits are to be avoided include the following:

- A large current account deficit means a net outflow of money leaving the UK economy (though this may be matched by a surplus on the financial and capital account balances).
- A current account deficit may indicate a weakness in the country's export industries. For example, outdated technology, poorly trained workers and little investment in research and development may mean a country struggles to produce exports which are in demand.
- If the exchange rate is fixed, a deficit may persist. With a floating exchange rate, a current account deficit could lead to a fall in the currency's value, which would help to boost exports, thus reducing the deficit.
- A persistent deficit on the current account not matched by a surplus on the capital and financial account balances will lead to a fall in the government's foreign currency reserves. Eventually these will run out and the government will be forced to borrow. Some governments would have to increase interest rates or negotiate special terms in order to attract borrowed funds.

However, there are reasons why a current account deficit should not matter. These include the following:

- Imports are likely to rise when economic growth is high and the current account deficit may just be the result of high economic growth and increases in people's incomes.
- As long as the deficit on one component of the balance of payments is matched by the surpluses on the other components, the individual deficit should not matter.
- Although a current account deficit may appear to be large, it will matter only if it is large when expressed as a percentage of the economy's GDP. Even then, if the deficit is short-lived, it still might not matter.
- If a government has plenty of foreign currency reserves, or has plenty of lenders willing to supply capital if need be, the deficit should not matter.

Implication of current account imbalances

REVISED

If a major economy or group of economies attempts to improve the current account, there will be implications for other economies.

Any policy adopted will reduce demand for exports from other countries, which will have an adverse effect on output and employment and, in turn, may also lead to reduced global demand for the exports from other economies. For example, protectionist policies adopted by the USA are likely to reduce the demand for EU exports to the USA, which may also lead to lower incomes in the EU as job losses increase.

Policies of this form are sometimes referred to as 'beggar thy neighbour' policies, where action taken by one country to improve an economy worsens the performance of other economies. The problem here is that other economies will retaliate with their own policies and all economies end up worse off.

Exam tip

The importance of the current account balance really does depend on the country. Less developed countries will have to pay more attention to the deficit due to the need to borrow to finance a deficit.

Exchange rate systems

Exchange rates are expressed, for example, as follows: £1 = €1.30. This shows us how many euros one pound would buy or how much one pound costs in terms of euros. This could also be expressed as €1 = £0.769 (the reciprocal of the exchange rate — i.e. 1/1.30).

A higher exchange rate means that £1 will buy more foreign currency and a falling exchange rate means it will buy less. Rising exchange rates are often referred to as strengthening (or strong) currencies, and falling exchange rates are often expressed as weakening (or weak) currencies.

> **Exchange rate:** the price of one currency expressed in terms of another currency.

> **Typical mistake**
>
> Always remember which way you are quoting an exchange rate in terms of price and in terms of which currency (e.g. is it €s per £ or £s per €?).

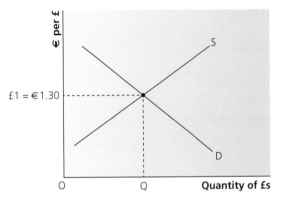

Figure 14.3 The exchange rate is determined by the demand for and supply of a currency

The exchange rate is determined by the forces of demand and supply (see Figure 14.3), with the equilibrium being the current exchange rate.

Determinants of the exchange rate

REVISED

A **floating exchange rate** will rise and fall due to market forces (i.e. the conditions of demand and supply for the currency). These are likely to include the following.

> **Floating exchange rate:** one where the government makes no attempt to influence the value of the currency.

Interest rate movements

If UK interest rates increase relative to those of other economies, there will be an inflow of short-term 'hot money' into the UK to take advantage of higher interest rates offered by UK financial institutions. This means increased demand for the pound, which, as shown in Figure 14.4, leads to a rise in the value of the currency.

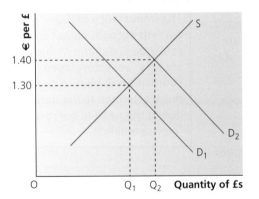

Figure 14.4 A rise in the demand for the pound will lead to a rise in the exchange rate

- Higher (relative) interest rates normally mean a rise in the exchange rate.
- Lower (relative) interest rates normally mean a fall in the exchange rate.

Foreign trade

Increased demand for imports would mean an outflow of pounds in order to buy the foreign currency needed to purchase the imports. This increases the supply of pounds, and therefore will lead to a fall in the exchange rate. This is shown in Figure 14.5.

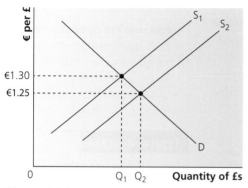

Figure 14.5 An increase in imports will increase the supply of pounds and lead to a fall in the exchange rate

Alternatively, higher UK exports mean more demand for the pound (needed to buy our goods and services), which will lead to a rise in the currency's value. In general:
- higher imports/falling exports will normally lead to a fall in the exchange rate
- reduced imports/rising exports will normally lead to a rise in the exchange rate

Relative inflation

If UK inflation is higher than the economies of our trading partners, our exports become less price-competitive. This will reduce demand for exports and will lead to a lower exchange rate — it will normally result in a greater supply of pounds and reduced demand for pounds.

Foreign direct investment

Increasing FDI to the UK will increase the demand for the currency and, as we can see in Figure 14.4, this would lead to a rise in the exchange rate.

Expectations

If we think the price of a good is likely to rise soon, we may decide to 'beat' the price change by buying now. Exchange rates move similarly. If any of the determinants are expected to change in the near future (say, a rise in interest rates), we may buy currency now in anticipation of a rise in the exchange rate.

Exchange rates are often determined by expectations of events occurring, rather than the actual event itself. For example, often after an interest rate rise, the exchange rate does not change — because the interest rate rise was anticipated and the buying of the currency happened before the rise.

Typical mistake

Foreign currency transactions arising out of trade are now a very small proportion of total foreign currency transactions.

The case for floating exchange rates

The UK government has let the exchange rate float for more than 20 years. Clearly there are benefits in allowing the exchange rate to float.

Advantages of floating exchange rates

- Monetary sovereignty — where interest rates are set on the needs of the UK economy alone (e.g. to manage levels of inflation or unemployment) rather than having to change them to stabilise the exchange rate.
- Automatic adjustment to the current account balance — a large deficit on the current account would see an outflow of pounds, which should lead to the exchange rate falling, thus automatically leading to restoring export competitiveness.
- There is no need for the government to hold extensive stocks of foreign currency for **open market operations** to influence to currency's value.

> **Open market operations**: direct intervention into the foreign currency market to influence the demand for and supply of that currency.

Disadvantages of floating exchange rates

- Uncertainty for businesses — not knowing the value of the currency makes it harder for businesses to plan ahead for leaky prices, profit margins and possible sales volume.
- Over-valued/under-valued currency — the exchange rate may remain high or low due to speculators deciding to either buy or sell the currency. An over-valued currency makes it difficult for those wishing to export, while an under-valued currency would generate cost-push inflation.

> **Typical mistake**
>
> The adjustment process of the exchange rate to current account deficits (or surpluses) is unlikely to be as smooth as theory suggests — exchange rate determination is more complex than this.

Fixed exchange rates

The government can intervene in the foreign exchange market. This is usually done to attempt to influence the exchange rate's value. The methods of intervention would be as follows:

- Monetary policy — changes in interest rate deliberately enacted to alter the demand for the currency.
- Open market operations — buying and selling reserves of foreign currency to influence the demand and supply of the currency.
- Capital controls — restrictions on the quantity of currency that can leave or enter an economy.

Most countries no longer impose capital controls. This means that there are no restrictions on the flows of hot money into and out of a currency. As a result, any government wishing to **fix the exchange rate** is going to have to match the interest rates of the economy whose currency it wants to fix against (otherwise there would be a tendency for money to flow into the currency with the higher interest rates, thus pushing up the exchange rate).

> **Fixed exchange rate**: where the government intervenes in the foreign exchange market to stabilise a currency's value against one or more other currencies.

The UK government has fixed the exchange rate during periods in the past 70 years. The periods from the late 1940s to the early 1970s and between 1990 and 1992 saw the pound fixed against other currencies.

Advantages of fixed exchange rates

- Easier trading for businesses — making it likely there will be an expansion of trade between those with fixed rates against one another.

- Monetary discipline — keeping interest rates in line with those of the economy that the currency is being fixed against gives monetary policy added credibility. This means there are less likely to be cuts in interest rates which might be inflationary purely to boost a government's popularity.

Disadvantages of fixed exchange rates

These disadvantages are similar to the benefits of having a floating exchange rate. These include:
- loss of monetary sovereignty — interest rates cannot be used for domestic purposes and have to be kept at the same level as those in the economy whose currency the exchange rate is being fixed against
- large reserves of foreign currency may be needed for government intervention (especially given that the quantity of internationally mobile 'hot money' far outweighs the size of most governments' foreign reserves)
- lack of adjustment to current account imbalances

> **Now test yourself**   TESTED ☐
>
> 6 Draw a demand and supply diagram showing how government intervention in the foreign exchange market may keep an exchange rate fixed between two narrow bands.
>
> Answer on p. 232

Currency unions   REVISED ☐

Some members of the EU share a common single currency, the euro. These countries are often referred to as belonging to the **eurozone**. The UK chose not to join this **currency union**, though there are arguments in favour of membership.

Arguments in favour of joining a currency union

- Greater certainty for businesses that trade with members of the currency union.
- No costs involved in converting currencies between members.
- No worries about the exchange rate being over-valued or under-valued against other members.
- Greater price transparency for consumers.

Arguments against joining a currency union

- Monetary policy has to be conducted for the currency union as a whole — individual countries lose the right to set their own monetary policy.
- Businesses may be unable to compete with lower-cost producers that are members of the union and cannot benefit from a falling exchange rate.
- Fiscal policy needs to be used more widely to correct for imbalances across the currency union area (this is unpopular in the EU).
- Countries may have to 'bail out' other members that run into problems financing their government debt.

Economic growth and development

The difference between economic growth and development

REVISED ☐

Economic growth refers to the increase in the level of national income over time, measured in either actual or potential terms. Development, meanwhile, is a multidimensional concept and is believed to depend on a number of criteria being achieved, such as:

- income — which will come from economic growth
- availability of basic goods and services for survival — food, shelter, warmth and so on
- freedom of individuals to make choices on a social and an economic level

There is a connection between economic growth and development. However, higher income alone will be insufficient for an economy to reach development. Development, then, can come only from progress being made in a variety of areas.

Characteristics of less developed economies

REVISED ☐

Less developed economies are diverse in terms of their location, their size and other social and economic characteristics. However, less developed economies are bound to share similar characteristics. These common characteristics include:

- low levels of real GDP per capita
- dependence on primary products for export revenue
- fast population growth and a low median age for the population as a whole
- a high proportion of the population based in rural areas and likely to be employed in agriculture
- higher than average size for the informal economy
- poor levels of infrastructure
- poorly developed financial markets

Indicators of development

REVISED ☐

Given its multidimensional nature, the statistics used to measure development also make use of multiple indicators. The most commonly used measure is the Human Development Index (HDI).

Human Development Index

The HDI is issued by the United Nations each year and assigns each country a development score. The HDI scores on three dimensions of development:

- real national income per capita — based on PPP exchange rates
- health of the population — based on life expectancy at birth
- education of the population — based on mean years of schooling and expected years of schooling

The three scores are combined to give an overall score for the HDI. Countries are ranked and classified as exhibiting very high, high, medium or low levels of human development.

The HDI measure has limitations, as it fails to include other characteristics of development, such as the level of freedom enjoyed by the population, but it remains the most widely used statistic for measuring development.

Other measures of development

Although the HDI is widely used, other measures are also used to assess the level of development in an economy. These include:

- Human Poverty Index — measures which look at a range of indicators, including life expectancy, poverty rates and literacy rates
- Gender-related Development Index (GDI) and Gender Empowerment Measure (GEM) — measures which are similar to the HDI but also consider gender gaps in development
- social indicators — individual statistics which look at levels of social development (e.g. education levels, access to health and education, literacy rates and so on)

Factors affecting growth in development

REVISED

Long-run growth comes from outward shifts of the PPC. However, for development to take place, this growth needs to be achieved in a way which will allow further growth to be sustained into the future.

- Investment adds to both short-run and long-run growth within an economy. Investment in infrastructure — transport links, sewerage systems, public services, etc. — would be more useful for development than, say, increased military investment.
- Education and training will add to short-run growth and should also move the economy closer to development. Education adds to the economy's intellectual capacity — e.g. boosting literacy rates helps development. Training increases workers' employability, either boosting productivity or increasing the range of jobs they can perform.

Barriers to economic growth and development

REVISED

Even with investment and increased emphasis on education and training, an economy may still fail to reach developed status. There are plenty of barriers which prevent development. These include:

- poor infrastructure — e.g. lack of transport links or telecommunications networks
- corruption — especially in public office, which makes a country a less attractive place to locate in terms of FDI
- inadequate human capital — lack of investment in education and training means the population is not adequately equipped for development of a business sector, or will be unattractive to MNCs looking for an appropriate workforce
- lack of property rights — businesses depend on ownership of assets and contracts being upheld by law, and if this is not happening, enterprise is less likely to flourish and the country will find it difficult to attract FDI
- primary product dependency — many primary products have seen their price fall over the last 50 years in real terms and these are generally income inelastic products

- volatile earnings from commodities — over-reliance on one or two commodity exports (e.g. oil) makes foreign currency earnings unpredictable and budgeting for the future becomes difficult
- an undeveloped financial system — this means that those looking for capital cannot access the funds needed to set up or expand business operations
- institutional factors — a lack of certain institutions, such as stable government, a viable health service and a legal system, makes it much harder for development to take place

Now test yourself

TESTED

7 Explain why income inelastic demand for primary products is bad for those countries relying on them for exports.

Answer on p. 232

Policies to promote economic growth and development

REVISED

The best way of achieving economic growth is through sound monetary, fiscal and supply-side policies. However, growth alone does not lead to development. Thus other policies will be needed in conjunction with macroeconomic policy.

Market-based strategies include:
- trade liberalisation — removing or decreasing trade barriers
- removal of subsidies — often found on import substitutes
- policies to attract inward investment — such as removing legal barriers to foreign ownership
- allowing the price mechanism to work more freely — i.e. cancelling minimum and maximum prices in individual markets

Now test yourself

TESTED

8 Explain two limitations of trade liberalisation in promoting development.

Answer on p. 232

Interventionist strategies include:
- infrastructure investment — e.g. in transport, in technology and in basic facilities (e.g. sanitation and health)
- education and training investment
- investment in tourism and other services
- overseas aid
- debt cancellation
- state investment in the welfare system

Now test yourself

TESTED

9 Explain why debt cancellation might not be a good idea.

Answer on p. 232

The role of aid and trade in promoting growth and development

An inflow of foreign currency will help governments in less developed economies fund development strategies, such as the construction of infrastructure projects or the development of health and education systems.

Economists disagree on whether trade or aid is the best way to promote development and generate foreign currency for development.

Trade

Allowing free trade helps development as countries benefit from specialisation in industries where they have comparative advantage. As long as trade takes place between other countries with minimal barriers, the gains from specialisation can be shared between all.

Some economists have argued that in reality governments of developed economies will protect their own industries from low-cost competition in less developed economies by claiming that these countries have an 'unfair' advantage in terms of low costs.

Aid

International **aid** can take many forms. It is usually provided by developed countries for less developed countries. Common forms of aid include:

- money — either unconditional transfers or ones that are tied under some set condition (i.e. they must be spent on certain products) or in the form of a '**soft loan**'
- goods and services — often for a particular cause (sometimes labelled 'disaster relief'), such as food in times of famine or clothing when populations have been displaced due to military conflict or natural disasters

> **Aid:** this can refer to money, goods and services, as well as loans at favourable interest rates given to a less developed country.
>
> **Soft loans:** loans to less developed countries at less than market interest rates or with favourable payback conditions.

Aid can be helpful if it comes with few or no conditions attached to it. Aid in monetary form can be used to fund capital investment in infrastructure or social programmes. However, aid can be inappropriate for development in a number of ways:

- Money may get channelled into benefiting a small group of people in the less developed country (this will depend on the level of public corruption).
- Conditional aid may largely benefit the developed economy granting the aid, if it has to be spent on goods from the developed economy.
- The systems for distributing aid (especially if in the form of goods and services) may not be present, which may mean few benefit from the aid.
- Goods and services may not be suitable for the needs of the population.
- Those receiving the money may not have the expertise to spend it wisely, which can lead to expenditure on inappropriate programmes (e.g. road and airport developments which are not needed and remain largely unused).

Conclusion

It is likely some combination of trade and aid is going to be helpful. Certainly, money with few conditions attached to the donation is more use than aid with conditions. Exports of goods which are in demand and are not income inelastic are also useful.

Cancellation of debt or restructuring of the terms of payback of any outstanding debt will also help. However, even debt relief is not without its criticisms as some feel it has made it easier for corrupt regimes to remain in power.

Exam practice

Between 2009 and 2015 the pound gradually rose in value against the euro, a currency used by many countries in the EU. The rise in the pound's value accelerated in the first half of 2015.

Table 1	Value of £1
January 2009	€1.06
August 2015	€1.41

Although a rising currency may appear favourable for some, the rise in the pound's value has been linked to the sizeable current account deficit in the UK. The large deficit has also been linked to slow economic growth in the EU.

Table 2	UK balance of trade in goods (in £ billions)	
2015	With EU countries	With non-EU countries
August	–7.1	–3.8
September	–7.1	–1.7
October	–7.7	–3.6
November	–8.2	–2.5

Being a member of the EU allows the UK to benefit from free trade with other members. However, there are some who feel the free trade has not benefited the UK. Recent closures of factories producing steel in the UK have been linked by some to free trade.

Others feel that the UK should change its emphasis on who it trades with away from the EU and towards other parts of the world. They would use evidence of the value of UK exports to non-EU countries to support their case. The UK government is said to be keen on the EU signing more free trade agreements with non-EU countries.

Although the 2016 referendum supported the UK leaving the EU, the UK is likely to remain a member of the EU until 2018 at least.

1 Using Table 1, calculate the percentage change in the £/€ exchange rate between January 2009 and August 2015 to two decimal places. [3]
2 Using Table 2, explain two problems for the UK economy following a rise in the value of the pound. [10]
3 Using the information in Table 1, analyse reasons why the UK has a large current account deficit. [12]
4 'The UK government is said to be keen on the EU signing more free trade agreements with non-EU countries.' Using Table 1, evaluate the impact on the UK if the EU were to sign more free trade agreements with non-EU countries. [25]

Answers and quick quiz 14 online

ONLINE

Summary

You should have an understanding of:
- The causes and characteristics of globalisation.
- The consequences of globalisation for less developed and for more developed countries, and the role of MNCs.
- The distinction between comparative and absolute advantage.
- The reasons for changes in the pattern of trade between the UK and the rest of the world.
- Protectionist policies, such as tariffs, quotas and export subsidies, and the causes and consequences of these policies.
- The main features of a customs union and of the Single European Market (SEM).
- The consequences for the UK of its membership of the European Union (EU).
- The role of the World Trade Organization (WTO).
- The sections of the balance of payments.
- The factors that influence a country's current account balance, such as productivity, inflation and exchange rates.
- Policies that might be used to correct a balance of payments deficit or surplus and the implications for the global economy of deciding to take corrective action on these deficits or surpluses.
- The significance of current account deficits and surpluses.
- How exchange rates are determined in freely floating exchange rate systems.
- How governments can intervene to influence the exchange rate and the advantages and disadvantages of fixed and floating exchange rate systems.
- Advantages and disadvantages for a country of joining a currency union, e.g. the eurozone.
- The difference between growth and development and the main characteristics and indicators of less developed economies.
- Factors that affect growth and development, such as investment, education and training, and the barriers to growth and development.
- Policies that might be adopted to promote economic growth and development.
- The role of aid and trade in promoting growth and development.

Now test yourself answers

Chapter 1

1   B   All other answers are positive economic statements because they can be tested and subsequently declared to be true or false. Answer B is a normative statement since it is a subjective opinion, or value judgement: the word 'should' often suggests that a statement is an opinion.

2   C   Oil in the North Sea is a naturally occurring resource, which economists classify as the factor of production known as land; A and D would be classed as capital equipment; B would be classed as labour.

3   Because the vast majority of resources are limited in supply, i.e. they are scarce. Individuals, firms and governments also have finite incomes.

4   In a free market economy, consumers will send signals via the strength of demand to firms in order to determine what will be produced. Firms will then aim to maximise profits and so attempt to produce goods and services in the most productively efficient way. Who gets the goods and services produced will be determined by consumers' ability to pay for them. In a centrally planned economy, all decisions will be made by the government.

5   D   £8000. This question contains lots of extra information designed to test whether you understand the essence of the concept of opportunity cost. The only relevant information is that John can either keep or sell the car, missing out on £8000 if he chooses the former.

6   (a) Point Z is productively inefficient, since it is inside the economy's PPC. Output of one or both of consumer goods and capital goods could be produced with existing resources. There is a waste of scarce economic resources arising from unemployment of one or more factors of production.

    (b) Points A and B are both on the PPC and so are productively efficient. Maximum possible output combinations are being produced at any point on the PPC, including A and B. At either point, it is not possible to increase the output of one type of good without reducing output of another.

    (c) Point Y may be achieved in the future if the PPC shifts outwards sufficiently. This means economic growth is necessary, arising from an increase in quantity and/or improvement in productivity of one or more factors of production.

    (d) The opportunity cost, for example, of increasing the output of consumer goods by the amount RS is the loss of ML capital goods.

7   (a) An outward shift of the PPC due to more productive land.

    (b) An inward shift of the PPC due to a smaller population.

    (c) An outward shift of the PPC in the long run due to increased productivity of capital equipment in producing all goods and services.

    (d) An outward shift of the PPC in the long run due to more productive labour.

Chapter 2

1   D
2   B
3   D
4   C
5   D

Chapter 3

1   (a) A leftward shift of the demand curve.

    (b) A rightward shift of the demand curve.

    (c) A leftward shift of the demand curve.

    (d) A rightward shift of the demand curve.

2   (a) 0.5 (inelastic).

    (b) 2.5 (elastic).

    (c) 3.3 (elastic).

3   PED is 0.5 (inelastic). Initial total revenue is 3000 × £1.50 = £4500. New total revenue is 3300 × £1.20 = £3960. Overall revenue has fallen by £540.

4   Total revenue will fall, depending how price elastic holidays to the Maldives are.

5   Milk can be considered price inelastic.

6   (a) −3 (inferior).

    (b) 2.5 (normal/luxury).

    (c) 4 (normal/luxury).

7   (a) 0.75 (substitutes).

    (b) −0.8 (complements).

8   Excess supply.

9   Firms would have to reduce the price of the good in question in order to sell all their stocks. This would lead to both a contraction along the supply curve, as firms have less of a profit incentive to produce the good, as well as an extension along the demand curve, as more of a good is demanded at a lower price. Eventually the forces of supply and demand achieve a state of balance and a new, lower equilibrium price is reached which 'clears' the market of any excess supply.

10(a) The demand curve shifts to the right, leading to an increase in price and quantity.

(b) The supply curve shifts to the right, leading to a fall in price and an increase in quantity.

(c) It depends! If cars become more popular, the demand curve for petrol will shift to the right, leading to a rise in price and quantity. However, if there is an overall reduced need for petrol, the opposite will happen.

(d) The supply curve shifts to the right, leading to a fall in price and a rise in quantity.

11(a) e.g. fish and chips.

(b) e.g. lamb chops and wool.

(c) e.g. land may be used for building houses or shopping centres.

(d) e.g. the demand for pilots is derived from the demand for long-distance travel for holidays and business trips.

12 D

Chapter 4

1 Production refers to total output, whereas productivity refers to the rate at which output is produced.

2 450 / 3 = 150 cups of coffee per employee per day.

3 D

4 C

5 A

6 A

7 C

8 Relevant points for analysis include:
- definition(s) of monopoly, perfect competition, average revenue, marginal revenue
- relevant diagram(s), e.g. monopoly, perfect competition
- features of perfect competition that determine slope of curves: perfect information, homogeneous product, freedom of entry and exit, leading to perfectly elastic demand, average revenue and marginal revenue
- features of monopoly that determine slope of curves: barriers to entry and exit, ability to set price or output

9

Quantity of footballs sold	Total revenue £	Total fixed costs £	Total variable costs £	Total costs £	Profit £
10	50	100	20	120	−70
20	100	100	40	140	−40
30	150	100	60	160	−10
40	200	100	80	180	20

Chapter 5

1 Imperfect information about costs and revenues, actions of competitors, stakeholder pressures, managerial theories such as satisficing, 'the quiet life' and X inefficiency.

2 C 　　　　　5 B

3 C 　　　　　6 D

4 B

Chapter 6

1 D

2 A

3 Factors include: (i) higher MRP for surgeons, driven by higher-level qualifications, experience, productivity and higher 'priced' work; (ii) more inelastic demand for surgeons, driven by fewer available substitutes; (iii) lower supply of surgeons, driven by fewer candidates able to achieve the high levels of educational attainment required to embark upon medical training, along with fewer people willing to work long, unsociable hours (net disadvantage); (iv) more inelastic supply of surgeons, driven by length of training and qualification period. Factors may be considered from standpoint of nurses, surgeons or both. Factors lead to higher earnings for surgeons compared with nurses.

4 B

5 C

6 D

Chapter 7

1 B

2 C

3 B

Chapter 8

1 C

2 C

3 C

4 D

5 B

6 D

7 A

8 B

9 C

10 Measures include: privatisation, deregulation, breaking up of monopolies, price controls, measures to increase contestability.

11 D

Chapter 9

1 2.5%.

2 It has risen but at a slower rate.

3 UK = $46,016, Norway = $96,154.

4 Possible answers include:
- It's a sign that the population is enjoying a higher standard of living.
- Taxation revenue will increase, enabling tax cuts elsewhere.
- More government can be financed through higher taxation revenue.
- Any budget deficit can be reduced through reductions in welfare expenditure.

5 They are still rising but at a slower rate (3% down to 2% rate of increase).

6 Possible reasons:
- People may not qualify for benefits who are still looking for work.
- People may not wish to claim benefits for personal reasons.

7 Possible reasons:
- Motivation at work may fall (due to low pay, poor conditions).
- Inappropriate training provided to workforce.
- Teething problems with new technology.
- Rapid turnover of employment (people moving between jobs, etc.).

8 Index numbers are useful when it is the change in a price that matters more than the actual price of a good. Index numbers make it easier to see the magnitude of changes in the variable and can also be used to contrast with other variables that have been translated into an index number.

9 Possible reasons:
- Inflation does not account for quality improvements.
- Trends in what we actually buy may change before the basket used is updated.
- Personal spending habits may differ significantly from what is in the weighted basket.

10 (a) Those items have the highest weights mainly because they are more significant elements in what the typical household spends its money on.

(b) Trends in spending habits change — as incomes rise over time, the proportion spent on essentials should decline, which should mean the weights used need to alter. Additionally, as new products emerge, this may mean we switch to buying these products.

11 Possible answers include:
- comparisons between expenditure and income data — expenditure will be higher than income if income is unrecorded
- estimates of illegal activity based on crime statistics

- anonymous surveys covering unrecorded activity to elicit 'honest' responses that may be unreported otherwise

12 ($4/£3): £1 = $1.33

13 Relevant issues for explanation include:
- degree of income inequality
- amount committed to military expenditure by government
- amount invested in merit good provision
- degree of welfare expenditure
- non-financial factors, e.g. environmental issues, individual freedoms, etc.

Chapter 10

1 Total expenditure and total income should be the same as they are looking at the same set of transactions but from different points of view. When we spend our money we are generating incomes for the supplier of whatever we are spending our money on. If we stopped spending our income, this would lead to falls in income elsewhere.

2 (a) £840 billion.

(b) 5%.

3 Possible problems with the data are:
- They don't take into account the distribution of income.
- They don't take into account welfare provision for the poorer members of society (which determines their standard of living).
- How government spending is distributed will affect living standards (e.g. spending large amounts on national defence doesn't directly contribute to most people's living standards).
- Living standards will depend on the provision of public and merit goods.
- Non-financial factors, such as freedom of speech, democratic rights and so on, will matter.
- Environmental degradation may be serious and will not show up in national income statistics.

4 It is not in equilibrium. Total injections add up to £800 billion whereas total withdrawals add up to £765 billion. As it stands, national income will rise to bring the economy back into equilibrium.

5 (a) Rightward shift in AD.

(b) Leftward shift in AD.

(c) Leftward shift in AD.

(d) Rightward shift in AD.

6 Although extra spending will generate income and this in turn leads to more spending, this process is finite. Any extra income received will not all be spent. Initially the extra income will be taxed. Out of this now smaller amount of extra (disposable) income, some may be chosen to be saved, and even

if it is spent, some of this extra spending may leave the domestic circular flow as it is spent on imports. Therefore, with each extra 'round' of the multiplier process, a smaller amount is passed on and this will mean the rises in income quickly fall to small amounts after an initial boost.

7 (a) 4, (b) 5, (c) 3, (d) 2.5.

8 (a) Increase of £200 m. (b) Increase of £80 m.
   (c) Decrease of £200 m.

9 A higher MPC means a higher proportion of consumption is spent from any additional income received and this will be passed on, creating income elsewhere. With a higher MPC, more is passed on at each stage of the process, leading to an overall greater increase in income than would occur with a smaller MPC.

10 (a), (b) and (c) Rightward shift in SRAS.
    (d) Leftward shift in SRAS.

11 Possible answers include:
    – easier access to government grants for starting up businesses
    – reductions in paid holiday requirements for employees
    – reduction in power of trade unions
    – easier access to business advice/information
    – reduction in legislative requirements on setting up companies

12 Reduced subsidies for childcare will make it more expensive to put children into childcare. This will make working (and using childcare) less attractive, especially for those who have recently returned to work after looking after young children. This will reduce the number of people willing to participate in the labour market and therefore this reduced labour supply will mean less can be produced at full capacity (hence the leftward shift in the LRAS).

13 Diagram will contain a Keynesian AS curve and at least three AD curves all shown as shifted to the right. The equilibrium points will initially show how an increase in AD leads to higher GDP with negligible (or no) effects on the price level. As the AD shifts further to the right, the impact on GDP is reduced but the increase in the price level will increase the further to the right AD shifts.

14 (a) D
    (b) C
    (c) B

15 An AD/AS diagram should show both a rightward shift in AD and a rightward shift in LRAS leading to a new equilibrium position with higher real GDP — which should lead to lower unemployment.

    Unemployment will fall due to the expansion of AD — the extra spending by the government on education will have a multiplier effect on the economy and lead to a greater increase in

spending, meaning there is a greater demand for output and more workers are required.

Unemployment may also fall due to an expansion of the productive capacity of the economy (rightward shift in the LRAS). This is because the investment in education should increase occupational mobility of labour and increase its productivity (though these effects may take time to fully work).

16 There would be a leftward shift in the AD curve caused by a negative wealth effect. This is likely to have negative multiplier effects in the economy. As households feel less wealthy, they will cut back on consumption and will borrow less to finance credit-related consumption. This means there is likely to be a rise in unemployment due to the reduced AD. The government's budget is likely to move closer to, or further into, deficit.

Chapter 11

1 (C) and (E).

2 The rise in investment will lead to a rightward shift in the LRAS as well as a rightward shift in AD. The government will encourage investment because:
   – higher investment raises the productive capacity of the economy (increased LRAS), which means the economy can be expanded with less risk of generating inflationary pressure
   – more investment will boost AD and have multiplier effects on the economy (leading to reduced unemployment and higher GDP)
   – higher investment may also boost efficiency, which will lead to more exports potentially

3 Benefits for government of achieving growth include:
   – higher living standards for the population (which may increase the government's popularity)
   – lower unemployment — achievement of objective for government
   – increased tax revenue
   – less need for welfare expenditure — which could be spent elsewhere or fund tax cuts
   – greater international status for the government

4 Drawbacks of growth for individuals might include:
   – increased negative externalities (e.g. congestion, pollution — both arising out of increased output)
   – potential for greater inequality if growth is unevenly shared out
   – higher inflation if growth is of a short-term nature

5 Ways to promote sustainable growth may include:
   – subsidies for 'green' forms of investment/ development

- taxes on non-renewable sources of production
- rules and regulations
- grants/incentives

6 It is most likely to achieve:
- minimising unemployment
- economic growth
- reduced budget deficit

It is unlikely to achieve:
- stable inflation
- balance on the current account of the balance of payments

7 Possible explanations of the 2008–09 recession include:
- asset price bubble
- speculation
- herding
- excessive build-up in credit

8 (a) Structural — occupational immobility
(b) Cyclical
(c) Structural — geographical immobility
(d) Frictional

9 When there is a positive output gap, actual growth is higher than trend growth. This means spending (AD) is above long-term rate of growth. In this case there will be increased demand for output to be produced and this would mean more workers are required. Hence, unemployment would fall.

10 There is an element of value judgement in this answer. To some extent the worker is voluntarily remaining unemployed as they could complete any relevant training which they need to obtain this job. However, until they are trained it would be easier to justify that they are involuntarily unemployed — it depends on how easy it is for the worker to obtain this job. If it is regional immobility, again it could be classed as voluntary unemployment if they are choosing not to move, but this would be hard to justify if it is impractical for relocation to take place.

11 Effects for the economy of a significant increase in the minimum wage include:
- reduction in voluntary unemployment (or frictional)
- reduction in relative poverty
- reduction in poverty trap
- higher real-wage unemployment

12 Deflation refers to a fall in the average level of prices. Low inflation refers to a period in which prices are rising but at a low rate.

13 A leftward shift in AD can lead to deflation. This is due to lower demand leading to lower real output — there will be less demand-pull pressure on prices and firms may cut prices in order to sell surplus stock.

A rightward shift in SRAS can lead to deflation. A fall in the cost of production (e.g. falling material costs) will mean firms are willing to supply more at any price level and this will lead to a surplus of output and therefore firms cut prices in order to clear this.

14 Appropriate policy would be to control the money supply through either interest rate policy or control of credit available in the economy.

15 Reasons for sticky wages might include:
- money illusion of workers
- trade union pressure
- contracts which fix wages

16 A negative output gap will see growth being below average and, as a result, unemployment is likely to rise. This may be associated with a reduced current account deficit, an increased budget deficit and falling inflation.

A positive output gap will see above-average growth and as a result there is likely to be inflationary pressure. Unemployment should be falling and the budget deficit will also be falling. However, the current account deficit will be widening as imports rise with spending.

17 Increases in wages generate higher costs for businesses, which may increase prices to restore profit margins. Hence changes in wage rates may lead to higher inflation if sufficiently high (and not backed up with productivity gains).

18 If inflation is demand-pull in cause, then attempts to reduce this will involve reductions in the level of aggregate demand. In this case, this will take spending out of the economy. Lower spending will mean less demand for output and therefore fewer workers will be required and we will see (cyclical) unemployment rise. Hence, there will be a conflict in this case.

Chapter 12

1 Gold is scarce and is accepted by plenty of people. It has no intrinsic value but people seem to accept that gold has 'worth' — probably due to its price rising and the fact that throughout history it has served as the basis for money in many economies across the world.

2 E, B, F, A, D, C.

3 Reasons include:
- to make a profit — i.e. speculative motive
- as insurance against an unfavourable move expected in the exchange rate
- future need of currency and not wanting to wait for value to change

4 Motives for buying shares:
- capital gains
- dividends

5 If the bond paid a sufficiently high rate of interest then it would be attractive — a bit like an annuity.

6 Yield would be (a) 5%, (b) 3.33% and (c) 2.5%.

7 Likely reason would be to maximise profits. It could also be argued that there are economies of scale in being a 'bigger' bank and also that it spreads risks by operating in two distinct markets.

8 Holding assets in liquid form (notes and coins, for instance) is unprofitable as it generates more return. Profits can be obtained from making loans to others — often the riskier the lending, the higher the return that can be obtained, but clearly this profitable use of money means it is not held in a liquid form.

9 Any of the following:
   – higher consumption due to lower monthly mortgage repayments
   – higher consumption as credit-financed consumption is cheaper
   – higher consumption due to saving being less rewarding
   – higher investment as the cost of borrowing to invest is reduced
   – potentially a boost to exports as lower interest rates are likely to lead to a lower value of sterling

10 The MPC will look at a variety of factors. Reasons for the decrease in the bank rate despite rising inflation could be:
   – The rise in inflation is due to one-off cost-push pressure (such as a rise in indirect taxes) and is not expected to lead to ongoing rises in inflation.
   – The inflation rate is still below target and therefore lower interest rates are still needed to boost AD (and raise inflation back to target).
   – The rise in inflation is not expected to last and the forecast over the next two years is for there to be downward pressure on inflation — remember that changes in interest rates can take up to two years to work fully.

11 Any AS curve can be used (as long as it is correct). The AD curve will shift to the right and will lead to either higher GDP or higher prices (or both).

12 Giving the Bank of England independence over monetary policy was meant to give greater credibility in monetary policy. As a result, it was hoped that inflation expectations would be reduced, which would lead to lower wage claims and therefore lower actual inflation in the medium to long term.

13 The government believes that the economy needs a viable banking system for it to function efficiently. If banks were allowed to fail, people would be reluctant to place their money in bank accounts. This guarantee should satisfy most customers that their money is 'safe'.

14 £50 billion.

Chapter 13

1 (a) (i) £800, (ii) £3800, (iii) £7200.
   (b) (i) 5.3%, (ii) 12.7%, (iii) 16%.
   (c) The system is progressive as the average amount of tax paid rises as the individual's income rises.

2 A regressive tax is one where people on lower incomes pay a higher proportion of their income in that tax. If VAT is placed on essential goods, it cannot be avoided, and given that VAT is a flat rate (of 20% in most cases), it will account for a higher proportion of a poorer person's income.

   Some would disagree though and say that essential goods are usually subject to zero VAT and as a result poorer households would be unaffected. For example, food, prescription charges and children's clothing are zero rated, while electricity and gas bills have a lower rate of VAT (5%) attached to them.

3 Higher direct taxes make working less attractive as they mean less income is retained for each extra hour worked — they increase the attractiveness of not working. Higher taxes on profits (another direct tax) reduce a company's incentive to strive for profits — they also may mean a firm takes steps to avoid paying tax if too high.

4 The cut in income tax should lead to higher consumption, thus shifting the AD curve to the right. It should, according to supply-side theory, lead to a rightward shift in the LRAS curve as more people will be willing either to work longer hours or to enter the labour force as a result, thus increasing the productive potential of the economy.

5 If the debt is expressed as a percentage of national income, rising prices (i.e. inflation) would reduce the value of this debt. Debt is expressed in nominal terms, whereas national income is expressed in real terms, and this means that the significance of the debt will diminish over time due to rising inflation.

   Another possibility is that as long as the budget deficit is smaller than the growth in national income, the addition to the national debt will be smaller than the growth in the national economy — i.e. both will grow in size but the denominator (the national debt) will grow faster, shrinking the ratio.

6 Possible reasons why it is undesirable include:
   – could lead to demand-pull inflation
   – more will need to be borrowed in the future
   – interest payments will increase
   – credit rating may worsen

7 Macroeconomic effects are on aggregate demand — it will increase disposable income and should increase consumption. Microeconomic effects are on the incentive to supply labour. A

cut in direct taxes should lead to a higher labour supply due to increased incentives to work.

8 Possible reasons include:
   – reduce relative poverty
   – reduce the unemployment trap, i.e. increase the replacement ratio
   – increase popularity of government
   – take away a share of supernormal profits from monopsony employers

9 Possible reasons include:
   – industry is a natural monopoly
   – market is not contestable
   – regulation is not in place
   – regulatory capture
   – time lags in policy and improvement

10 Reasons include:
   – training would be underprovided in a free market
   – it reduces occupational immobility
   – it increases worker productivity

11 The natural rate is probably lower in the UK because of these factors:
   – less generous unemployment benefits in the UK
   – less protection for workers in the workplace in the UK
   – more powerful trade unions in France
   – less generous pensions in the UK
   – less generous occupational benefits, such as sick pay and holiday pay, in the UK

Chapter 14

1 Any numerical example will show that there are no gains to be made from specialisation and trade if the opportunity cost ratios are identical. The following table is one example which illustrates that:

	Food (units)		Clothing (units)
Country A	100	and	300
Country B	25	and	75
World total	125	and	375

2 Diagram would look like this:

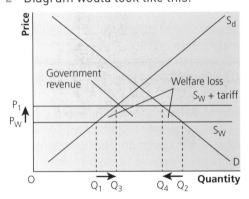

3 Tariffs can vary on different products but are the same for each product across the EU. If tariffs were different then this would lead to goods and services being imported into the EU through the country with the lowest tariff and then re-exported across the EU.

4 (a) improve
   (b) improve
   (c) worsen
   (d) worsen
   (e) worsen
   (f) improve

5 £38,552 million.

6

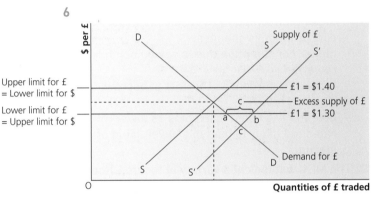

This figure shows how the government would need to buy up an excess supply of £s if the £/$ exchange rate looked like falling below the lowest permitted level (of £1 = $1.30). If the £ was likely to breach the upper band, it would need to sell £s (and buy $s).

7 Income inelastic demand means that as income rises, the demand for the product will rise by a proportionally smaller amount. This means as global incomes rise, the demand for these products will not rise as quickly and any earnings from these will also not rise quickly.

8 Limitations include:
   – cost of negotiation
   – likely impact on developed countries as established industries cannot compete with low-cost producers in less developed economies
   – likely harm to less developed economies, whose industries may be small and unable to compete with firms in other countries which may benefit from economies of scale
   – possible dumping effects on economy

9 Debt cancellation may be a bad idea because it:
   – may encourage wasteful spending by less developed economy
   – may prop up a corrupt government in power
   – reduces incentives to lend further money to less developed economy